The Spread of Modern Humans

Fully modern humans evolved in Africa, probably between 200 000 and 100 000 years ago. By 30 000 years ago, they had colonized much of the globe. Rising temperatures at the end of the last Ice Age allowed plants and animals to become more abundant, and new areas were settled. By 8000 B.C., larger populations and

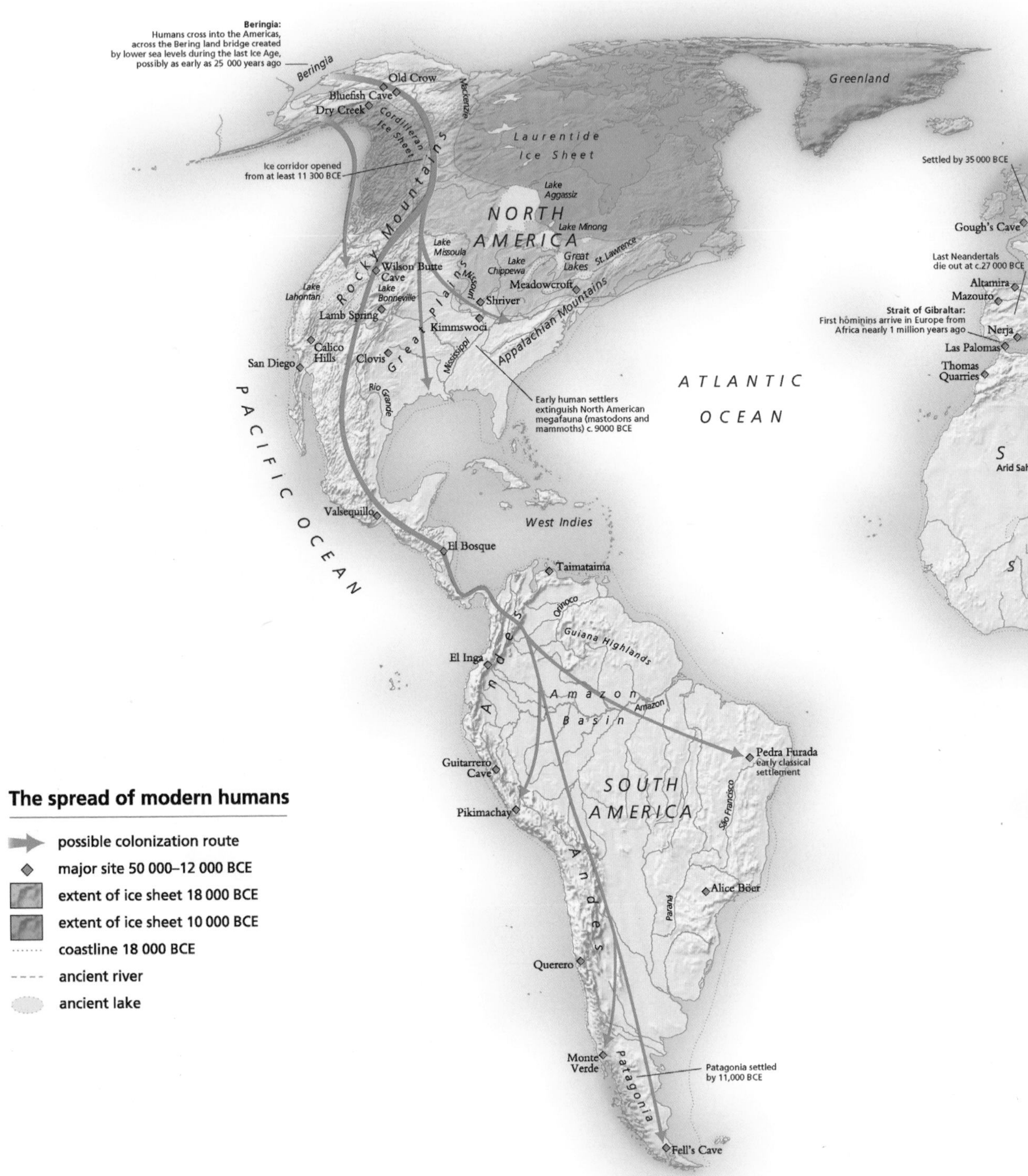

intense hunting had contributed to the near extinction of large mammals, such as mastodons and mammoths. In the Near East, groups of hunter gatherers were living in permanent settlements, harvesting wild cereals, and experimenting with the domestication of local animals. The transition to agriculture was under way.

The Spread of Agriculture

The appearance of farming transformed the face of the Earth. It was not merely a change in subsistence, it also transformed the way in which our ancestors lived. Agriculture, and the vastly greater crop yields it produced, enabled larger groups of people to live together, often in permanent villages. After agriculture emerged, craft, religious, and political specialization became more likely, and the first signs of social

inequality appeared. In 5000 B.C., only a limited number of regions were fully dependent on agriculture. In many parts of the globe, small-scale farming began to supplement hunting and gathering, the first steps in the gradual transition to the sedentary agricultural way of life.

The First Civilizations

The period between 5000 and 2500 B.C. saw the development of complex urban civilizations in the fertile river valleys of the Nile, Tigris, Euphrates, and Indus. Mesopotamian city states formed small kingdoms, which competed with one another. A literate elite ruled over each civilization, and their artisans experimented with new technologies such as bronze and copper metallurgy. Many village societies developed important ritual centres or buried their dead in communal sepulchres.

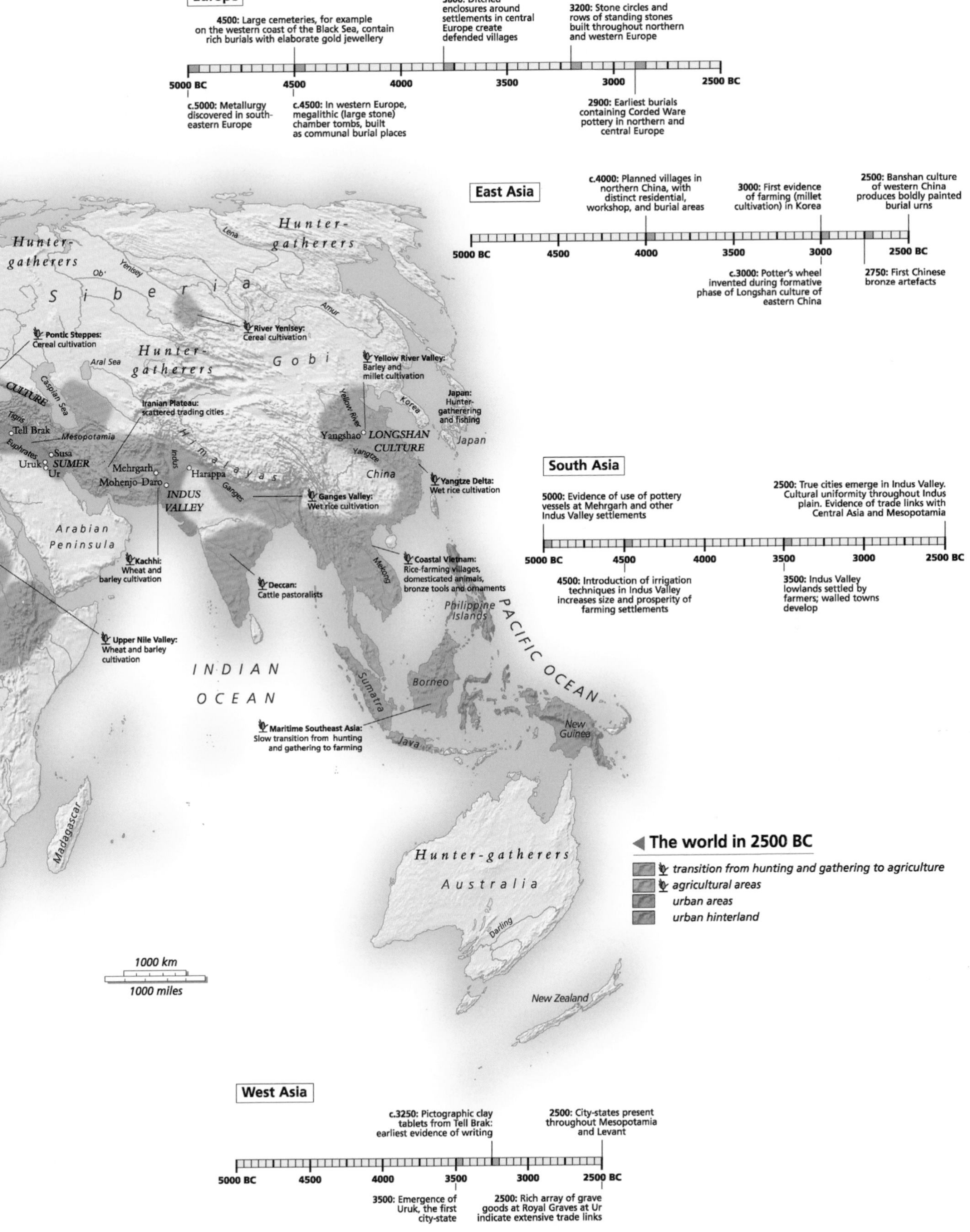
Europe
4500: Large cemeteries, for example on the western coast of the Black Sea, contain rich burials with elaborate gold jewellery
3800: Ditched enclosures around settlements in central Europe create defended villages
3200: Stone circles and rows of standing stones built throughout northern and western Europe
5000 BC
4500
4000
3500
3000
2500 BC
c.5000: Metallurgy discovered in south-eastern Europe
c.4500: In western Europe, megalithic (large stone) chamber tombs, built as communal burial places
2900: Earliest burials containing Corded Ware pottery in northern and central Europe
East Asia
c.4000: Planned villages in northern China, with distinct residential, workshop, and burial areas
3000: First evidence of farming (millet cultivation) in Korea
2500: Banshan culture of western China produces boldly painted burial urns
5000 BC
4500
4000
3500
3000
2500 BC
c.3000: Potter's wheel invented during formative phase of Longshan culture of eastern China
2750: First Chinese bronze artefacts
South Asia
5000: Evidence of use of pottery vessels at Mehrgarh and other Indus Valley settlements
2500: True cities emerge in Indus Valley. Cultural uniformity throughout Indus plain. Evidence of trade links with Central Asia and Mesopotamia
5000 BC
4500
4000
3500
3000
2500 BC
4500: Introduction of irrigation techniques in Indus Valley increases size and prosperity of farming settlements
3500: Indus Valley lowlands settled by farmers; walled towns develop
West Asia
c.3250: Pictographic clay tablets from Tell Brak: earliest evidence of writing
2500: City-states present throughout Mesopotamia and Levant
5000 BC
4500
4000
3500
3000
2500 BC
3500: Emergence of Uruk, the first city-state
2500: Rich array of grave goods at Royal Graves at Ur indicate extensive trade links
Hunter-gatherers
Hunter-gatherers
Siberia
Lena
Yenisey
Ob'
Amur
River Yenisey: Cereal cultivation
Pontic Steppes: Cereal cultivation
Hunter-gatherers
Aral Sea
Gobi
Yellow River Valley: Barley and millet cultivation
Japan: Hunter-gatherering and fishing
Caspian Sea
CULTURE
Iranian Plateau: scattered trading cities
Korea
Yellow River
Tigris
Tell Brak
Mesopotamia
Euphrates
Susa
Uruk
SUMER
Ur
Himalayas
Indus
Yangshao
LONGSHAN CULTURE
Japan
Yangtze
Mehrgarh
Harappa
China
Mohenjo-Daro
INDUS VALLEY
Ganges
Ganges Valley: Wet rice cultivation
Yangtze Delta: Wet rice cultivation
Arabian Peninsula
Kachhi: Wheat and barley cultivation
Coastal Vietnam: Rice-farming villages, domesticated animals, bronze tools and ornaments
Mekong
Deccan: Cattle pastoralists
Philippine Islands
PACIFIC OCEAN
Upper Nile Valley: Wheat and barley cultivation
INDIAN OCEAN
Sumatra
Borneo
Maritime Southeast Asia: Slow transition from hunting and gathering to farming
Java
New Guinea
Madagascar
Hunter-gatherers
Australia
Darling
New Zealand
1000 km
1000 miles
The world in 2500 BC
transition from hunting and gathering to agriculture
agricultural areas
urban areas
urban hinterland

PEARSON ALWAYS LEARNING

Carol R. Ember • Melvin Ember • Peter N. Peregrine
Robert D. Hoppa

Physical Anthropology and Archaeology

Custom Edition for University of Toronto

Taken from:
Physical Anthropology and Archaeology, Third Canadian Edition
by Carol R. Ember, Melvin Ember, Peter N. Peregrine
and Robert D. Hoppa

Cover Art: Courtesy of PhotoDisc and Getty Images.

Taken from:

Physical Anthropology and Archaeology, Third Canadian Edition
by Carol R. Ember, Melvin Ember, Peter N. Peregrine and Robert D. Hoppa

Published by Prentice Hall
Toronto, Ontario

This special edition published in cooperation with Pearson Learning Solutions.

Pearson Learning Solutions, 501 Boylston Street, Suite 900, Boston, MA 02116
A Pearson Education Company
www.pearsoned.com

Printed in Canada

1 2 3 4 5 6 7 8 9 10 V0YA 16 15 14 13 12 11

000200010270775837

CT

ISBN 10: 1-256-34151-7
ISBN 13: 978-1-256-34151-2

Contents

UNCOVERING THE PAST: TOOLS AND TECHNIQUES

CHAPTER OUTLINE

Reconstructing the past using archaeological and palaeoanthropological evidence requires a firm understanding of the methods for acquiring data. This chapter deals specifically with the associated methods of site identification and recovery. The methods discussed are broadly applicable to both palaeoanthropological and archaeological research; in some instances issues are more relevant to one field than the other. The material covered in this chapter forms part of the foundation for subsequent chapters, which go on to introduce the biological and cultural evolution of human populations, through the archaeological and palaeontological record.

Understanding past life from the archaeological and palaeontological record requires expertise in a variety of areas. First, specialized methods, mostly borrowed from geological sciences and physics, have been developed to augment the traditional anthropological methods to locate *archaeological sites*—areas of human habitation or where fossil remains are found. Second, archaeological techniques are used for the excavation of remains—whether fossil remains of a hominin (a human, or the direct ancestor of a human), a prehistoric cemetery, or an entire settlement—so as to maximize and preserve the information that can be derived from the excavation of a site.

An important fact to remember is that archaeological remains are the most valuable source of data when the information about where they were buried in relation to all other remains is preserved—something called **provenience**. This is why it is so important that illegal or amateur excavation of sites must be prevented. Archaeology, by its very nature, is destructive—once material has been removed, all information regarding its burial environment is lost. As a result, archaeologists have developed extremely rigorous methods for recording this information before and while remains are excavated from a site.

Reconstruction of the past is not an easy task. It requires the careful analysis of the environment in which the materials are found in order to say something about the circumstances by which that material came to be there. **Material culture**—the objects that people have and make—is a direct reflection of human culture and behaviour. Archaeologists and their colleagues in related disciplines attempt to understand a complex process as it is reflected in the remains of the everyday belongings of past peoples. For example, if we want to understand how a community changed over the course of its history, we need to recognize that those changes would have been influenced by a variety of factors. These would include changes in the environment, the population numbers, religion, and culture, to name just a few. However, unravelling these factors is sometimes difficult, which is why the researcher has to pay careful attention to the context in which material culture is found. Further, while material culture is a direct reflection of past culture, the archaeological record is not always a direct reflection of material culture. A number of factors can affect where the remains of material culture are found and the patterns of deposition. The archaeologists must be able to recognize these influences.

Site Formation Processes

The archaeological record is not simply a sterile snapshot of society as it once was. Material culture is subjected to a host of **site formation processes**, including environmental and cultural, that affect how and where materials are deposited. Cultural factors can be as simple as past populations dumping waste in the same area for a long duration of time. This creates a garbage heap or **midden** as it is called in the archaeological record. The materials contained within a midden are waste products of the human population that produced them. However, examining the kinds of materials that were being produced and how they were being produced and contemplating their possible functions

Provenience: the location of an artifact or feature within a site. Also called provenance.
Material Culture: objects that people have and make.

Site Formation Process: environmental and cultural factors that affect how and where materials are deposited at an archaeological site or fossil locale.
Midden: a pile of refuse, often shells, in an archaeological site.

Modern landfill sites provide a cross-section of human material culture today.

are fundamental aspects of archaeological reconstruction. Imagine what archaeologists 1000 years in the future might be able to say about life today by excavating a modern landfill site. Think about what a stranger could infer about your own life by what you throw out each week.

Similarly, how a community constructed its dwellings might have an impact on the formation of an archaeological site, such as whether its people were nomadic, moved around in an annual pattern, or lived a more sedentary life, building permanent or semi-permanent dwellings. Locations where a community lived continuously over long periods tend to have layers of accumulated materials left by successive occupations, and these layers are superimposed on one another—people tend to build or rebuild on the rubble left from the dwellings of the previous occupants of a site. A community constantly on the move affects the quantity and distribution of the materials left in any one area. If a site is a product of seasonal habitation, the kind of material culture left behind will not be random, but will reflect the activities occurring at one time of the year but not another. Further, the composition and position of materials within the archaeological record can affect preservation of those remains. For example, in the contact period in Canada—when Europeans were first meeting with and interacting with Aboriginal populations—burials that contain copper artifacts tend to show increased preservation of organic materials that are in direct association with the copper. Coffins provide a different burial environment for bodies than does burial directly in the soil.

People also reuse materials and trade materials over distances. Old timber may be used in the construction of a new house. Material from another region may be imported and valued for its rarity. For example, we see in the archaeological record the movement of native copper from northern Wisconsin and northwestern Canada into the interior regions of western Canada, where it was used by people who otherwise would not have had access to it.

Material culture can have functional, social, and aesthetic purposes. Consider the number of items that were once utilitarian in your own home that serve no functional purpose today. Pottery is a good example. Old glass and earthenware containers such as glass milk jugs or hand-thrown pottery that were used as everyday items in homes in the past might

Finding fossil hominins requires patience and endurance.

be used as decorative items within modern households. Fine ceramics may not be routinely used for food processing, storage, or service, but they do serve important social functions. These functions may be embedded in the meaning imparted to the vessels. Fine ceramics might be family heirlooms, or expensive icons of social prestige. Such items might "function" to impart social messages about affluence and social position. So it can be difficult to untangle the many cultural processes that contribute to the formation of an archaeological site.

Natural physical processes can affect the survival of artifacts. Deposits from wind erosion and water can cover or submerge whole communities, depending on the environmental conditions at the time that they were occupied. Those same natural processes can cause erosion, exposure, and destruction of archaeological sites. Soil chemistry, temperature, water level, and bacterial action can all affect the rate of decay of organic and inorganic material. As a result, the archaeological record tends to favour the presence of inorganic materials, such as stone, metals, and baked clay, but under good preservation conditions organic materials such as bone, shell, hair, paper, and even soft muscle tissue can survive for extended time periods.

Locating Sites

The first and most important aspect of archaeology is actually finding the remains of the past. Archaeologists have developed specialized techniques, some borrowed from other disciplines, to accurately identify, map, and excavate sites. However, identification of **archaeological sites**, that is, locations of human occupation, and *fossil locales* where fossilized remains of once living organisms are found, requires somewhat different prospection strategies.

Fossil Locales

Fossil locales are those places where the fossilized remains of animals are found. For the most part, a locale has no bearing on the life of the animal but is a product of a series of processes that affect the remains following death. Candidate locations for fossil sites are identified based on the environment that would have existed tens of thousands or even millions of years ago. Once identified, it is a long and tedious process of field survey on foot, carefully looking for telltale signs in the hopes of finding that rare fossilized specimen. Oftentimes a whole field season can pass by without any new discoveries. Sometimes though, the combination of skill and luck prevails, and the remains of a fossilized specimen are discovered.

What Are Fossils?

A fossil may be an impression of an insect or leaf on a muddy or other surface that now is stone. Or it may consist of the actual hardened remains of an animal's skeletal structure. It is this second type of fossil—bone turned to stone—that has given palaeoanthropologists the most information about the evolution of primates.

Fossilization. When an animal dies, the organic matter in its body quickly begins to deteriorate. The teeth and skeletal structure are composed largely of

Archaeological Site: areas of past human habitation or where fossil remains are found.
Fossil Locales: places where fossilized remains of once living organisms are found.

inorganic mineral salts, and soon they are all that remains. Under most conditions, these parts eventually deteriorate too. But once in a great while conditions are favourable for preservation—for instance, when volcanic ash, limestone, or highly mineralized groundwater is present to form a high-mineral environment. If the remains are buried under such circumstances, the minerals in the ground may become bound into the structure of the teeth or bone, harden, and thus make them less likely to deteriorate. This process of **fossilization** leaves a combination of inorganic bone and mineral, while retaining microscopic detail of the original material. Fossilization requires very specific environmental conditions—organisms need to be at the right place at the right time before there is even a chance of their remains becoming fossilized. Further, the process takes considerable time—more than 10 000 years, depending on soil chemistry and other factors. In fact, given the relative rarity of fossilization, palaeontologists have collected an exceptional amount of information about hundreds of past species from various periods.

Unfortunately, we have fossil remains only of some species and sometimes only fragments from one or a few individuals. So the fossil record is very incomplete. Robert Martin estimates that the earth has probably seen 6000 primate species; and remains of only 3 percent of those species have been found. While this seems small, given the relative rarity of fossilization we should not expect to have as much information from the fossil record as we do. Nevertheless primate palaeontologists continue to explore the evolutionary connections between early and later fossil forms. The task is particularly difficult with small mammals, such as the early primates, which are less likely to be preserved in the fossil record than are large animals (Bilsborough, 1992).

Palaeoanthropologists have a more narrow interest in terms of the kinds of species they look at—primates at the broadest level, and more often hominins alone. Given these factors, it is

Fossilization: the process of becoming a fossil by the replacement of organic materials with an inorganic mineral matrix.

The fossil of a trilobite from the Cambrian period, 500 million years ago.

amazing how much information we have actually accumulated regarding human evolution.

What Can We Learn from Fossils?

Palaeontologists can tell a great deal about an extinct animal from its fossilized bones or teeth, but that knowledge is based on much more than just the fossil record itself. Palaeontologists rely on comparative anatomy to help reconstruct missing skeletal pieces as well as the soft tissues attached to bone. New techniques, such as electron microscopy, CT scans, and computer-assisted biomechanical modelling, provide much information about how the organism may have moved, the microstructure of bone and teeth, and how the organism developed. Chemical analysis of bone can suggest what the animal typically ate. Palaeontologists are also interested in the surroundings of the fossil finds. With methods developed in geology, chemistry, and physics, palaeontologists use the surrounding rocks to identify the period in which the organism died. In addition, the study of associated fauna and flora can suggest what the ancient climate and habitat were like (Klein, 1989).

Since most of human evolution predates human material culture, palaeoanthropologists have only the biological remains of human ancestors from which to infer hominin behaviour. Because the environment in which these hominins lived and died was very different from that of today, palaeoanthropologists have turned to the expertise of geologists to interpret geological phenomena that reflect the environments that existed millions of years ago. Many fossils result from organic remains being deposited in lakes or rivers where they were quickly covered with sediment. Over time, lakes may have dried up, rivers may have changed course, and the land may have been uplifted. The old lake floors or riverbeds could now be represented by eroding sediments on hilltops. Consequently, the majority of fossil hominin remains found by palaeoanthropologists have been subject to long-term environmental processes before being found.

Taphonomy. The processes that affect an animal's remains following its death are important for understanding the context in which fossil remains are found. The study of the processes that affect the body of an animal following its death, known as **taphonomy**, is literally the science of burial. Taphonomic processes are certainly an important consideration in archaeological contexts, and palaeoanthropology requires an extensive understanding of them. For example, the distribution of bones observed in an area may reflect predation by a carnivore and subsequent disturbance by scavengers. This is relevant to the study of early hominins in particular, many of whom were often the prey for large carnivores rather than predators themselves. A carnivore may have brought a skull to a cave, for example, and it may be preserved because of the cave environment, yet the rest of the skeleton is missing from the cave. Of particular concern to palaeoanthropologists are any physical distortions to the fossil hominin remains. Skulls, for example, can be slowly crushed over the course of the fossilization process, leading to a distorted morphology, or form. Palaeoanthropologists need to try to determine the original morphology of the specimen in such instances.

Finding Archaeological Sites

Archaeological sites are generally viewed as geographic areas that contain evidence of past human behaviour and activity. An archaeological site can range from a small campsite to a large city, a place for growing food or killing game, a place for mining or processing raw materials, or a place of worship or a place of burial. All of these activities can leave varying degrees of evidence in the archaeological record. Further, some sites may be clearly identifiable, such as the Great Pyramids of Egypt, or go relatively unnoticed for long periods.

Although many archaeological sites are discovered accidentally, the process of finding a site still remains an important aspect of archaeology. Most development plans in Canada require an archaeological assessment to ensure that cultural heritage is not being destroyed by modern development. By building archaeological research into the environmental assessment, the protection and investigation of these fragile non-renewable resources can be more carefully managed. Even with this level of planning, many archaeological sites are discovered by accident. Whether a site is discovered accidentally or as a consequence of a deliberate search, one of the first phases of archaeological investigation involves documenting the boundaries of a site. This enables the most efficient use of time and resources for site investigation. In most cases, only a portion of a site can be excavated, and proper survey techniques can help identify the areas of greatest interest to the archaeologist.

Site Prospection

Detection of human modification of the landscape will depend on the scale of human activities. In the case of subtle landscape modifications, such as a single house or a burial, even a trained archaeologist may have difficulty recognizing the changes associated with these features. Often intuition, experience, and subsurface inspections will aid in the initial discovery of archaeological sites. The identification of a site is based on methods that can be broadly divided between *surface* and *subsurface surveying techniques* that can involve remote sensing or be intrusive, such as digging.

Surface Techniques. **Surface techniques** include *field walking* and *field surveying.* Much like the

Taphonomy: the study of changes that occur to organisms or objects after being buried or deposited.

Surface Techniques: archaeological survey techniques for finding and assessing archaeological sites from surface finds.

palaeoanthropologist, an archaeologist will patiently walk and survey the surface of a location for signs of artifacts or surface irregularities that may indicate structures. Surface inspection is appropriate in situations where disturbances have exposed archaeological materials. These disturbances could be natural processes like erosion. Human activities like cultivation, construction, or clearing of forests are examples of modern practices that might reveal the presence of material culture from the past. Artifacts collected as part of field walking provide important clues about the potential distribution and boundaries of the disturbed archaeological materials, and can aid in identifying areas that remain undisturbed.

Field surveying can be as simple as the archaeologist walking through an area and carefully watching for sometimes subtle clues that indicate the presence of material culture, or as complex as the systematic survey of a region aided by local histories of land use and occupation by local residents. Once the archaeologist identifies an area of increased density of recovered surface artifacts or specific structures, he or she will use subsurface techniques to define where more comprehensive excavations will proceed.

Past changes to the landscape on a larger scale, such as irrigation systems for fields or whole cities, may still be sufficiently distinct to be identified through field inspection or the examination of air photographs or satellite images. *Aerial photography* and *satellite imaging* can even provide clues to the remains of structures buried under thick accumulations of sediment, particularly if the underlying cultural deposits alter the soil chemistry or soil moisture to the point that can change the pattern of vegetation. Areas disturbed by past human occupation may produce differences in the kinds of vegetation that cover the area, and these may be detectable only from the air. Even when large-scale alterations to the landscape have been reduced through natural processes such as erosion or artificial processes such as plowing, they can leave distinct topographical patterns on the surface that are distinguishable from the air. Satellite imagery provides a similar tool, although the cost of using it and the observable level of precision make it currently impractical for archaeologists except for the documentation of large-scale disturbances such as roads, canals, irrigated fields, or large communities with monumental architecture.

Archaeological test pits and trenching (shown here) help define the boundaries of a site.

Subsurface Techniques. In most cases, surface surveying is not the most efficient means for locating archaeological sites. Those sites that have not yet been exposed, or whose distribution or pattern is not clearly recognizable on the surface, require other kinds of surveying techniques.

Subsurface techniques can be mechanical or electronic. Mechanical techniques tend to be invasive and include *shovel shining, test pitting,* or *trenching.* Electronic techniques tend to be non-invasive and allow the archaeologist to survey or map below the surface without actually disturbing the site.

Shovel shining is a simple method where the edge of a shovel is used to scrape off thin layers of the

Subsurface Techniques: archaeological survey techniques that map features beneath the surface.

A grid system is used at archaeological sites to accurately record the position of artifacts and features during excavation.

immediate and usually disturbed surface layer to reveal undisturbed soil. This method is suitable for unearthing features like post moulds, hearths, house foundations, or refuse that can be identified through their different soil colour and composition. Shovel shining is also used to systematically explore a site that has been disturbed, perhaps through cultivation, for intact deposits that remain below the disturbed zone. The site is then further assessed by systematically removing layers of the surface from a small, contained area. This approach is most effective where the approximate extent and cultural identity of a disturbed site has been defined through a field-walking survey and surface collection.

Where a newly discovered site is relatively undisturbed, the excavation of test pits at intervals across the site might offer a better and less destructive understanding of the site's extent and its artifacts. Such test pits are usually excavated with a shovel, are generally quite small (about 50 cm in diameter), and spaced at regular intervals across the site. The size, depth, and spacing of the test pits vary with the nature of the site deposits, the research objectives, and the resources available to the archaeologist. Each test pit should provide a sample of artifacts that can aid in dating the site's age and function. The density and position of what is recovered, that is, the recoveries, may aid in determining the size and shape of the site. As each test pit is associated with a specific location within the site, the archaeologist can use the shovel test pit data to examine the changing pattern and density of recoveries across the site. This serves as a useful preliminary assessment tool in planning a full-scale excavation.

In instances where material is suspected to be at great depths beneath the surface, boring and core samples can be taken to retrieve a column that reflects the overall layering of a small but deep area. This technique is being employed by archaeologist Aubrey Cannon of McMaster University in his analysis of middens from prehistoric Northwest Coast sites (Cannon, 2000a; Cannon, 2000b). The method has the advantage of providing a snapshot of all the layers within a site without the need for a complete excavation. The primary assumption of this method is that the distribution of artifacts within the core will be representative of the distribution within the immediate surrounding area. The same technique may be used to sample sediments that aid in reconstructing past environments. For example, how and when deposits were laid down may be inferred from sediment particle size, or pollen recovery can indicate past climatic conditions and vegetation cover.

Non-invasive site inspection techniques have been borrowed from a variety of disciplines and applied to archaeological survey. These include *ground-penetrating radar*, or methods based on *magnetic* or *electrical resistance* of subsurface features. Since archaeology is itself destructive, archaeologists would ideally like to obtain as much information as possible about the composition of a site without the need for excavation. Ground-penetrating radar involves radar waves that map subsurface sedimentary layers and buried archaeological features. Radar waves will "reflect" off subsurface features and produce pulses that can be detected on the surface. The speed at which the radar waves penetrate the surface varies due to soil composition, but when the velocity is known and the time between pulses recorded, the depth of features below the surface can be calculated. The radar can provide a subsurface map of the relative locations and depths of features over a large area.

Electrical resistivity meters measure differences in the ability of sediments and other materials beneath the surface to conduct electricity. For example, features like stone or brick walls are less conductive than the surrounding deposits. Alternatively, a concentration of metallic objects or a pit that has filled over time and has different soil moisture levels may be more conductive than the surrounding deposits. When soil resistivity is measured along controlled grids, patterns of variation in electrical conductivity can be detected and mapped to aid in site interpretation. Similarly, a *magnetometer* can measure the relative magnetism of items below the surface. Clay when fired acquires a small magnetic field that can be detected with this instrument. Rocks with trace amounts of iron in them or iron metal objects can also be detected. By examining the patterns in variation in sediment magnetism, the archaeologist can identify zones of particular interest that can be investigated through subsurface excavation.

Excavation

Once a site has been identified, excavation can begin. Before, during, and after excavation, the archaeologist follows a series of methods to maintain maximum control over the relationships between items in the three-dimensional space of the site. To begin with, *site evaluation* involves an assessment of the size of the site, depth of the deposits, site formation processes (including taphonomic processes that may bias site integrity such as scavenger activity, water, etc.), and function. While horizontal control is important, vertical control of the excavation process can be critical when there are dramatic differences in the time that various layers of sediment took to accumulate (see discussion of *stratigraphy for relative dating* below). A preliminary assessment of the information from the site evaluation is critical for planning an appropriate research design that includes budgeting for the costs of excavation and analysis, and implementing detailed excavation. Detailed excavation is generally conventional. However, because excavation is destructive, permanent (once an artifact is out of the ground, its context is lost), and expensive in terms of both time and money, archaeologists try to obtain a sample of deposits that they hope is representative of the whole site.

How a sample is chosen is based on a careful analysis of preliminary survey information regarding the distribution and function of the site. For example, determining the sampling strategy at a buffalo jump site like Head-Smashed-In Buffalo Jump in southern Alberta depends on the kinds of research questions that people have. If the researcher is interested in the antiquity, seasonality, and cultural association of a stratified sequence of bison kill events, then a deep excavation focused at the base of the jump would be appropriate. In contrast, if you are interested in the full sequence of events involved in the communal bison drive of past populations, then a broader perspective and more diverse sampling strategy would be warranted.

The first step of a controlled excavation is choosing a datum point. The **datum** represents a fixed, permanent reference point within or near the site.

Datum: a fixed, permanent reference point within or near an archaeological site used to define the location of all information and specimens collected from the site. As the datum is a permanent fixture, future investigations can be spatially related to all previous work at the site.

This fixed reference point defines the location of all information and specimens collected from the site. As the datum is a permanent fixture, future investigations (perhaps using new, innovative techniques) can be spatially related to all previous work at the site. This enables an ongoing synthesis of information. Once a datum has been decided, a *grid system* is laid out, usually dividing the site into 1- or 2-metre squares. Under special circumstances, like cave archaeology or underwater archaeology, extra control over depth is necessary. Each square is defined by its location within the grid, and more detailed mapping and documentation of recoveries within the square is relative to the grid location of the control square. The careful recording of all information within the grid allows for all data to be incorporated into a single system at the end of the excavation, even though different people may have excavated certain grid squares at different times.

Depending on the scale of the excavation, archaeologists apply different techniques and equipment. For example, a backhoe or bulldozer might be used to remove disturbed or culturally sterile topsoil or sod from a location. Once this top disturbed layer has been removed, much finer excavation techniques using small hand tools are needed. In some circumstances, shovels are used to remove sediment. When beginning to excavate an area of interest most archaeologists use small mason's trowels, whisk brooms and paintbrushes, root cutters, teaspoons, and dental picks to carefully remove the sediment and expose and recover the artifacts. This care is necessary to preserve and record the spatial context of recovery, prevent damage to the specimens, and enable discovery and documentation of features that might be represented by subtle shifts in sediment colour, texture, and degree of compaction.

Depending on the context and research objectives, sediment removed from the excavation unit is examined for minute objects that might have been missed during excavation. This involves removing the backdirt—or pile of soil left from excavating an area—in buckets, and sifting it through fine screens to identify small artifacts. The mesh size of the screen depends on the objectives of the researchers and the time and fiscal resources for the project. At most modern excavation projects, sediment is screened through at least 5 mm (1/4-inch) hardware cloth, and a 2 to 3 mm (1/8-inch) screen size is routinely used at many projects. While the smaller screen size dramatically increases the rate of recovery of minute artifacts, there is a significant increase in associated time and costs of excavation and analysis. If the coarser 5 mm screen is used, then the archaeologist will often monitor artifact loss rates by regularly screening subsamples with the finer mesh.

Soil samples may also be bagged and labelled for future analysis. This might involve documenting sediment particle size, soil pH, charcoal and other organic materials, or the concentrations of chemicals such as phosphorus and nitrogen. The presence of *patterned variation*—systematic trends in the way in which material is distributed—of such materials may reflect the nature and intensity of past human activity, and is also very useful for reconstructing the past environmental context of the site. Such soil samples can also be useful for the recovery of minute organic materials. These could be charcoal and preserved wood fragments, carbonized seeds and other preserved plant parts, microscopic pollen, and **phytoliths** (microscopic granules of silicon dioxide that enter a plant's cells and take their shape), as well as land snails and other minute indicators of past climatic and vegetation conditions.

Throughout a site, the remains of human culture are represented by **artifacts**—items manufactured by people, **ecofacts**—natural objects that have been used or affected by humans, and **features**—the non-portable portions of a site, some of which can include artifacts. Artifacts are tools like projectile points or bone tools, and items like clay pots or stone figurines. Ecofacts include bone from animals, seeds, and pollen. Features include things like hearths or fireplaces, burials, houses, fences, or middens. For the archaeologist, the most important aspect of an excavation is the proper mapping and recording of the

Phytolith: microscopic granules of silicon dioxide that enter a plant's cells and take their shape.
Artifact: item manufactured by people and found in archaeological contexts.
Ecofacts: natural objects that have been used or affected by humans.
Feature: the non-portable portions of an archaeological site, some of which can include artifacts.

ANTHROPOLOGY IN ACTION

Anthropologist at Work: Priscilla Renouf

Archaeologist Priscilla Renouf in the field.

In 1984 Priscilla Renouf, now a professor and Canada Research Chair in North Atlantic Archaeology at Memorial University, Newfoundland, investigated two sites on the west coast of the Island of Newfoundland—Port au Choix and Point Riche—for Parks Canada. For her this investigation began what would become a career of excavating Palaeo-Eskimo sites, significantly expanding on previous research in this area. The term Palaeo-Eskimo refers to groups of Native peoples who inhabited the eastern Arctic from approximately 900 to 4000 years ago. They were distinct from the modern Inuit, who are not their direct descendants. Remains of Palaeo-Eskimo settlements have been found from Greenland and Ellesmere Island to the shores of Hudson Bay and Labrador, and as far south as the Island of Newfoundland.

Port au Choix, which is now a National Historic Site, is located on limestone bedrock. This has allowed for the preservation of organic materials, providing archaeologists with a glimpse at the burial customs, subsistence practices, and skeletal biology of Palaeo-Eskimo and more recent Native groups.

Late Palaeo-Eskimo (also known as *Dorset*) sites like Port au Choix are quite large and show evidence of a long-term occupation. Priscilla Renouf has excavated large quantities of harp seal bones at Port au Choix, suggesting that this was a prime location for the hunting of these animals. The peoples' sophisticated hunting technology may be the reason why Dorset sites are so numerous on the Island of Newfoundland—they were perhaps even the most numerous Aboriginal people ever to occupy the island. Nevertheless, Dorset culture seems to have disappeared from the island by about 1200 years ago, and from Greenland and the Canadian Arctic shortly thereafter. Perhaps the people were displaced by the ancestors of modern Inuit—the Thule people.

In 1990 Priscilla Renouf continued with her investigations at Port au Choix. While a large Maritime Archaic Indian cemetery had been discovered in the 1960s at Port au Choix, no associated habitation site had been identified. In 1996 Priscilla Renouf and colleagues developed a model that utilized aspects of relative sea level, palaeogeography, and cultural history to predict a site location for occupation. The next year they found the site exactly where the model had predicted. Radiocarbon dating confirmed its contemporaneity with the Maritime Archaic Indian cemetery. Her ongoing research at Port au Choix continues to document 4500 years of occupation at the site.

Sources: Renouf MAP, Bell T. Searching for the Maritime Archaic Indian Habitation Site at Port au Choix, Newfoundland: An Integrated Approach Using Archaeology, Geomorphology, and Sea Level History. Reports on file with the Government of Newfoundland and Labrador, Provincial Archaeology Office Culture and Heritage Division, Department of Tourism, Culture and Recreation.

Renouf, MAP. 1991. The Newfoundland Museum Notes #5, 1991.

provenience or location of all features and artifacts. This is critical as the **association** of artifacts or features with one another is important for understanding past life at the site. Association is extremely important, for example, in the study of early hominins and the first appearance of manufactured stone tools. Unless the artifacts and fossils can be shown archaeologically to have been associated in the same *depositional context*, that is, from the same time period, one cannot assert that the tools were produced and used by that particular hominin species.

Association: the relationship between artifacts and features within archaeological sites.

Artifacts

Anything made or modified by humans is an artifact. The book you are reading now, the chair you are sitting in, the pen you are taking notes with are all artifacts. In fact, we are surrounded by artifacts, most of which we will lose or throw away. And that is exactly how things enter the archaeological record. Think about it: How much garbage do you produce in a day? What kinds of things do you throw away? Mostly paper, probably, but also wood (from the ice-cream bar you had at lunch), plastic (like the pen that ran out of ink last night), and even metal (the dull blade on your razor). Into the garbage they go and out to the dump or landfill. Under the right conditions many of those items will survive for future archaeologists to find. Most of the artifacts that make up the archaeological record are just this kind of mundane waste—the accumulated garbage of daily life that archaeologists may recover and examine to reconstruct daily life long ago.

By far the most common artifacts from the past are stone tools, which archaeologists call **lithics**. Indeed, lithics are the only artifact available for 99 percent of human history. Humans started using stone tools more than 2.5 million years ago, and some stone tools (grinding and polishing stones, for example) are still used today. Stone has been used for making almost any object you can think of, from cutting tools to oil lamps, but hunting, butchering, and hide-processing tools were commonly made from stone. Another common kind of artifact is **ceramics** (pots and other items made from baked clay). Humans started making ceramics about 10 000 years ago, and ceramic objects such as storage and cooking vessels quickly became widespread. Because they are both fragile and relatively easy to make, ceramics show up frequently in the garbage that makes up the archaeological record. Wood and bone artifacts are common too, and tools for hide working, cooking, hunting, and even butchering were made of these materials. Humans have used wood and bone tools at least as long as stone tools, but unlike stone tools, these tend not to survive well in the archaeological record. In some places metals and glass are common artifacts. These survive well in the archaeological record, and hence they are often found where they were used.

Lithics: the technical name for the tools made from stone.
Ceramics: objects shaped from clay and baked at high temperature (fired) to make them hard. Containers such as pots and jars are typical ceramics, though they can take on many forms and uses.

A ceramic pot from China, dating to the period when agriculture first developed there—some 6000 years ago.

Ecofacts

Ecofacts are natural objects that have been consumed or affected by humans. A good example are the bones of animals that people have eaten. These bones are somewhat like artifacts, but they haven't been made or modified by humans, just used and discarded by them. Another example is pollen found at archaeological sites. Because humans bring plants back to their homes for a number of reasons, pollens from many plants are commonly found. These pollens may not have come from the same location. The only reason they are together is that they have been brought together by human use. Yet another example are the remains of insect and animal pests that associate with humans, such as cockroaches and mice. Their remains are found in sites because they associate with humans and survive by taking advantage of the conditions that humans create. Their presence is in part caused by the human presence, and thus they are considered ecofacts too.

Features

Features are a kind of artifact, but archaeologists distinguish them from other artifacts because they cannot be easily removed from an archaeological site. Hearths are a good example. When humans build a fire on bare ground, the soil becomes heated and is changed—all the water is driven out of it and its crystalline structure is broken down and re-formed. It becomes hard, redder, and even slightly magnetic (as we discuss later). When an archaeologist finds a hearth, what exactly is found? An area of hard, reddish soil, often surrounded by charcoal and ash. Here, then, is an artifact—an object of human manufacture. But it would be very hard, if not impossible, for the archaeologist to pick the hearth up and take it back to the lab for study like a lithic or ceramic. A hearth is really an intrinsic feature of a site—hence the name *feature.*

Hearths are common features, but by far the most common features are called *pits.* Pits are simply holes dug by humans that are later filled with garbage or eroded soil. They are usually fairly easy to distinguish because the garbage or soil they are filled with is often different in colour and texture from the soil the pit was dug into. *Living floors* are another common type of feature. These are the places where humans lived and worked. The soils in these locations are often compacted through human activity and are full of minute pieces of garbage—seeds, small stone flakes, beads, and the like—that became embedded in the floor. A large or very deep area of such debris is called a *midden.* Middens are often the remains of garbage dumps or areas repeatedly used over long periods of time, such as caves. Finally, *buildings* are a common feature on archaeological sites. These can range from the remains of stone rings that once held down the sides of tents to palaces built of stones that had been shaped and fitted together. Even the remains of wooden houses (or parts of them) have been preserved under some conditions. Features are a diverse array of things that can provide lots of information about the past.

Dating Techniques

One must know the age of archaeological sites and fossils in order to reconstruct the evolutionary history of humans and their ancestors. For some time *relative dating methods,* that is, methods that could state that a fossil was older or younger than those from another area of the site, were the only methods available. These techniques generally addressed the sequence of layers by referring to the sedimentary context. The last 50 years have seen important advances in **absolute dating** or *chronometric dating*—methods that can estimate the age of a specimen or deposit in years—including techniques that allow the dating of the earliest phases of primate evolution (Bilsborough, 1992). **Relative dating** allows the age of a specimen or deposit relative to another specimen or deposit to be determined.

Relative Dating Methods

The earliest and still the most common method of relative dating is based on **stratigraphy**, the study of how different layers of sediments and soils, artifacts, and fossils are laid down in successive deposits, or *strata.* The **law of superposition** states that older layers are generally deeper or

Absolute Dating: a method of dating fossils in which the actual age of a deposit or specimen is measured. Also known as chronometric dating.
Relative Dating: a method of dating fossils that determines the age of a specimen or deposit relative to a known specimen or deposit.
Stratigraphy: the study of how different rock formations and fossils are laid down in successive layers or strata. Older layers are generally deeper or lower than more recent layers.
Law of Superposition: a law that states that older layers at an archaeological site are generally deeper or lower than more recent layers. The law of superposition provides a framework with which to make inferences regarding the relationship and relative date of cumulative layers of different strata.

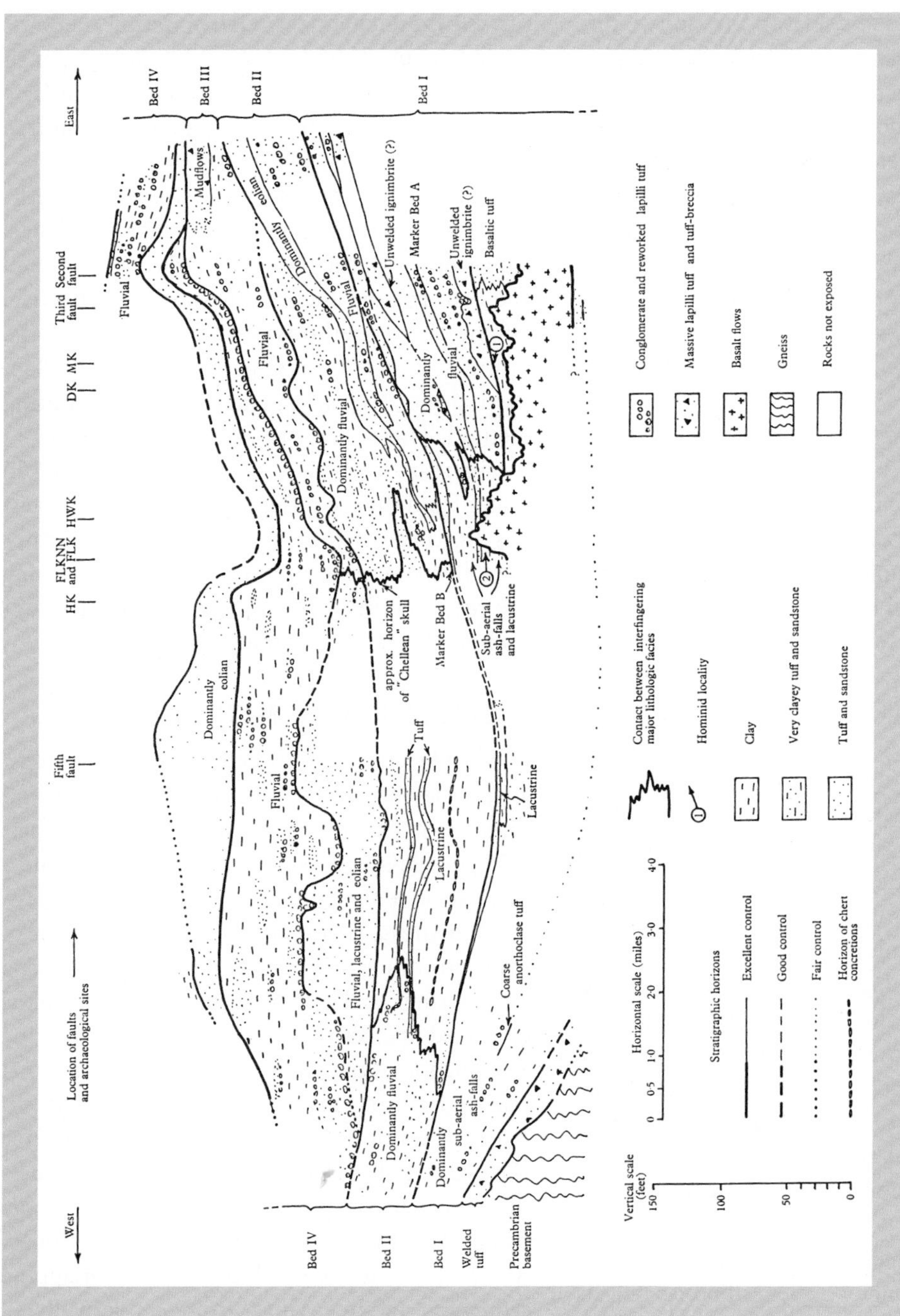

Figure 2–1 Stratigraphy of Beds I–IV along Olduvai Main Gorge

Notice how complex the four stratigraphic layers are—each has numerous layers of soil and rock within them. Index fossils, particularly those of pigs, along with a series of potassium-argon dates, allowed the researchers to identify the four major strata of the site, which correspond to four major periods of human occupation.

Source: Fagan BF. In the Beginning: An Introduction to Archaeology. Upper Saddle River, NJ: Prentice-Hall, 2000, p 218. Reproduced with permission from Prentice Hall.

lower than more recent layers (see Figure 2–1). On the basis of this law, researchers can make inferences about the relationship and relative date of cumulative layers of different strata.

Animals (*fauna*) and plants (*flora*) that spread widely over short periods, died out fairly rapidly, or evolved rapidly provide the most suitable indicator fossils for establishing a stratigraphic sequence for the relative dating of new finds. These life forms help in the relative dating of less well-known specimens found in association with them. Different animals and plants can serve as indicators of relative age in different areas of the world. In Africa, the fossils of elephants, pigs, and horses have been particularly important in establishing stratigraphic sequences. Once the stratigraphy of an area is established, the relative ages of two different fossils in the same or different sites are indicated by the associated flora and fauna (Klein, 1989). Major transitions in flora and fauna define the epochs and larger units of geologic time. The dates of the boundaries between such units are estimated by absolute dating, described below.

If a site has been disturbed, stratigraphy will not be a satisfactory way of determining relative age. A site may be disturbed in various ways: remains from different periods may be washed or blown together by water or wind, or a landslide may superimpose an earlier layer on top of a later layer. Still, it may be possible using chemical methods to estimate the relative age of the different fossils found together in a disturbed site.

Three of the chemical methods used in the relative dating of fossil bones are the fluorine, uranium, and nitrogen tests, sometimes known as the **F-U-N trio** (Oakley, 1963). All are based on the same general principle: bones and teeth undergo a slow transformation in chemical composition when they remain buried for long periods, and this transformation reflects the mineral content of the groundwater in the area in which they are buried. Fluorine is one mineral present in groundwater; therefore, the older a fossil is, the higher its fluorine content will be. Uranium, like fluorine, is also present in groundwater, so the longer the time that bones or teeth remain in the ground, the greater their uranium content. The relationships are reversed for nitrogen: the older the fossil, the smaller the amount of nitrogen present in it. Thus, older bones have relatively higher concentrations of fluorine and uranium and less nitrogen than do recent bones.

However, a problem can arise with the F-U-N tests because the mineral content of bones reflects the mineral content of the groundwater in the area. A 30-million-year-old fossil from a high-mineral area may have the same fluorine content as a 50-million-year-old fossil from a low-mineral site. So these chemical relative dating methods cannot be used to compare the relative ages of specimens from widely separated sites. The F-U-N tests are restricted, then, to specimens from the same site or from neighbouring sites.

Each of the chemical relative dating methods, used alone, can give only tentative evidence. However, when the three methods are combined and confirm one another, they are very effective. Of the three methods we have discussed, the uranium test is by far the most reliable when used alone. It is not strictly a relative dating method. There seems to be some consistency in the increase in radioactivity with age, even in bones from different deposits. The uranium test has another distinct advantage over the other tests. Because uranium is radioactive, measuring the radioactivity does not require the destruction of any part of the sample in testing.

F-U-N Trio: fluorine (F), uranium (U), and nitrogen (N) tests for relative dating. All three minerals are present in groundwater. The older a fossil is, the higher its fluorine or uranium content will be, and the lower its nitrogen content.

Absolute Dating Methods

Dendrochronology. Through **dendrochronology**, an archaeologist can estimate the age of wood samples by examining the annual growth rings. A.E. Douglass first used it in the 1920s to date a prehistoric settlement in New Mexico (Douglass, 1929). During each year of its life, a new layer of wood grows in a tree's trunk and branches, creating annual rings that can be seen when the trunk is examined in cross-section. The nature of each ring is a function of the growing conditions during that year, and the rings act as a kind of fingerprint of climatic conditions during the life of the tree (Douglass, 1947). Dendrochronology becomes useful as an archaeological dating technique if a *master chronology* of tree ring patterns can be developed. A chronology is the result of linking overlapping sequences of tree rings from modern living trees with those in ancient trees found in palaeontological or archaeological contexts. With the establishment of a regional master chronology, analysts then examine the archaeologically recovered wood sample of unknown age and seek to match

Dendrochronology: an absolute dating technique based on counting annual tree rings in wood.

the ring pattern to one observed in the master sequence. Since the master sequence counts back from the modern period, the calendrical date of the archaeological wood sample can be calculated. Dendrochronology obviously is limited to the dating of wood and wood products, and has a limited temporal range. It is generally only useful at a regional level, reflecting local climatic conditions. The most useful dendrochronological sequences have been developed for arid areas. While most individual trees do not live for thousands of years, dendrochronological research has been considerably furthered by the study of very long-lived trees such as the bristle cone pine (see Figure 2–2). In this way, dendrochronology is useful for measuring the age of wood that may be several thousand years old or before present (B.P.).

Many of the absolute dating methods are based on the decay rate of a radioactive isotope. The age of the specimen can be determined by measuring the remaining quantity of the isotope in the sample since the rate of decay or **half-life** is known, and the original concentration of the isotope can be estimated, within a range of possible error. Radiocarbon, or carbon-14 (^{14}C), dating is perhaps the most popularly known method of determining the absolute age of an organic specimen.

Radiocarbon Dating. **Radiocarbon dating** is a reliable method for dating remains up to 50 000 years old (Brown, 1992). It is based on the principle that all living matter possesses a certain amount of a radioactive form of carbon (^{14}C). Radioactive carbon is produced when atmospheric nitrogen-14 is bombarded by cosmic rays. This material is absorbed from the air by plants and then ingested by animals that eat the plants. After an organism dies, it no longer takes in any of the radioactive carbon (see Figure 2–3 on page 37). Carbon-14 decays at a slow but steady pace and reverts to nitrogen-14. (By "decays," we mean that the ^{14}C releases a certain number of beta radiations per minute.) The rate at which the carbon decays is known: ^{14}C has a half-life of 5730 years. In other words, half of the original amount of ^{14}C in organic matter will have disintegrated 5730 years after the organism's death; half of the remaining ^{14}C will have disintegrated after another 5730 years; and so on.

To discover how long an organism has been dead—that is, to determine how much ^{14}C is left in the organism and therefore how old it is—we count the number of beta radiations given off per minute per gram of material. Modern ^{14}C emits about 15 beta radiations per minute per gram of material, but ^{14}C that is 5730 years old emits only half that amount (the half-life of ^{14}C) per minute per gram. So if a sample of some organism gives off 7.5 radiations a minute per gram, which is only half the amount given off by modern ^{14}C, the organism must be 5730 years old (Hole and Heizer, 1973). This is why radiocarbon dating usually is not accurate for anything more than 50 000 years old—the amount of ^{14}C remaining in the organic matter is too small to permit reliable dating.

Is it really that simple though? Unfortunately, the answer is no. One of the problems with radiocarbon dating is that it assumes the relative level of ^{14}C present in the atmosphere remains constant over all time. In fact we now know that this is not true, and that there are fluctuations because of variation in the intensity of solar radiation. The question is then, how do we compensate for these unknown fluctuations when estimating age using carbon-14 dating? The solution is to calibrate the expected values against observed values using dendrochronology. By taking samples of wood that can be dated accurately using dendrochronology and radiocarbon dating, we can assess any deviation between the two dates. By plotting the distribution of these two dates for many different samples that span the last several thousand years, we can create a *calibration curve* (see Figure 2–4). Then, we can calculate the radiocarbon date of organic archaeological material, and the date can be calibrated against the curve. This method provides a calibration curve with a time range of about 9000 years ago for carbon-14 dating (Brown, 1992).

Half-life: the time it takes for half of the atoms of a radioactive substance to decay into atoms of a different substance.

Radiocarbon Dating: a dating method that uses the decay of carbon-14 to date organic remains. It is reliable for dating once-living matter up to 50 000 years old.

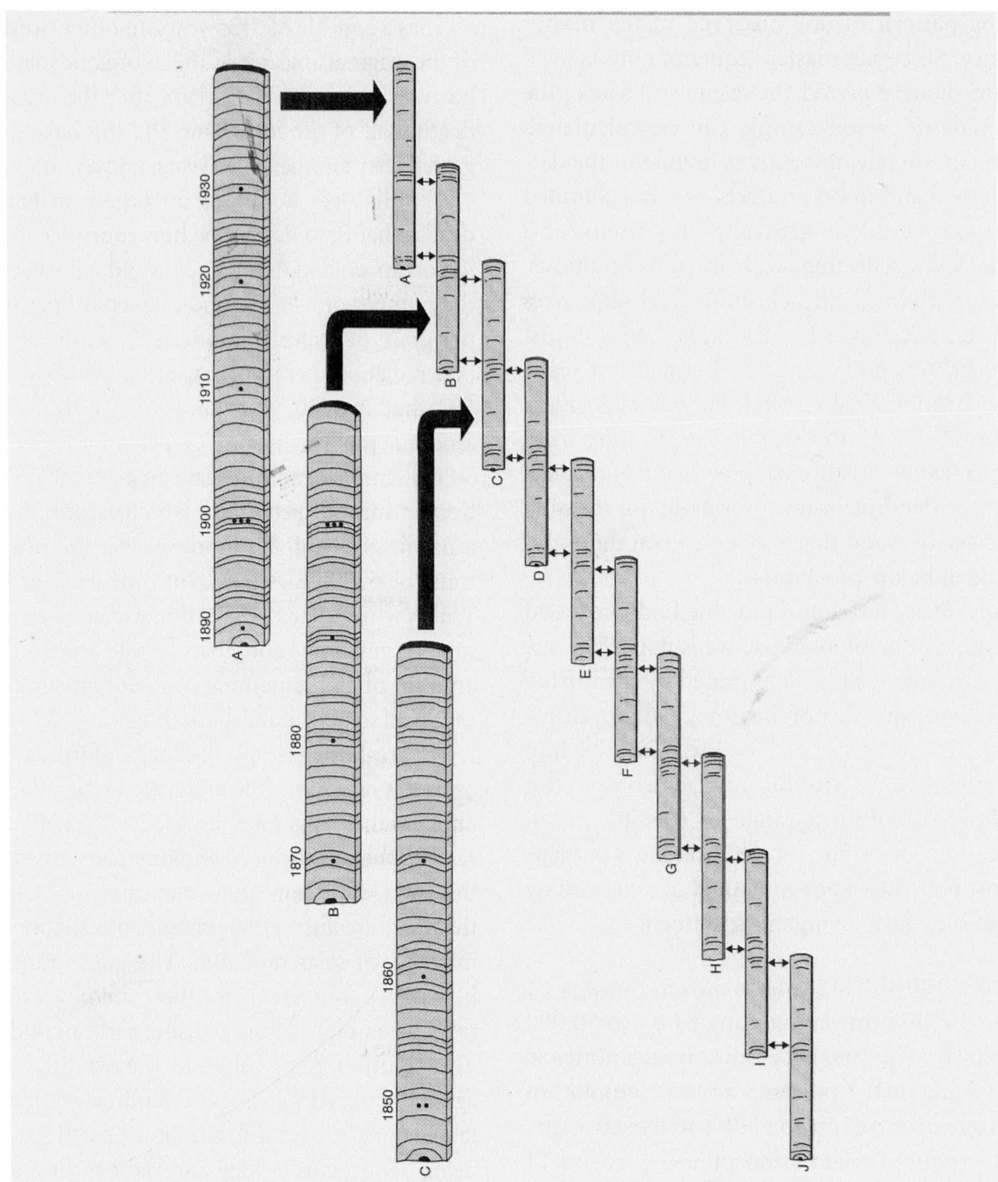

Figure 2–2 Dendrochronology

In order to establish a tree-ring chronology, core samples are removed from living trees, and the annual rings established. Wood specimens taken from other sources are matched up with specific years from the control cores in order to establish a date. In a similar manner, cores from trees of varying, overlapping ages can be compared in order to push back the dendrochronological record even farther into the past.

Source: Fagan BF. 2000. In the Beginning: An Introduction to Archaeology. Upper Saddle River, NJ: Prentice Hall. p 142. Reproduced with permission from Prentice Hall.

Accelerated mass spectrometry (AMS) radiocarbon dating provides a number of advantages over traditional radiocarbon dating, and has revolutionized the dating of archaeological specimens. First, this new method can date specimens that are up to 80 000 years old because it is more capable of accurately measuring minute quantities of ^{14}C (Brown, 1992). It also has the advantage of requiring

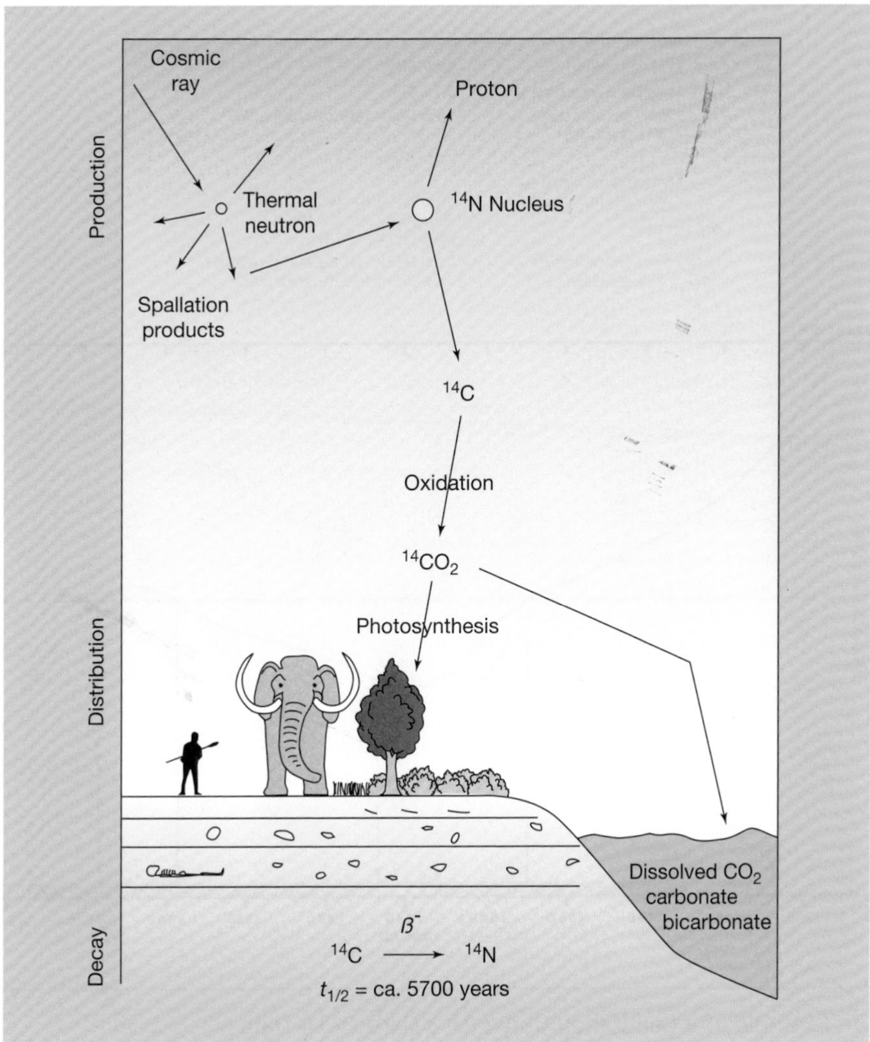

Figure 2–3 The Carbon-14 Cycle

Source: Taylor, RE. 1997. The Carbon-14 Cycle, Radiocarbon Dating. In: Taylor RE, Aitken, MJ, editors. Chronometric Dating in Archaeology. New York: Plenum. Copyright © 1997 by Plenum Publishers. Reprinted by permission of Plenum Publishers.

considerably less raw material to generate a useful date. Since the material to be dated is destroyed in the testing process, the smaller the sample required, the smaller the portion of the archaeological specimen that needs to be sacrificed. Taking only a very small sample is crucial when dating extremely rare items like a unique Northwest Coast atlatl (spear-throwing tool) (Fladmark et al., 1987). The reduced sample size also enables the dating of carbon that clearly derives from the organic component of bone (*collagen*). This greatly reduces the risk of sampling and dating carbon that may have percolated into the bone from groundwater.

Potassium-Argon Dating and Argon-Argon Dating. Potassium-40 (^{40}K), a radioactive form of potassium, decays at an established rate and forms argon-40 (^{40}Ar). The half-life of ^{40}K is a known quantity, so the age of a material containing potassium can be measured by the amount of ^{40}K it contains compared with the amount of ^{40}Ar (Gentner and Lippolt, 1969) that it also contains.

^{40}K (Potassium-40): a radioactive form of potassium that decays at an established rate and forms argon-40 used in K-Ar dating.

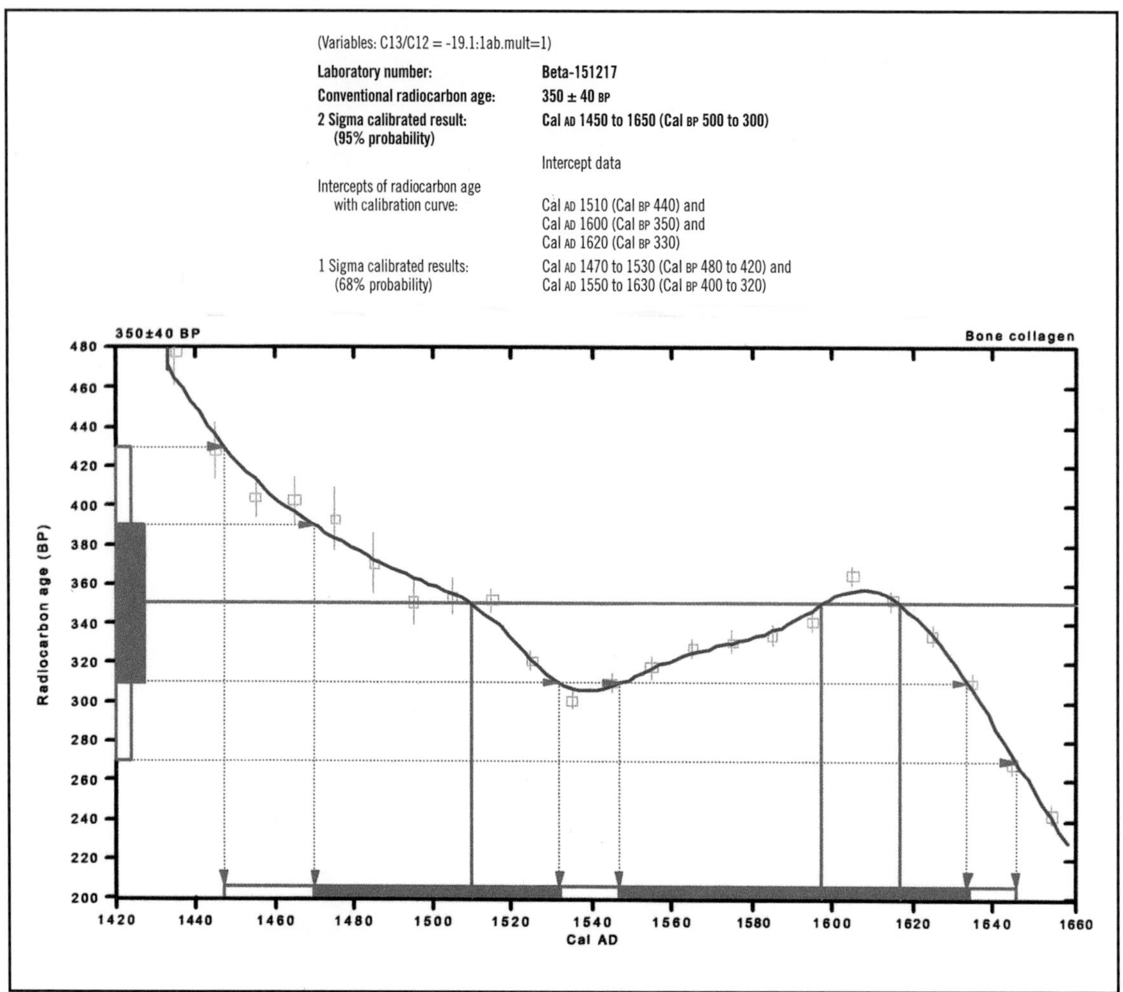

Figure 2–4 An Example of a Calibration Curve for a Carbon-14 Date

This example is based on AMS dating of collagen extracted from bone. Here a conventional radiocarbon age of 350 ± 40 years ago is obtained. In order to calibrate this age, the estimate and its outer limits (40 years on either side for a 66-percent probability and 80 years on either side for a 95-percent probability of being correct) are plotted against the C-14 dates taken on wood dated by dendrochronology. The resultant fluctuations reflect variations in atmospheric carbon during this time period. By examining the points at which the C-14 date limits cross the calibration curve, we come up with a calibrated estimate of the age of the specimen. In this case, the C-14 date of 350 years B.P. crosses the calibration curve at three different points—the years 1510, 1600, and 1620. As a result, the calibration makes the estimate less well defined with the specimen being between 300 and 500 years old or from between A.D. 1450 and A.D. 1650.

Source: Courtesy of Beta Analytic Inc., Miami, Florida.

Radioactive potassium's (^{40}K's) half-life is very long—1330 million years. This means that **potassium-argon (K-Ar) dating** may date samples from 5000 years old up to 3 billion years old.

The K-Ar method is applied to date potassium-rich minerals in rock, not the fossils that may be found in the rock. While it is an absolute dating technique, it is nevertheless indirect in that it is used

Potassium-Argon (K-Ar) Dating: a chronometric dating method that uses the rate of decay of a radioactive form of potassium (^{40}K) into argon (^{40}Ar) to date samples from 5000 to 3 billion years old. The K-Ar method dates the minerals and rocks in a deposit, not the fossils themselves.

to date geological deposits or layers that temporally surround the fossils or artifacts of interest. Very high temperatures, which for example occur during a volcanic event, drive off any original argon in the rock. Such volcanic events might involve the deposition of lava, or the accumulation of volcanic dust over top of the fossil-bearing strata. Therefore, the amount of argon that accumulates afterward from the decay of radioactive potassium is directly related to the amount of time since the volcanic event has passed. This type of dating has been extremely useful in East Africa, where volcanic events have occurred frequently since about 24 million years ago (Klein, 1989). If the material to be dated is not rich in potassium, or the area did not experience any high-temperature events, other methods of absolute dating are required.

One problem with the K-Ar method is that the amounts of potassium and argon must be measured from different rock samples, so that researchers must assume that the potassium and argon are evenly distributed in all the rock samples from a particular stratum. Researchers got around this problem by developing the **^{40}Ar-^{39}Ar dating** method. After measuring the amount of ^{40}Ar, a researcher, by using a nuclear reactor, converts another kind of argon, ^{39}Ar, to potassium so that the potassium/argon ratio can be measured from the same sample (Brown, 1988; Bilsborough, 1992).

Fission-Track Dating. The **fission-track dating** method is another way to determine the absolute age of fossil deposits (Fleischer et al., 1965). Like the K-Ar method, it dates minerals contemporaneous with the deposit in which fossils are found and it also requires the prior occurrence of a high-temperature event, such as a volcanic eruption. The kinds of samples it can date—such as crystal, glass, and many uranium-rich minerals—include a much wider variety than those that can be dated by the K-Ar method. The age range of fission-track dating, like that of K-Ar dating, is extensive—20 years to 5 billion years (Fleischer and Hart, Jr., 1972).

How does it work? This method is basically the simplest of all the methods discussed here. It entails counting the number of paths or tracks etched in the sample by the fission, or explosive division, of uranium atoms as they disintegrate. Scientists know that ^{238}U, the most common uranium isotope, decays at a slow, steady rate. This decay takes the form of spontaneous fission, and each separate fission leaves a scar or track on the sample, which can be seen through a microscope when chemically treated. To find the age of a sample, one counts the tracks, then measures their ratio to the uranium content of the sample.

The fission-track method was used to date Bed I at Olduvai Gorge in Tanzania, East Africa, where some early hominin remains were found (Fleischer et al., 1965). And the results corroborated earlier K-Ar estimates that the site dated back close to 2 million years. That the K-Ar and fission-track methods use different techniques and have different sources of error makes them effective as checks on each other. When the two methods support each other, they provide very reliable evidence.

Palaeomagnetic Dating. Most fossils of interest to anthropologists occur in sedimentary rocks, but the potassium-argon and argon-argon methods are suitable only for dating igneous rocks. When rock of any kind forms, it records the ancient magnetic field of the earth, which has reversed itself many times. **Palaeomagnetic dating** can identify the geomagnetic patterns in rocks and therefore date the fossils within those rocks. Strictly speaking,

^{40}Ar-^{39}Ar Dating Method: used in conjunction with potassium-argon dating, this method gets around the problem of needing different rock samples to estimate potassium and argon. A nuclear reactor is used to convert the ^{39}Ar to ^{39}K, on the basis of which the amount of ^{40}K can be estimated. In this way, both argon and potassium can be estimated from the same rock sample.

Fission-Track Dating: a chronometric dating method used to date crystal, glass, and many uranium-rich materials contemporaneous with fossils or deposits that are from 20 to 5 billion years old. This dating method entails counting the tracks or paths of decaying uranium-isotope atoms in the sample and then comparing the number of tracks with the uranium content of the sample.

Palaeomagnetic Dating: a method used to identify the geomagnetic patterns in rocks, and to date the fossils within those rocks.

palaeomagnetic dating is not an absolute dating method, but geomagnetic time periods have been dated absolutely in conjunction with potassium-argon dating. Palaeomagnetic dating has been used to date primate finds from the Eocene and Miocene epochs (Kappelman, 1993).

Uranium-Series Dating. The decay rates of two kinds of uranium, ^{235}U and ^{238}U, into other isotopes (such as ^{230}Th, thorium) have also proved useful for dating *Homo sapiens* (modern human) sites, particularly in caves where there are stalagmites and other calcite formations. Because water that seeps into caves usually contains uranium but not thorium, the calcite formations trap uranium. The time that has elapsed since the formation of the materials can be estimated from the ratio of those isotopes—a process called **uranium-series dating**. The thorium-uranium ratio is useful for dating cave sites less than 300 000 years old where there are no volcanic rocks, which could be dated using the potassium-argon method. Early *Homo sapiens* from European cave sites in Germany, Hungary, and Wales were dated this way (Brown, 1992; Schwarcz, 1993).

Thermoluminescence Dating. Many minerals emit light when they are heated (*thermoluminescence*), even before they become red hot. This so-called "cold light" comes from the release under heat of "outside" electrons trapped in atoms within the crystal structure of the material. **Thermoluminescence dating** (Aitken, 1985) is based on the principle that if an object is heated to a high temperature during its production or use, it will release all its trapped electrons. This is the process that clay undergoes when it is fired to produce a pot. Subsequent to heating, the object continues to trap electrons from radioactive elements (potassium, thorium, uranium) found in the sediments around it. The greater the time interval subsequent to its last firing, the greater the accumulation of electrons.

The amount of thermoluminescence emitted when the object is heated during testing allows researchers to calculate the age of the object. Of course, the analyst must have a sample of sediment that was associated with the object (for example, the surrounding soil in which a clay pot is found). This will determine the kind and amount of radiation that the object has been exposed to subsequent to its last heating event. Thermoluminescence dating is well suited to samples of ancient pottery, brick, tile, or terracotta that were originally heated to a high temperature when they were made. This method can also be applied to burnt flint tools, hearth stones, lava or lava-covered objects, meteorites, and meteor craters (Aitken, 1985).

Electron Spin Resonance Dating. **Electron spin resonance dating** is a technique that, like thermoluminescence dating, measures trapped electrons from surrounding radioactive material. In this case, the method is different. The material to be dated is exposed to varying magnetic fields, and a spectrum of the microwaves absorbed by the tested material is obtained. Since no heating is required for this technique, electron spin resonance is especially useful for dating organic material such as bone and shell, which decompose if heated (Aitken, 1985).

Amino Acid Racemization. **Amino acid racemization** is a non-radiometric technique

Uranium-Series Dating: a technique for dating *Homo sapiens* sites that uses the decay of two kinds of uranium (^{235}U and ^{238}U) into other isotopes (such as ^{230}Th—thorium). Particularly useful in cave sites. Different types of uranium-series dating use different isotope ratios.

Thermoluminescence Dating: a dating technique that is well suited to samples of ancient pottery, brick, tile, or terracotta, which (when they were made) were heated to a high temperature that released trapped electrons from radioactive elements around it; the electrons trapped after manufacture emit light when heated, so the age of the object can be estimated by measuring how much light is emitted when the object is heated.

Electron Spin Resonance Dating: like thermoluminescence dating, this technique measures trapped electrons from surrounding radioactive material. The material to be dated is exposed to varying magnetic fields in order to obtain a spectrum of the microwaves absorbed by the tested material. Because no heating is required for this technique, electron spin resonance is especially useful for dating organic materials, such as bone and shell, that decompose if heated.

Amino Acid Racemization: a non-radiometric technique for dating materials that can be applied to organic material such as bone, mollusc shells, and eggshells.

Table 2–1 Summary of Dating Techniques Available to Archaeologists

Name	Age Range	Materials Dated
Relative		
Stratigraphy		anything between two clearly defined sediment layers
F-U-N trio		bone and teeth
Absolute		
Amino Acid Racemization	2000 to 1 million years ago	bone, charcoal, other organic material
Dendrochronology	Up to 9000 years ago	wood
Electron Spin Resonance	Up to 1 million years ago	bone and shell
Fission-Track	20 to 5 billion years ago	crystal, glass, and many uranium-rich minerals
Obsidian Hydration	Up to 800 000 years ago	volcanic glass
Palaeomagnetic	Up to 10 000 years ago	geological deposits
Potassium-Argon (K-Ar)	5000 to 3 billion years ago	volcanic rock
Radiocarbon (^{14}C)	Up to 50 000 years ago	bone, mollusc shells, eggshells
Thermoluminescence	Unlimited	baked clay, pottery, and burnt rocks
Uranium-Series	Less than 300 000 years ago	calcite formations

that can be applied to organic material such as bone, mollusc shells, and eggshells. It is useful for dating materials from a few centuries old to several hundred thousand years old. Most amino acids in protein occur in one of two forms termed *D-* and *L-isomers.* Both have the same molecular structure, but are mirror images of one another.

Only L-isomers are found in living organisms. When an organism dies, maintenance of the L-form ceases and there is a slow process toward equal distributions of the L- and D-isomers. This process of change in composition of the amino acids is called *racemization,* and can be applied to dating prehistoric shell and bone—the older a fossil shell or bone, the further along the process of racemization should be.

Obsidian Hydration. *Obsidian* is naturally formed volcanic glass, used by many prehistoric populations for the production of extremely sharp-edged tools. When a piece of obsidian is newly exposed to the atmosphere through natural forces or human activity, that surface begins to absorb water. This process is known as **obsidian hydration**. The layer that is being weathered is invisible, but its thickness can be measured. The thickness will depend on the time it has been exposed, as well as the amount of moisture available, and what kind of sediment surrounded the artifact (Fagan, 2000). Obsidian hydration can be used as both a relative and an absolute dating technique for tools fashioned from obsidian.

Each dating technique has its own benefits (see Table 2–1). Which ones are used will be determined by the material available and the expected age of the remains to be tested. Overall, anthropologists, whether examining archaeological sites or palaeoanthropological locales, use the techniques we have described to gather information about remains that they find. In the next chapter we will look at ways in which they interpret this information to reconstruct the past.

Obsidian Hydration: the absorption of water by a piece of obsidian when it is newly exposed to the atmosphere through natural forces or human activity. The layer that is being weathered is invisible, but its thickness can be measured and will depend on the time it has been exposed.

Summary

1. Understanding past human life from the archaeological record requires expertise in a variety of areas. Archaeological techniques for the excavation of remains are used so as to maximize the amount of information gained during the excavation of a site.
2. Archaeological context, or the association of artifacts and features with one another, is a crucial aspect of archaeological interpretation. Without controlled provenience, archaeological data are of little value.
3. The formation of sites is an important aspect for understanding what they represent. The study of taphonomy—post-depositional changes to remains—is critical for reconstructing the past.
4. The process of fossilization is a relatively rare process in which the organic components of an organism are replaced with minerals percolating through the surrounding environment over a period of thousands of years.
5. Site prospection includes a variety of techniques including surface and subsurface surveying, field walking, test pitting, and trenching.
6. Excavation requires control over spatial aspects of a site, which can be accomplished by establishing a grid system, with more detailed mapping and documentation of recoveries within subunits relative to the grid location of the control square. The careful recording of all information within the grid allows for all data to be incorporated into a single system at the end of the excavation.
7. Both relative and absolute dating techniques can be employed to assess the age of a site. Relative techniques like stratigraphy provide a basis on which to determine whether a feature or object is younger or older than other features in adjacent layers. Absolute dating techniques provide methods for assessing the age of an object or site in actual years.

Glossary Terms

Critical Questions

1. Why is careful mapping and recording of archaeological sites so crucial for interpreting the past?
2. How do relative dating methods differ from absolute dating methods? Are there circumstances when one technique is more appropriate than another? Explain your answer.

Internet Exercises

1. Go to the webpage for the Canadian Archaeological Association at **www.canadianarchaeology.com**. Explore the resources available there, and make some constructive criticisms about this public face of the CAA.
2. Visit and review archaeological field techniques at the Parks Canada site at **http://www.pc.gc.ca/docs/pc/guide/fp-es/tdm-contents_e.asp**
3. Go to **http://www.archaeolink.com/dating_archaeological_sites_arti.htm** and explore how various archaeological projects are using different kinds of dating techniques.

Suggested Reading

Bahn PG. 2001. Archaeology: Very Short Introduction. Oxford, UK: Oxford University Press. A survey of the technological developments in the field of archaeology, and how archaeology can be used. This popular book explores the main areas of archaeological research today, and the origin and development of the field.

Collis J. 2004. Digging Up the Past: An Introduction to Archaeological Excavation. Stroud: Sutton Publishing. An introduction to archaeological excavation techniques.

Peregrine PN. 2001. Archaeological Research: A Brief Introduction. Upper Saddle River, NJ: Prentice Hall. This concise yet thorough introduction to archaeological research presents students with the basic methods of data collection, analysis, and interpretation. Focusing on the research process itself, the text explores why archaeologists choose particular methods over others, along with the varying circumstances of their research. It also provides a brief overview of archaeological literature and legal and ethical issues in the fields.

RECONSTRUCTING THE PAST: ANALYSIS AND INTERPRETATION

CHAPTER OUTLINE

The relationship between humans and their environment has long been a focus of study, particularly among archaeologists and physical anthropologists. To reconstruct how past populations lived, researchers examine evidence from the archaeological record. They draw upon a variety of related disciplines to help reconstruct former ecological conditions, determine what people ate and how and where they obtained their food, and study the diseases of the past. Analysis of human remains is important for determining diet and disease, as well as revealing demographic information, such as lifespan and infant mortality. Settlement patterns are another focus of study, specifically, where people established permanent and seasonal dwellings, as well as the size of the settlements, how many people lived there, and how long the sites were occupied. The archaeological record can also give clues about the society itself—whether some people had a higher socio-economic status than others, for example, and what the patterns of resource distribution and allocation were. In this chapter, we explore some of the anthropological methods for reconstructing these aspects of lives of past populations.

Reconstructing the past is not an easy task. It is not enough to simply dig up material left behind by people who once lived in a place. Rather, it requires the careful analysis of the environment in which the materials are found in order to say something about the circumstances by which that material came to be there. Archaeologists and others attempt to understand a past society as it is reflected in the remains of the everyday belongings of past peoples. For example, if we want to understand how a community changed over the course of its history, we need to recognize that those changes would have been influenced by a variety of factors, including changes in the environment, in population numbers, and in culture, to name a few. However, unravelling these factors is sometimes difficult. The archaeologist has to pay careful attention to the context in which material culture is found. Further, while material culture is a direct reflection of past culture, the archaeological record is not always a direct reflection of material culture. A number of factors can affect where the remains of material culture are found in the archaeological record and the patterns of deposition. The archaeologist must also be able to recognize the influence of these factors.

Analyzing Artifacts

Conservation is the process of treating artifacts, ecofacts, and in some cases even features to stop decay and, if possible, even reverse the deterioration process. Some conservation is very simple, involving only cleaning and drying the item. Some conservation is highly complex, involving long-term chemical treatments and, in some cases, long-term storage under controlled conditions. The so-called "Ice Man," for example, the frozen remains of a man who lived 5000 years ago found in 1993 in the Italian Alps, is kept in permanently glacial-like conditions after investigators found to their dismay that warming the remains for study induced the growth of mould. The archaeologists removed the mould, but decided that his remains would have to be kept under the same conditions that preserved them in the first place, and so a complex storage facility had to be built to recreate the glacial environment in which he was originally found (Nash, 2001; Makristathis et al., 2002; Dickson et al., 2003; Murphy, Jr. et al., 2003).

Reconstruction is like building a puzzle—but a three-dimensional puzzle where you're not sure which pieces belong and you know not all of the pieces are there. First, materials have to be sorted into similar types. For example, to reconstruct ceramics from a site, all the ceramics have to be sorted into types with similar colour, decoration, and shapes. Then the similar pieces are compared to see if any seem to come from the same vessel. Once all the pieces thought to be from the same vessel are located, they can be assembled. Reconstruction is clearly a long, difficult process—in some cases taking years.

What Can We Learn from Artifacts?

Once conservation and reconstruction are complete, the archaeologist or paleoanthropologist can begin to analyze the artifacts they've found. Archaeologists

Conservation: techniques used on archaeological materials to stop or reverse the process of decay.

A conservator applying preservative to a decaying Alaskan totem pole.

have developed specific and often unique ways to analyze the many different types of artifacts. Stone tools are examined in different ways from ceramics, and both are examined differently from bone. But there are some commonalities in the way artifacts are analyzed, regardless of what they are made of.

First, archaeologists typically examine the *form* of an artifact—how it is shaped. For most common artifacts, such as lithics and ceramics, forms are known well enough to be grouped into typologies. Placing artifacts into a **typology** is often the primary purpose of *formal analysis*, because typologies allow archaeologists to place a particular artifact into context with other artifacts found at the site or even at other sites. Typologies often provide a lot of information about an artifact, including its age, the species or culture with which it is affiliated, and in some cases even how it was made, used, or exchanged in the past. Second, archaeologists often measure artifacts, recording their size in various, often strictly defined, dimensions. Such analysis is used to group artifacts into a typology. Figure 3–1 shows the standard measurements taken from projectile points.

Typology: a way of organizing artifacts in categories based on their particular characteristics.

Third, archaeologists often attempt to understand how an artifact was made. By examining the material the artifact is made from and how that material was manipulated, archaeologists can learn about the technology, economy, and exchange systems of the peoples who made the artifact. For example, if the material is not locally available, that means the people traded for it. Archaeologists can also study present-day peoples and how they make similar artifacts in order to understand how ancient artifacts were made.

Finally, archaeologists attempt to understand the function of an artifact. Knowing the function of an artifact allows the archaeologist a direct window into ancient life. Since this information is so important, a number of sophisticated techniques

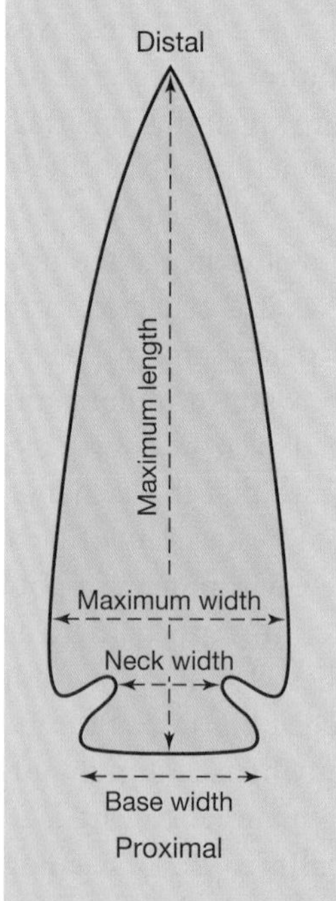

Figure 3–1 Standard Metrical Measurements of Chipped Stone Tools

have been developed to determine how artifacts were used. For stone, bone, and wood tools, a technique called *use-wear analysis* has been developed, which can determine how a tool was used through the careful examination of the wear on its edges. For ceramic vessels, techniques have been developed to extract residues trapped in the clay and determine what the vessel held.

But what can archaeologists really learn by placing artifacts in typologies through formal and metric analysis, or by learning how an artifact was manufactured and used? Knowing how an artifact was made allows the archaeologist to understand the technology and technical abilities of peoples in the past. Artifacts and their context with other features can help inform us about the social organization of a past people and may also reveal religious beliefs. Even gender roles can be explored archaeologically (see New Perspectives on Gender, "Women in the Shell Mound Archaic").

Analyzing Human Remains

Osteology or skeletal biology is the specialized subdiscipline of physical anthropology that deals with the biological remains of humans from past populations. Osteological reconstruction contributes a significant amount of information to our understanding of the past. The analysis of demographic structure (palaeodemography), health and disease (palaeopathology), diet and nutrition (palaeonutrition), as well as population affinity are just a few of the areas that skeletal biology can contribute to.

The first step to any analysis is identifying skeletal remains as being human. While this is relatively straightforward for well-preserved samples, this can be a difficult task for small fragmentary skeletal remains. For early hominins the task of identification and classification becomes increasingly difficult. Estimation of the age and sex of individuals within a skeletal sample is the first step toward interpretation.

Estimation of Age

The age of an adult skeleton can be estimated using a variety of techniques. These methods are referred to as **skeletal age-indicator techniques**. These techniques depend on both *macroscopic*—visible by naked eye—observation and *microscopic* changes in the shape and structure of bone for estimating the age of an individual. Many macroscopic techniques focus on the pattern of age-related degeneration of bone. These include examination of the pubic symphysis and auricular surface on the hipbone, the closure of sutures between bones on the skull, and the ends of the fourth rib (see Figure 3–2). Other methods focus on **remodelling** to see how microscopic fractures may occur normally from everyday wear and tear. The physical anthropologist is trained to evaluate several criteria that indicate age, and then estimate an overall age range for the individuals within the sample.

The estimation of age from the skeletal remains of children is based on the development of dental and skeletal tissues—that is, the growing bones and developing teeth (see Figure 3–3 on page 51). Age estimation for a child is much easier and more accurate than age estimation for an adult. While there are fewer specific techniques that can be used, these methods have a smaller range of error than do most adult aging techniques. Overall, estimation of age of a juvenile is accurate to within a range of about half a year.

Sex Determination

It is widely recognized by physical anthropologists that the pelvis or hipbone is the most reliable part of the skeleton for determination of sex. Both metric (based on measurements) and non-metric or morphological (based on size and shape) techniques are better than 95 percent accurate for correctly

Osteology: the study of the form and function of the skeleton.
Skeletal Age-Indicator Techniques: osteological techniques that are used to estimate the age at death of an individual from skeletal remains.

Remodelling: occurs after growth has ceased and replaces old tissue with new formed bone to maintain bone strength from microscopic fractures from normal biomechanical stress.

NEW PERSPECTIVES ON GENDER

Women in the Shell Mound Archaic

One of the main issues addressed by archaeologists interested in gender is how we can learn about and understand gender roles in prehistoric cultures. Gender roles might seem impossible to study in archaeological contexts. How is gender preserved in the archaeological record? How can knowledge about gender roles be recovered? Information about gender roles can be recovered if one maintains an awareness of how material culture that is associated ethnographically with particular gender roles changes over time. Archaeologists argue that such an awareness leads not only to a better understanding of gender in prehistory but can also lead to a fuller understanding of prehistoric cultures overall.

An example is Cheryl Claassen's work on the Shell Mound Archaic culture of the Tennessee River valley. The Shell Mound Archaic represents the remains of people who lived in Tennessee and Kentucky between about 5500 and 3000 years ago. They were hunters and gatherers who lived in small villages, and probably moved seasonally between summer and winter communities. The most distinctive feature of the Shell Mound Archaic is the large mounds of mollusc shells they constructed for burying their dead. Tens of thousands of shells were piled together to create these mounds. Yet, around 3000 years ago, shellfishing and thus the creation of shell burial mounds stopped abruptly. Claassen wondered why.

Suggested explanations include climate change, overexploitation of shellfish themselves, and emigration of shellfishing peoples from the area. None has proven wholly satisfactory. In contemporary cultures shellfishing is typically done by women and children, and Claassen wondered whether an approach that considered gender roles might be more productive. She decided to approach the problem through the perspective of women's workloads, since it would have been women who would have most likely been the ones shellfishing. The end of shellfishing would have meant that women would have had a lot of free time—free time that could have been put to use in some other way. What might have

determining sex (see Figure 3–4 on page 52). Accuracy rates based on other parts of the skeleton are usually lower than those using the hipbone.

Unfortunately, determination of sex from the skeleton is restricted to remains of sexually mature adults. A variety of studies have investigated traits that might be **sexually dimorphic**—showing size and shape differences between males and females—in infants and juveniles, but only a few studies of such traits have demonstrated sufficient levels of accuracy to warrant applying these traits in osteological analyses. More promising, but still restricted by costs, are methods of sex determination that are based on *ancient DNA* extracted from the bones or teeth of individuals.

Ancient DNA

The ability to extract DNA from prehistoric remains has become an important aspect of anthropological research. Determination of sex was one of the first areas of study for the application of DNA techniques to human skeletal samples. The ability to accurately identify sex from DNA is relatively straightforward now, although the time and cost associated with this methodology is still prohibitive for large samples. Another area of focus has been on population affinity or identification of maternal biological lineages through the analysis of mitochondrial DNA, from analysis of DNA extracted from skeletal samples. And most recently, researchers have begun trying to identify the DNA of agents associated with diseases that can be identified in the skeletal remains of individuals from the past. All of these areas, and those that have yet to be explored, will greatly enrich our understanding of past populations and how they lived.

A variety of researchers in Canada have been working in the field of ancient DNA for over a decade now. In 1996, the Paleo-DNA lab was established at Lakehead University. A number of projects have resulted from research and collaborations at this facility including studies of the evolution of diseases (Donoghue et al., 2004, 2005; Larcombe et al., 2005; Spigelman et al., 2002), the bioarchaeology

Sexually Dimorphic: refers to a species in which males differ markedly from females in size and appearance.

changed to lead women to stop shellfishing? Would something else have perhaps become more important, so that women's labour was needed more for those other tasks?

Women's labour might have been redirected toward domesticated crops. There is archaeological evidence that about 3000 years ago several productive but highly labour-intensive crops became widely used. For example, *chenopodium,* one of the more plentiful and nutritious of these new crops, has tiny seeds that require considerable labour to harvest, clean, and process. Women were likely the ones burdened with such work. They not only would have harvested these crops but also would have been the ones to process and prepare meals from them. Thus, the emergence of agricultural economies would have required women to undertake new labour in food production and processing that may well have forced them to stop other tasks, like shellfishing.

The development of agricultural activities might also have brought about changes in ritual and ceremonialism. The shell burial mounds were clearly central to Shell Mound Archaic death ceremonies. Considerable labour, mostly by women, would have been required to collect the shells and to build these mounds. Later societies in the region buried their dead in earthen mounds. Could this be a reflection of the new importance earth had in an emerging agricultural economy? If so, what role did women play in ceremonies of death and burial? If they were no longer the providers of the raw materials needed for burial, does that mean their status in society as a whole changed?

We may never know exactly why the Shell Mound Archaic disappeared, or how women's work and women's roles in society changed. But as Claassen points out, taking a gender perspective provides new avenues along which to pursue answers to these questions, and interesting new questions to pursue.

Sources: Claassen C. 1991. Gender, Shellfishing, and the Shell Mound Archaic. In: Gero J, Conkey M, editors. Engendering Archaeology: Women and Prehistory. Oxford: Blackwell. pp 276–300.

Claassen C. 2002. Gender and Archaeology. In: Peregrine PN, Ember CR, Ember M, editors. Archaeology: Original Readings in Method and Practice. Upper Saddle River, NJ: Prentice Hall. pp 210–224. Also in: Ember CR, Ember M, editors. New Directions in Anthropology. Upper Saddle River, NJ: Prentice Hall, CD-ROM, 2003.

of ancient Egyptians (Graver et al., 2001; Molto, 2001), and most recently, the forensic archaeological analysis of soldiers from Vimy Ridge in 2007. In 1999, Dr. Shelley Saunders, a Canada Research Chair in Human Disease and Population Origins, established the Institute for the Study of Ancient and Forensic DNA at McMaster University, now the McMaster Ancient DNA Centre directed by Dr. Hendrik Poinar. A variety of research has been undertaken at the lab including palaeopathological studies of humans and animals (Yang, Bathurst, and Barta, 2004), and forensic identification in historical archaeology (Dudar et al., 2003; Katzenberg et al., 2005). Dr. Poinar and his team continue to focus on a variety of areas including the evolution of HIV, the domestication of dogs in the New World (Schmutz et al., in press), early Archaic hunter-gatherers (Poinar et al., 2001) and evolutionary genetic relationships (Nielsen-Marsha et al., 2005; Poinar et al., 2006). In particular, he is interested in the preservation and extraction of ancient DNA from archaeological and forensic sources (Pääbo et al., 2004; Poinar, 1999, 2002; Poinar et al., 2006). At Simon Fraser University, Dr. Dongya Yang continues work on refining ancient DNA techniques begun at McMaster University (Yang et al., 1998, 2003; Yang and Speller, 2006; Yang and Watt, 2005) as well as recent analysis of archaeologically recovered fish and animal remains from archaeological sites on the Pacific Northwest Coast of North America (Cannon and Yang, 2006; Moss et al., 2006; Speller et al., 2005; Yang et al., 2004).

Palaeopathology

The study of palaeopathology seeks to answer questions concerning the origins, prevalence, and spread of diseases in past populations from human skeletal remains. The diagnosis and distribution of disease, within both individuals and the population, form the basis of interpretation for palaeopathological studies. Aided by macroscopic and microscopic examination, and some of the techniques already discussed, researchers attempt to identify and assess the prevalence of diseases

Palaeopathology: the study of health and disease in the past from skeletal evidence.

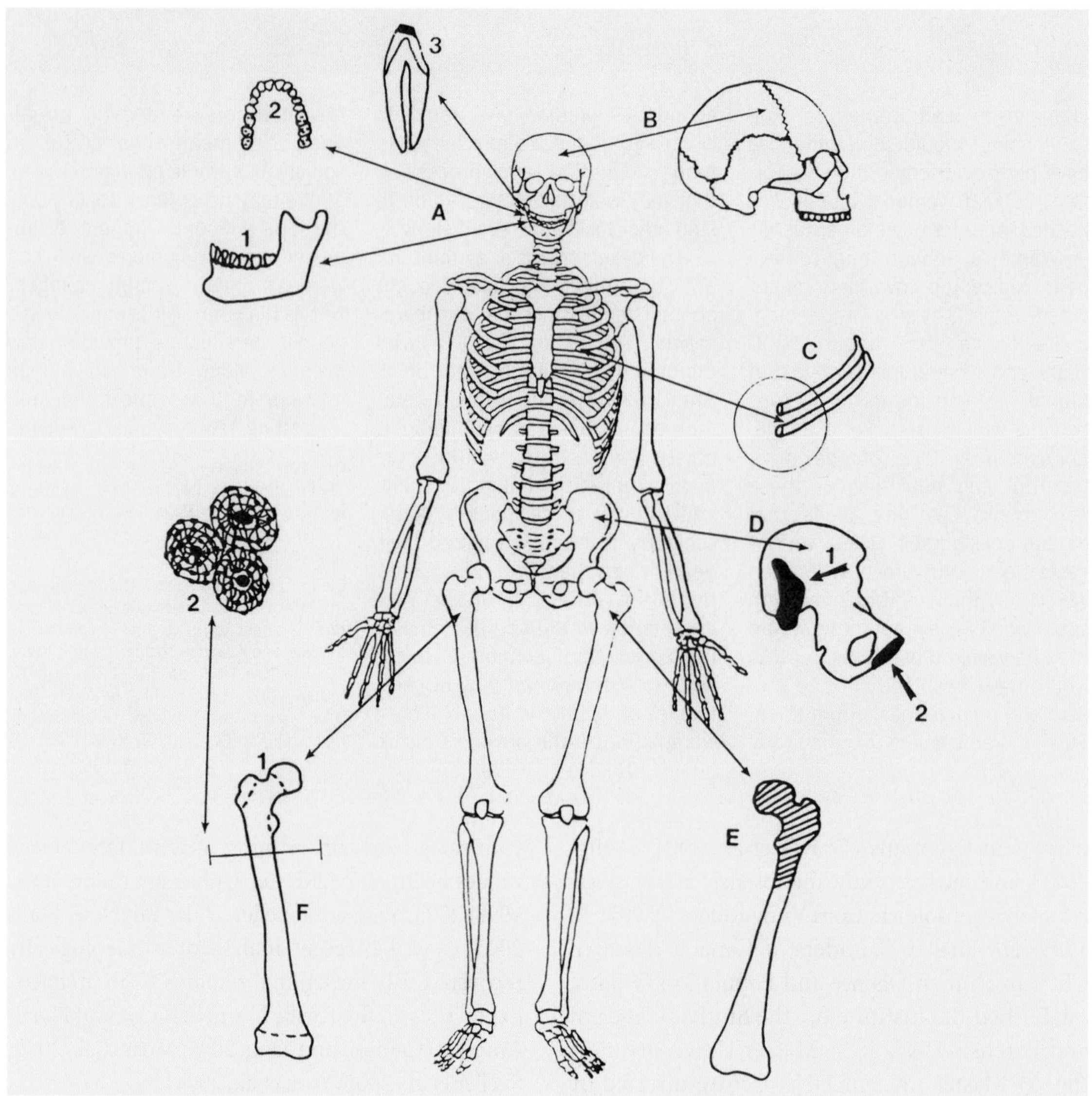

Figure 3–2 Commonly Used Skeletal Age-Indicator Techniques for Estimating the Age of Adult Remains

A: 1 dental development and eruption; 2 dental wear; 3 dental microstructure. **B**: cranial suture closure. **C**: sternal rib ends. **D**: 1 auricular surface; 2 pubic symphysis. **E**: radiographs of trabelucar bone from femur. **F**: 1 epiphyseal union; 2 cortical bone microstructure (osteon counting).

Source: Hunter J, Roberts C, Martin A. 1996. Studies in Crime: An Introduction to Forensic Archaeology. Chrysalis Books Ltd. Reprinted with permission.

within an archaeological sample. Then they may be able to draw conclusions about the prevalence of a disease within the population as a whole.

Like clinical medicine that deals with the whole person in his or her environment, palaeopathology must attempt to interpret the appearance, spread, and distribution of diseases in a biocultural context (Manchester, 1987). Increasingly, palaeopathologists have become aware that human behaviour and its social and cultural determinants play a prominent role in the distribution and spread of infectious diseases. As a result, temporal and spatial differences in most disease patterns are largely the result of cultural differences in behavioural and not biological variation (Dunn and Janes, 1986; Inhorn and Brown, 1990; Sattenspiel, 1990).

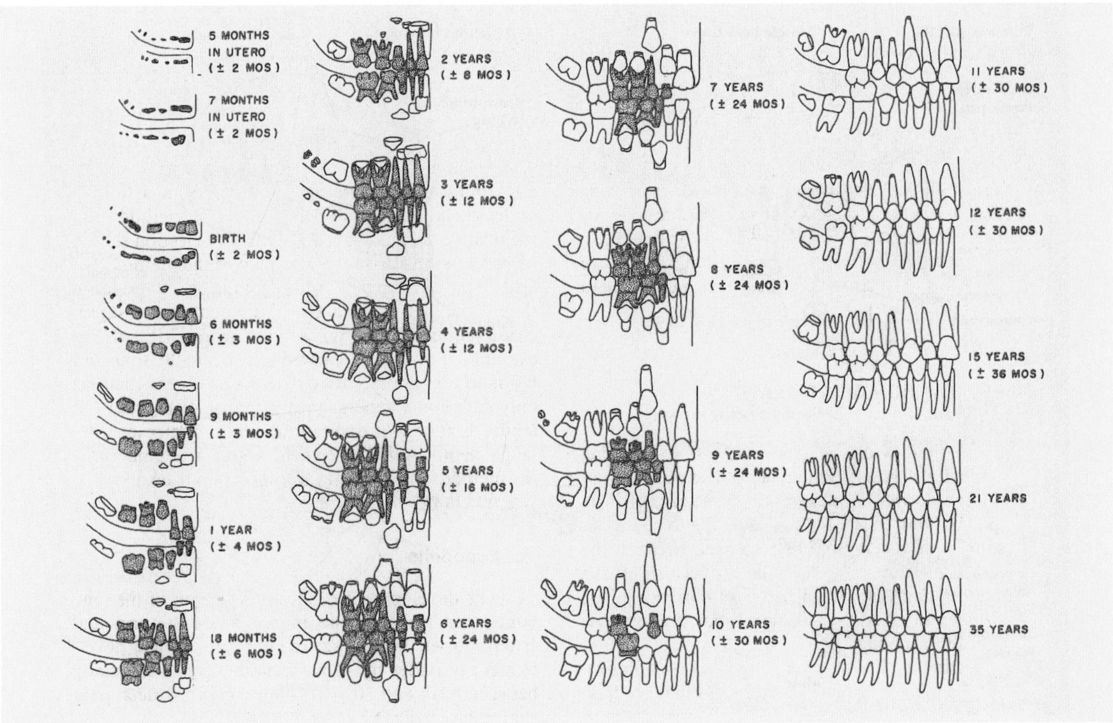

Figure 3–3 Pattern of Dental Development in Children

Age estimation in non-adult skeletons can be determined from dental development. Here a composite chart of development patterns is presented as a quick reference.

Source: Ubelaker D. 1989. Human Skeletal Remains: Excavations, Analysis, and Interpretation. Third edition. Washington: Taraxacum Press. Figure 71, p 64. Reprinted with permission.

A crucial aspect of palaeopathological studies has been to give precise descriptions and differential diagnoses from individual remains. **Differential diagnosis** is the process of listing each disease or condition that is consistent with the evidence observed, and then assessing which diagnosis is the most probable. The last few decades have seen a shift in emphasis to analysis of health and disease in populations. Interpretations of general population health from palaeopathological analyses have their limitations, however. First, only diseases that affect the hard tissues will generally be available for study, and of those, only a small percentage will actually result in changes to the skeleton. For example, pulmonary tuberculosis will affect the skeleton in only 3 to 7 percent of those individuals infected (Steinbock, 1976).

Differential Diagnosis: the assessment of potential diseases that are consistent with the observable traits/criteria on bones within an individual.

Skeletal evidence of health in the past is not limited to the effect of infectious diseases. Other conditions can leave distinct marks or lesions on bones and teeth, including but not limited to joint, autoimmune, and metabolic diseases as well as other more specific maladies such as Paget's disease. The frequency of lesions caused by any of these conditions within archaeological samples is affected by factors such as differential preservation, incomplete or biased excavation, and the age and sex distributions within the sample. Anthropologists must attempt to deal with these issues before they can make interpretations of general population health from skeletal samples.

A primary question that palaeopathologists must ask themselves is, what does the presence of infectious lesions on the skeleton mean, for both the health of the individual and the population from which such an individual comes (Ortner, 1991)? The basic assumption of palaeopathology is that there is a consistent relationship between the

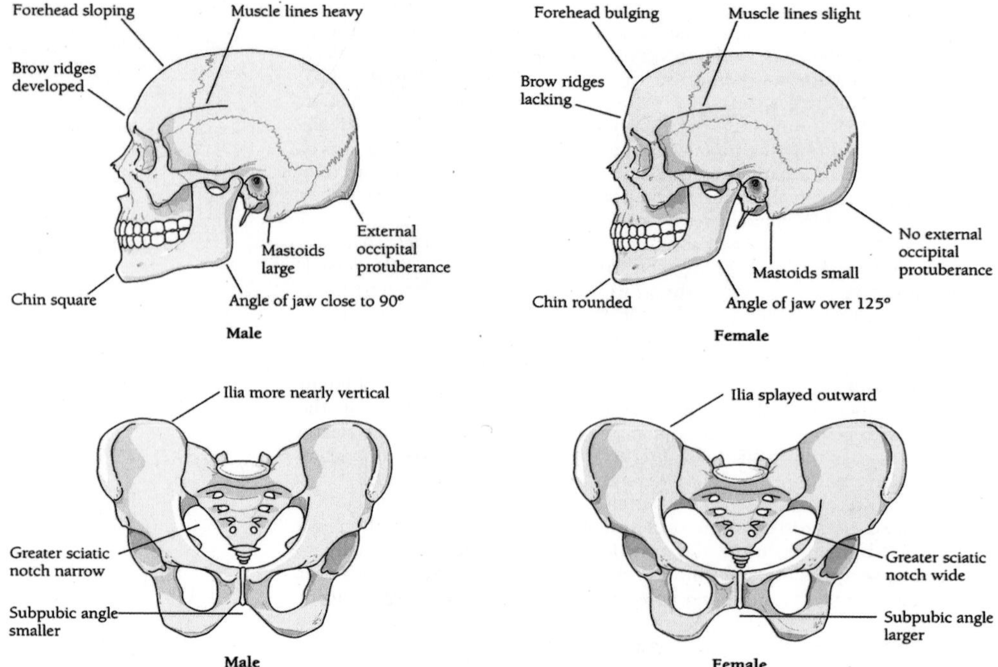

Figure 3–4 Common Traits of the Human Skeleton That Are Used to Assess Sex of Adults

Sex determination of the adult skeleton can be made from a variety of morphological techniques, as illustrated above. Determination of sex of children's skeletons cannot be done, as the growth process in children's skeletons is not yet complete.

Source: Feder KL, Park MA. 2007. Human Antiquity: An Introduction to Physical Anthropology and Archaeology. Fifth edition. New York: McGraw-Hill. Courtesy of the McGraw-Hill Companies.

presence of skeletal lesions produced by a specific disease process in the individual (infectious or otherwise), and the risks of sickness and death associated with that disease within the population as a whole (Ortner, 1991). Simply put, it is assumed that the more often you see evidence for a specific disease in the archaeological record, the greater the risk of illness or death from that disease for individuals in the living population who were exposed to it.

In the early 1990s, Jim Wood and colleagues cautioned palaeopathologists against drawing conclusions about past health based on this assumption (Wood et al., 1992). Palaeopathological interpretations of health assume that the individual immune response and environmental conditions do not influence the presence of skeletal lesions. Therefore, different levels of disease observed archaeologically must be related to cultural differences between populations (Cohen and Armelagos, 1984a; Goodman et al., 1984b; Cohen, 1989). Wood and co-workers, however, have strongly urged palaeopathologists to reconsider this supposition and critically examine the concepts of differential risk and susceptibility to disease and death within population samples. That is, each individual may or may not have the same chance of being exposed to a particular disease. Further, even when an individual is exposed, biological factors specific to the individual's immune response will result in some contracting the disease while others do not.

Many researchers have expressed concern over the fact that skeletal samples are intrinsically biased because they are the products of selective mortality (Cook and Buikstra, 1979; Cook, 1981; Saunders, 1992; Wood et al., 1992; Saunders and Hoppa, 1993). *Selective mortality* refers to the notion that skeletal samples represent not all the people who were susceptible (susceptibles) for a given age group, but only those individuals who died at that age. For example, 5-year-old individuals in a skeletal sample represent only those 5-year-olds who died and not all of the 5-year-olds who were alive in the population at risk; other surviving susceptibles continued to live, in effect contributing to, or

CORE CONCEPTS

Unlocking DNA

It appears in most living organisms that heredity is controlled by the same chemical substance, **DNA—deoxyribonucleic acid**. The possibility of extracting DNA from prehistoric bone or other tissues has, over the last decade, led to the development of intense research in the field of **ancient DNA (aDNA)**. It was first proposed in the 1980s that DNA could be successfully extracted from archaeologically recovered bone that was thousands of years old. Researchers around the world became excited by the possibilities of this new technology. However, like all new discoveries, several key methodological problems still had to be resolved. First, DNA is known to deteriorate over time. As a result, the actual quantity of DNA that might be present in a specimen could be very small and might represent comparatively fragmentary sections of the DNA sequence. Further, any DNA present might be damaged or degraded beyond the point of providing any useful information.

A significant advance in the field came with the discovery of the **polymerase chain reaction (PCR)** technique for the accurate recovery of ancient DNA. The major benefit of the PCR method is that it allows for the amplification of DNA sequences from trace amounts of the original genetic material. However, because the PCR method requires only a few molecules of DNA, it brought with it the heightened threat of sample contamination from both the burial environment and the laboratory environment. As a result, rigorous protocols have been developed to ensure the integrity of the original DNA sample, and minimize any possibilities of accidental contamination during the laboratory processing.

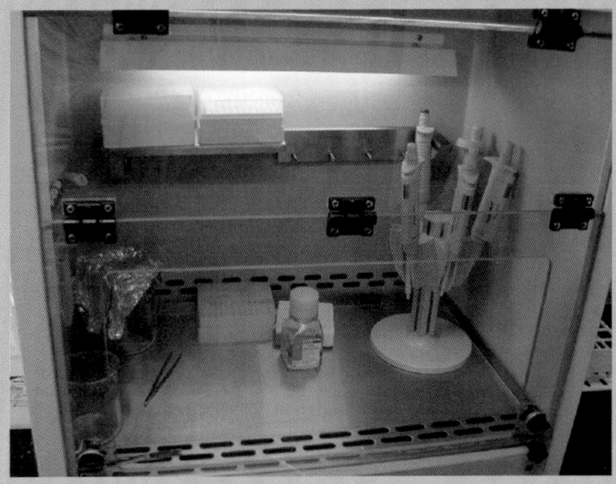

Processing ancient DNA requires meticulous control over the processing of samples. Seen here, an ultraviolet light is used to help prevent contamination.

being members of, older mortality groups (Wood et al., 1992). The obvious problem, then, is whether the evidence of disease in a skeletal sample accurately represents the real prevalence of infectious agents in the living population during the past.

A promising future direction is palaeopathological studies that seek to examine the epidemiology or the course taken by specific diseases (de Souza et al., 2003). For example, in order to better understand the true frequency of leprosy in Medieval Denmark, Jesper Boldsen demonstrated that both sensitivity and specificity of skeletal lesions had to be assessed (Boldsen, 2001). Using epidemiological concepts like this, researchers are better positioned to examine a variety of biocultural factors that might have influenced the population's response to the disease. This approach to past health has become an important focus of anthropological research.

Palaeodemography

Demography focuses on the age and sex structure of the population, and patterns of mortality, fertility, and population growth. **Palaeodemography** is the study of demographic structure in the past.

DNA (Deoxyribonucleic Acid): a long, two-stranded molecule in the genes; directs the making of an organism according to the instructions in its genetic code.
Ancient DNA (aDNA): DNA extracted from archaeologically recovered materials.
Polymerase Chain Reaction (PCR): technique for accurate recovery of ancient DNA. PCR requires only a few molecules for the amplification of DNA sequences from trace amounts of the original genetic material.
Palaeodemography: the study of demographic structure and processes in past populations from archaeological evidence.

Palaeodemographic studies have focused primarily on the interpretation of human skeletal samples recovered archaeologically. The basic assumption is that mortality statistics derived from the skeletal sample are sufficient to make inferences about the past population. As well, archaeological evidence for settlement size and distribution of settlements has been used to estimate population growth or to address broader questions of population structure in the past.

Anthropological demography of contemporary or recent historic hunter-gatherer and foraging populations can also provide us with models for prehistoric populations. This is known as **ethnographic analogy**. However, ethnographic analogy based on patterns of subsistence or mobility is extremely problematic. More recently, evidence from genetic studies has begun to be used to make inferences about long-term evolutionary changes in demographic structure in modern human populations that have lived over the past 250 000 years or so. In particular, genetic studies that examine variation within living human populations provide information on human demography since patterns of gene differences contain information about the demographic history of a species (Harpending et al., 1998).

Traditionally, palaeodemographers have used the abridged **life table** to place individuals into a series of age groups. They start by assuming that the past population numbers were **stationary**—in other words, that there was no in-migration or out-migration and the number of deaths equalled the number of births. They can then use the mean or average age-at-death in the skeletal sample to estimate life expectancy at birth. However, this assumption is not likely to apply in past populations, particularly over short periods and in small populations. In growing populations, age-at-death distributions are extremely sensitive to changes in birth rates but not to changes in death rates. Thus, if population numbers are not stationary—and changing populations never are—small variations in fertility have large effects on age-at-death distribution, while even quite large changes in mortality have virtually none (Wood et al., 1992). Recognizing this, many researchers have concluded that the age distribution of skeletal samples provides less information about mortality than it does about fertility. In fact, the same fertility and mortality patterns can produce different birth and death rates in populations with different age structures.

Two key factors that affect stationarity in populations are *growth* and *migration*. The immediate effects of migrations into or out of a population are obvious. People who move to a new location are not always representative of all age groups and therefore can affect birth and death rates unequally at the new location. Similarly, potential changes in the gene pool or genetic background of migrants can change the overall susceptibility to different kinds of diseases. The impact of such changes depends on the source of migration and the cultural forces that are propelling the migration. War or invasion, persecution, plague, and social, political, or economic factors can alter the demographic structure of a population in both the short and the long term. Failure to recognize the possible effects of migration on the age structure of past populations can distort conclusions (Johansson and Horowitz, 1986). If rates of population growth can be assessed independently of the skeletal evidence—that is, from other archaeological evidence—palaeodemographic analyses are less uncertain. However, such assessments are difficult to obtain (Moore et al., 1975; Milner et al., 1989).

In the 1970s, demographers expressed concern over the scant evidence on which to base palaeodemographic analyses. As a result, model life tables from modern demographic studies, linking death rates, birth rates, and age structure within a population, formed the basis upon which anthropological demographers began to assess life tables for past populations. Information from skeletal samples could then be compared with that in a model life

Ethnographic Analogy: method of comparative cultural study that extrapolates to the past from recent or current societies.

Life Table: a tool used by demographers to place individuals into age groups.

Stationary: in demography, a population is considered to be stationary when there is no in-migration or out-migration and the number of deaths equal the number of births per year.

table, and the fit between the model data and observed mortality distributions could then be assessed. Model life tables in anthropological demography have two functions. First, they provide a means of assessing or compensating for biased and incomplete data, and second, they allow for the estimation of fertility rates and construction of an initial population at risk—that is, all individuals alive at the time, not just those who died. In the early 1970s, Weiss developed a set of model fertility and mortality schedules derived from ethnographic samples of contemporary hunter-gatherer societies and prehistoric skeletal samples (Weiss, 1973). Many investigators agreed that demographic statistics derived from contemporary non-Western societies represented an accurate comparison to past populations. However, given the variety of conditions under which many contemporary populations live, it is difficult to be certain that ethnographic analogy will always be appropriate. Further, the application of ethnographic data to archaeological samples with sparse socio-cultural information further compounds the problem.

Ultimately, physical anthropologists have tried to improve methods for estimating age from the skeleton in order to combine individual estimates to create a demographic profile of the age structure. More recently, researchers have begun to estimate the age structure of a sample directly from the distribution of skeletal age indicator methods before assigning an age to each single individual (Hoppa and Vaupel 2002; Müller et al., 2001). While the difference is subtle, it is important. This approach attempts to avoid the broad range of error associated with estimates at the individual level. If you are interested in the pattern of distribution of mortality within a population (that is, who died at what age), then you must begin by estimating the overall age structure in the sample, and then estimate individual ages (Konigsberg and Frankenberg, 1994; Hoppa and Vaupel, 2002).

Reconstructing Past Diets

The only direct evidence for what people ate in the past is the preserved remains of the food itself. Such remains can be found in rare cases where mummified human remains may still have preserved stomach contents. Another form of direct evidence occurs in the form of *coprolites*—the fossilized remains of human feces. Other evidence for how people obtained their food and nutrition comes from a variety of sources. The study of the faunal or animal remains (*zooarchaeology*) and flora or plant remains (*palaeoethnobotany*) associated with settlement sites plays a major role in revealing the kinds of food people acquired and consumed. Evidence can also come from the analysis of human skeletons, that is, from biochemical analysis of bone.

Zooarchaeology

Zooarchaeology or *archaeozoology* is the study of animal remains from the archaeological record. The analysis of animal remains includes determining the number of different species represented, the minimum number of individuals of each species, and the age structure of those species. This information can provide clues about seasonal hunting strategies, specialized hunting practices, and the process of *domestication*—the modification of plants and animals for human use. However, it is critical to properly interpret the zooarchaeological data. For example, it is important to be able to distinguish between human-made butchering marks and marks from carnivore gnawing. Animals associated with human populations may reflect the kinds of foods that were consumed (including whether they were wild or domesticated, as we will see in Chapter 12). They may also reflect the strategies, such as big-game hunting techniques, used to acquire these food resources.

An example of the interpretation of animal remains is Aubrey Cannon's research on the Northwest Coast. Using zooarchaeological data from the site of Namu, downstream from Bella Coola on British Columbia's coast, Cannon has argued that the increased focus on catching fish on the Northwest Coast was not the result of population pressure or lack of food from land-based sources. Rather, **sedentism**—living in one place for a prolonged period—and intensive salmon fishing seemed to be independent of increased salmon

Zooarchaeology: the study of animals' remains from archaeological contexts.
Sedentism: settling in a single, permanent location.

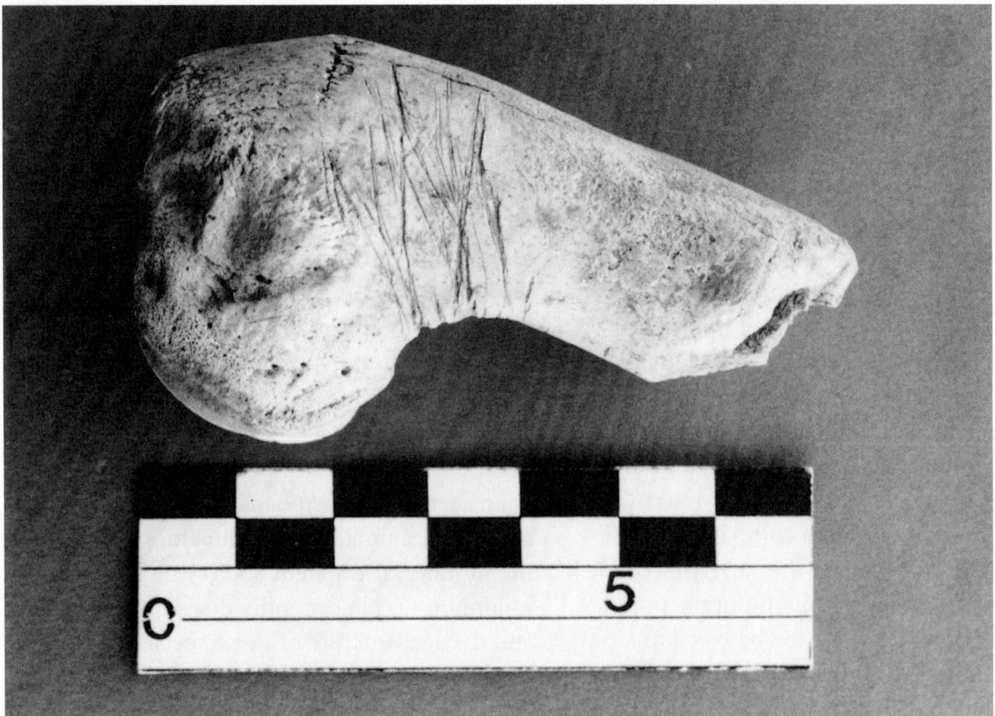

Interpreting butchering marks on animal bones helps us to reconstruct what people ate and how they procured and processed their food.

productivity and human population growth. He suggests that evidence of increased storage capacity associated with the development of wood plank housing, and social feasting could explain the apparent intensification of fishing economies on the Northwest Coast (Cannon, 1998). By examining when and how this behaviour developed in a region, we can better understand its importance in a complex society where social and political power are based on resource control by the elite.

However, faunal remains are not associated only with food consumption. Jim Savelle of McGill University has examined zooarchaeological assemblages of bowhead whalebone, which was a major component of house construction in Thule occupation sites throughout the Canadian Arctic around 1000 years ago. He has suggested that the use of whalebone in house construction is the primary reason that we find whalebone at all Thule sites (Savelle, 1997). This is of interest because most people would consider life in the Arctic, now as in the past, as involving small, widely dispersed populations of hunter-gatherers who are highly mobile, and follow an intensive seasonal economy and settlement pattern. However, Thule people lived in winter villages in pit houses composed of whalebone rafters and covered with skins and turf. The question is, why did these people invest in semi-permanent housing given what we might expect regarding their seasonal subsistence and mobility patterns? Part of the answer is that there was an increase in whale hunting associated with warmer climatic conditions during this period. With the intensification of this kind of subsistence strategy, people became more sedentary because they did not have the technology, population size, or need to move all that material around.

Experimental Archaeology

Experimental archaeology explores a variety of historical questions, especially those related to diet and subsistence. The goal of experimental archaeology is to reproduce or replicate technological traits and

Experimental Archaeology: a specialty within archaeology used to explore a variety of historical questions, especially those related to diet and subsistence by reproducing or replicating technological traits and patterns observed in the archaeological record.

patterns observed in the archaeological record. For example, many modern flint knappers attempt to reconstruct the process that would lead to the production of the kinds of chipped stone tools found in the archaeological record. Reconstruction may give the analyst insight into human behaviour and site formation processes. For example, animal carcasses were left to be scavenged to help palaeoanthropologists better understand the patterns in the distribution of bones found in sites associated with early hominins. The resultant tooth marks and distribution of bones were then analyzed and compared with that observed in the archaeological record (Hudson, 1993; Schick and Toth, 1994).

Similarly, Haskel Greenfield of the University of Manitoba is interested in food production and the origins of metallurgy. He has conducted experiments in which meat was butchered using replicas of stone tools and early metal tools, fabricated in a manner consistent with early metallurgy, so as to better understand how the transition from stone tools to early metal tools could be observed in the archaeological record. The results of this experiment will provide information for better understanding this technological evolution associated with food production.

The analysis of polishes or wear patterns and organic residues left on the tools used in food-related tasks by past populations is another relatively new area of research. Because of experimental archaeology, scientists now know that butchering an animal carcass and processing vegetable matter with stone tools lead to different microscopic wear patterns or polishes on the edge of the tools. Archaeologists can now look at the stone tools used by prehistoric peoples and examine them microscopically for patterns that are consistent with ones produced by experiment.

Even more exciting is the potential of **molecular anthropology**, which examines anthropological questions using genetic evidence. Researchers in molecular anthropology analyze and identify microscopic traces of organic material left on prehistoric tools (Loy et al., 1990; Loy et al., 1992; Loy and Hardy, 1992; Loy, 1998). New technology now allows stone tool edges to be examined for microscopic traces of blood from killed or butchered animals that might be preserved on such tools. Examples of success include blood retrieved from Australian stone tools, dated to 9000 years ago (Loy and Hardy, 1992), and mastodon blood on a tool found in Chile, dated to 13 000 years ago (Tuross and Dillehay, 1995). Blood residues of a variety of large mammal species, including mammoth, have also been detected on projectile points from Beringia, providing for the first time a direct association between the use of these tools and big-game hunting of Pleistocene mammals in Arctic and subarctic North America (Loy and Dixon, 1998). Residue analysis on the interior of clay vessels has formed an important part of reconstructing aspects of ancient diet (see Current Research and Issues, "Archaeology Helps Brew Ancient Beer").

Palaeoethnobotany

Palaeoethnobotany or archaeobotany is the study of the relationships between plants and people in prehistory. Palaeoethnobotanists are especially trained in the identification of seeds found, often burnt or carbonized, in ancient garbage heaps (middens), cooking vessels, and hearths at archaeological sites. Soil removed from a site must be processed to recover the seeds from the archaeological record. The soil is placed in a flotation device in which the light seeds and charcoal float to the surface of the water, where they are skimmed off for analysis. The heavier sediments such as clay, rock, and pebbles sink. Phytoliths, which are microscopic particles of silica from plants, can also be collected from archaeological remains, including artifacts, teeth, and feces, to provide clues as to the kinds of plants that were being processed and consumed. Gary Crawford and David Smith of the University of Toronto are examining sites at the western end of Lake Ontario and in the lower Grand River Valley in south-central Ontario that were occupied during the period from about A.D. 500 to A.D. 1100. They hope to gain an understanding of the transition from earlier seed crops to

Molecular Anthropology: the study of anthropological questions using genetic evidence.

Palaeoethnobotany: the study of plant remains from archaeological contexts.

maize (corn) agriculture in southern Ontario prehistory (Crawford and Smith, 1996; Crawford et al., 1997). As we shall see in Chapter 12, the analysis of carbonized seeds from the archaeological record provides us with clues as to the increasing dependence on seed crops at the beginning of the Neolithic era.

At Brandon University, Canada Research Chair in Archaeological Residue and Functional Analysis, Mary Malainey, is using gas chromatography to examine ancient fat (lipid) residues that remain from a variety of archaeological artifacts including pottery, cooking rocks, and food-processing tools. From her analysis, she is trying to answer questions about the diet of and activities performed by the ancient inhabitants of sites (Malainey et al., 1999).

Coprolites

Coprolites, or fossilized feces, provide evidence for diet because humans do not digest all food that they consume. Some of what an individual consumed can be identified in coprolites. Of course, this kind of evidence represents a snapshot of dietary intake. Coprolites occur most frequently in cave sites, where the dry air naturally desiccates, or removes the moisture from, organic material. Only foods consumed by a specific individual within a very narrow time frame will be present in preserved coprolites. However, if cave sites are frequently used by certain groups of people, there may be a sufficient sample of coprolites to provide a broader cross-section of the kinds of foods being consumed by the group. Similarly, the analysis of coprolites was used by Lin and Connor (2001) to compare the diet of a 500-year-old Greenland Eskimo relative to a contemporary Inuit diet.

Stable Isotopes and Trace Elements

Researchers are often interested in changes in nutrition for past populations. These changes may provide a link to broad biocultural adaptations, such as changes in the environment or in how people obtained their food. Researchers make inferences regarding the general levels of nutrition from skeletal samples through biochemical techniques, including the analysis of stable isotopes—isotopes of the same elements with different atomic masses—and trace elements—elements found in extremely small amounts within the body (Klepinger, 1984; Price, 1984; Boutton et al., 1991; Katzenberg, 1992; Sandford, 1992; Sandford, 1993; Schoeninger, 1995; Katzenberg, 2000) (see Current Research and Issues, "You Are What You Eat: Chemical Analyses of Bones and Teeth").

With respect to dietary reconstruction, the past consumption of two broadly different types of plants—tropical grasses and temperate climate plants—is commonly explored though stable isotope analysis. There are two types of photosynthetic pathways that plants can follow. The photosynthetic pathway for temperate-climate plants is different than the pathway for the tropical plants. Maize, like other tropical grasses, is a C4 pathway plant. Temperate climate plants are called C3 plants. C3 plants tend to absorb proportionately more carbon-12 (^{12}C) because they discriminate more strongly against the carbon-13 (^{13}C) isotope. In contrast, C4 plants produce more complex sugar molecules, and tend to more readily accept the ^{13}C isotope. This means that organisms that regularly consume C4 plants will display a different ratio of ^{13}C to ^{12}C than animals that routinely consume C3 plants. As a result, stable carbon isotope analysis on skeletal remains can be used extensively to assess the importance of maize in North American populations. Stable isotope analyses have shown the absence of maize in the diet of prehistoric Ontario populations prior to about A.D. 700 (Schwarcz et al., 1985; Katzenberg, 1993; Katzenberg et al., 1995). However, carbon isotope ratios increase after A.D. 1000 and peak around three to four centuries later, reflecting the adoption of maize agriculture in the region (Katzenberg et al., 1995). This is consistent with studies of other areas in eastern North America, although regional variations likely reflect a shorter growing season farther north.

Gas Chromatography: an analytical technique for determining the relative proportions of different substances within a sample.
Coprolites: the fossilized remains of feces.

Stable Isotopes: isotopes of the same elements with different atomic masses.
Trace Elements: elements found in extremely small amounts within the body.

CURRENT RESEARCH AND ISSUES

Archaeology Helps Brew Ancient Beer

Archaeological evidence from ancient civilizations in Mesopotamia and Egypt has shown some of the earliest evidence for the brewing of beer. At Godin Tepe, a site in the Zagros Mountains in Iran, excavators from the Royal Ontario Museum have found some of the earliest chemical evidence for beer. Clay pots have been identified; these were used for the storage and fermentation of beer. Grooves on the interior of these vessels below the shoulder are consistent with early Sumerian examples for beer storage. Further, residue analysis from the grooves of some of these vessels found the chemical remnants of calcium oxalate—a primary component of barley beer that settles on the surface of storage tanks during fermentation. These findings represent some of the earliest evidence of beer production in the fourth century B.C.

In the second century B.C., evidence for beer production from the New Kingdom period in Egypt can also be observed from the archaeological record. During this period, which covers the reign of the Pharaoh Tutankhamen, evidence includes residue from fermentation in vessels, and botanical remains. In 1990, the Egyptian Exploration Society approached Scottish and Newcastle Breweries in the United Kingdom to assist them in an investigation into beer making in ancient Egypt. Ancient Egyptian inscriptions and documents show that beer with bread was a daily food, giving nourishment to both the wealthy and poor. The established view of ancient Egyptian brewing, drawn from tomb scenes, was that beer loaves were made from a rich yeast dough, possibly with malt added. The dough was lightly baked and the resulting bread was then crumbled and strained through a sieve with water. Ingredients like dates or extra yeast might have been added at this stage. Fermentation occurred in large vats, and when complete, the liquid was poured into vessels and sealed for transportation.

Using a scanning electron microscope (SEM), researchers were able to examine residues on the interiors of fermentation pots, and have found evidence for yeast colonies and possibly lactic acid bacteria. In ancient Egypt, emmer and barley were the two major cereals for producing beer. Additional clues from SEM research on residues provide insight into the actual brewing process. For example, changes in the structure of starch granules, associated with starch being heated in water, can be observed in some residues. Comparisons between samples are difficult though, given that contamination of the residues over the last 3000 years can obscure analyses. However, there now seems to be enough evidence from microscopic analysis of pot residues to suggest the ancient Egyptians used a variety of techniques for brewing, and that bread probably did not play a role in the production of beer in the ancient world.

Sources: Armelagos G. 2000. Take Two Beers and Call Me in 1600 Years. Natural History, 109(4): 50–53.

Samuel D. 1996. Archaeology of Ancient Egyptian Beer. Journal of the American Society of Brewing Chemists, 54: 3–12.

Samuel D. 1996. Investigation of Ancient Egyptian Baking and Brewing Methods by Correlative Microscopy. Science, 273: 488–490.

Samuel D., Bolt P. 1995. Rediscovering Ancient Egyptian Beer. Brewers' Guardian, 124(12): 26–31.

Carbon isotopic analyses can also be used to study the diets of people who lived at coastal sites, particularly in determining the relative importance of marine versus terrestrial foods. Carbon absorbed by marine animals derives from dissolved carbonate, while terrestrial animals rely upon atmospheric carbon. As the relative abundance of ^{13}C is higher in marine environments than in the atmosphere, the entire marine food web reflects a high proportion of ^{13}C. This means the isotopic profile of human bones should show if past populations relied more heavily on marine foods than on terrestrial foods. For example, David Lubell and his colleagues have used this analysis to show an abrupt shift from marine to terrestrial food resources between Mesolithic and later Neolithic populations in Portugal (Lubell et al., 1994).

In the late 1980s researchers demonstrated that the ratio of stable isotopes of nitrogen could be used to detect the consumption of breast milk in an infant's diet (Fogel et al., 1989). The higher an organism is on the food chain, the more its tissues are enriched with the ^{15}N isotope. For example, carnivores that consume herbivores (plant-eating animals) have tissues enriched with ^{15}N. So we would expect that the tissues of breast-fed babies should be more enriched in ^{15}N than the tissues of their mothers. Many studies have explored

In ancient Egypt, figures were made depicting household activities such as bread and beer preparation. Above is a Middle Kingdom model.

whether high ^{15}N levels in infant skeletons, in contrast to decreased levels in older children, may reflect the weaning process (Katzenberg, 1991; Tuross and Fogel, 1994; White and Schwarcz, 1994; Katzenberg and Pfeiffer, 1995).

Annie Katzenberg, a physical anthropologist at the University of Calgary, and her colleagues have examined the issue of infant weaning, sickness, and mortality from a variety of skeletal samples. In a small protohistoric (around the time of contact with Europeans) sample from southern Ontario, Katzenberg and colleagues found that both carbon and nitrogen isotope ratios varied with age. This variation reflected a change in dietary intake associated with breast-feeding and weaning (Katzenberg et al., 1993). However, we must remember that infants and children in skeletal samples may reflect health and nutritional problems that prevented survival. As such, very young newborns might not have had the opportunity to nurse if very ill. Katzenberg analyzed skeletal samples of European descent from historic cemeteries. She found no difference in stable nitrogen ratios between newborns and adults, in contrast to very high levels among the infants and young children (Katzenberg, 1991).

In their analysis of the skeletal remains of 64 individuals from a historic Methodist cemetery in Newmarket, Ontario, Katzenberg and Pfeiffer observed that nitrogen isotope ratios rose rapidly from birth to about one year of age, after which they declined to adult levels by about two years of age (Katzenberg and Pfeiffer, 1995). In their study of infant mortality in a 19th-century pioneer cemetery in Belleville, Ontario, Ann Herring and colleagues suggested that the introduction of other food sources in relatively poor living conditions resulted in increased infant mortality by five months of age, even though breast milk remained a major component of infant nutrition until just over a year of age (Herring et al., 1998). It may be that the introduction of other foods in environments that were relatively unsanitary may have impacted on infant mortality and morbidity patterns, not nutritional decline associated with the weaning process itself (Katzenberg et al., 1996; Schurr, 1997; Herring et al., 1998).

Trace element analyses have also been used in reconstructing the diet of past populations. These studies have focused on identifying levels of calcium, strontium, and barium in bones. The pattern of absorption of strontium into the skeleton is opposite

CURRENT RESEARCH AND ISSUES

You Are What You Eat: Chemical Analyses of Bones and Teeth

Archaeologists study ancient diets in several ways, which are mostly indirect. They can infer indirectly some of what ancient people ate from recovered food wastes. For example, if you find a lot of corncobs, chances are that the people ate a lot of corn. Plant and animal foods can be identified in the charred remains of cooking fires and (when preserved) in the ancient people's feces. Such inferences are usually biased in favour of hard food sources such as seeds, nuts, and grains (which are likely to be preserved); rarely are the remains of soft plants such as bananas or tubers found. Archaeologists can also indirectly infer diet from the artifacts they find, particularly of course ones we can be pretty sure were used in obtaining or processing food. So, for example, if you find a stone with a flat or concave surface that looks similar to stones that some people use now in some places to grind corn, it is very likely that the ancient people also ground grain (or other hard things such as seeds) for food. However, plant remains or implements do not tell us *how much* people relied on particular sources of food.

There is a more direct way to study ancient diets. Anthropologists have discovered that in many ways "you are what you eat." In particular, chemical analyses of bones and teeth, the most common remains found in excavations, can reveal distinctive traces of the foods that metabolically went into the bones and teeth. One kind of informative chemical analysis involves the ratio of strontium to calcium in bone. This analysis can indicate the relative amounts of plant and animal food in the diet. So, for example, we know from strontium analysis of bones that just before the beginnings of cereal agriculture in the Near East, people were eating a lot of plant food, probably wild cereals that were intensively collected. Then there was a temporary decline in such collecting, suggesting overexploitation of the wild resources, or at least their decreasing availability. The cultivation and domestication (modification) of cereals presumably solved this problem.

Carbon isotope ratios also can tell us what types of plants people were eating. Trees, shrubs, and temperate-zone grasses (for example, rice) have carbon isotope ratios that are different from those of tropical and subtropical grasses (such as millet and corn). People in China were relying heavily on cereals about 7000 to 8000 years ago, but the cereals were not the same in the north and south. Contrary to what we might expect, the carbon isotope ratios tell us that an originally temperate-zone cereal (rice) was the staple in subtropical southern China; in the more temperate north, an originally tropical or subtropical grass (millet) was most important. The dependence on millet in the north was enormous. It is estimated that 50 to 80 percent of the diet between 5000 and 500 B.C. came from millet.

In the Americas, seed crops such as sunflower, sumpweed, and goosefoot were domesticated in eastern North America long before corn, introduced from Mexico, became the staple. We know this partly from the archaeology; the remains of the early seed crops are older than the remains of corn. Corn, an originally subtropical plant, has a carbon isotope ratio that is different from the ratio for the earlier, temperate-zone seed crops. Thus, the shift in carbon isotope ratios after A.D. 800 to A.D. 900 tells us that corn had become the staple.

Traditionally, non-chemical analyses of human bones and teeth were used by physical anthropologists and archaeologists to study similarities and differences between peoples in different geographic regions, between living humans and possible fossil ancestors, and between living humans and other surviving primates. Much of the research involved surface measurements, particularly of the skull (outside and inside). In recent years, physical anthropologists and archaeologists have begun to study the "insides" of bones and teeth. The new kinds of chemical analysis mentioned here are part of that trend. In NJ van der Merwe's pithy words, "The emphasis in studies of human evolution has shifted from a preoccupation with the brain to an equal interest in the stomach."

Sources: Larsen, CS. 1998. Bare Bones Anthropology: The Bioarchaeology of Human Remains. In: Ember CR, Ember M, Peregrine PN, editors. Research Frontiers in Anthropology. Upper Saddle River, NJ: Prentice Hall. Prentice Hall/Simon & Schuster Custom Publishing.

Van der Merwe NJ. 1992. Reconstructing Prehistoric Diet. In: Jones S, Martin R, Pilbeam D, editors. The Cambridge Encyclopedia of Human Evolution. New York: Cambridge University Press. pp 369–372.

to the absorption pattern for nitrogen isotope ratios—instead of increasing from plant to herbivore to carnivore, it decreases. This means that amounts of calcium and strontium in skeletal remains can be analyzed for reconstructing prehistoric diets in animals and hominins (Katzenberg, 1984). Herbivores have the highest levels of strontium in their skeletons, while carnivores have the lowest; and omnivores fall somewhere in between (Sandford and Weaver, 2000). Calculating the ratio of strontium and calcium (Sr/Ca) in infant skeletons has also been a method for detecting the beginning of the weaning process. This approach was based on the assumption that supplemental foods in the early weaning stage in past populations were cereals that were enriched in strontium. Because the infant digestive system is less able to discriminate against strontium, infant bones absorb more than you would expect, and researchers need to take this into consideration. In addition, issues of **diagenesis**—the artificial uptake of trace elements from the burial environment—produce additional methodological problems to this approach. As a result, current studies now rely on the analysis of stable isotopes for understanding infant feeding practices.

Reconstructing Past Environments

Archaeological reconstructions of past environmental conditions are derived from the analysis of soils, sediments, and remains of former life forms. These life forms include pollen, plant macrofossil remains of all kinds, invertebrates (including parasitic nematodes, insects and other arthropods, and molluscs), and vertebrates (Reitz et al., 1996; Evans and O'Connor, 1999; Dincauze, 2000). For example, sediment from West Coast shell middens have provided clear evidence of human intestinal parasitism (Bathurst,2005). Researchers can make inferences about environmental conditions through time and in different locations based on changes in the relative abundance of these life forms. Once researchers reconstruct the past environmental conditions, they can then address whether there are observable changes in the human populations living in the region that might be a function of the shifting environmental conditions.

Environmental Archaeology

Environmental archaeology is distinct from *palaeoecology*. Palaeoecology identifies and explains past ecological phenomena like changes in forest growth or the numbers of types of organisms living in a given location. Environmental archaeology is interested specifically in ecological and climatic conditions of the past as a means for better understanding how various peoples lived—what conditions they lived in and how those conditions affected their lives. While the ultimate goals of these two disciplines are somewhat different, their research tools are similar.

Environmental archaeology employs a number of methods to assess both general and specific ecological conditions in the past. This evidence can be divided into two broad classes: *biotic evidence*, which represents the remains of biological organisms from the past, and *abiotic evidence* or the remains of chemical components of sediments and their associated landforms. Biotic evidence includes the fossilized remains of bones, shells, seeds, and pollen. Abiotic evidence includes geological structures and the associated processes, soil sediments, and their chemical makeup.

Another source of evidence is **palynology**—the study of pollen from different periods. Pollen can be preserved within sediments and in water-saturated conditions. The relative abundance of different plant species can be inferred from the relative abundance of pollen grains. This will give some indication of vegetative conditions within a given region. If the materials are recovered in a dated

Diagenesis: chemical changes that occur in materials after deposition in the ground.
Environmental Archaeology: a field of study that is interested specifically in ecological and climatic conditions of the past as a means for better understanding how various peoples lived—what conditions they lived in and how those conditions affected their lives.
Palynology: the study of pollen from archaeological contexts.

stratigraphic context, the analyst can document regional vegetation change over time. Since certain kinds of plants thrive under specific climatic conditions, palynology can offer indirect evidence of the general environmental conditions that existed in the past. Like pollen, phytoliths can also be collected from the soil, artifacts, and human teeth, and analyzed to identify plant species.

Another source of evidence for reconstructing past climatic conditions at a global scale is measuring the ratio of oxygen isotopes. Sea water naturally contains both ^{18}O and the lighter ^{16}O. The lighter ^{16}O evaporates first, and when this water vapour falls as snow, some remains "locked up" as glacial ice in northern latitudes. Thus, the relative abundance of ^{18}O goes up. During warmer periods less precipitation falls as snow and glacial meltwater returns to the oceans, thereby reducing the relative abundance of ^{18}O. Past isotopic concentrations in sea water cannot be measured directly. Scientists use the fossilized remains of a small marine organism called *foraminifera* to measure these concentrations. Foraminifera absorb oxygen into its skeletal system, and its fossilized remains can be used as a proxy for broad changes in global temperatures.

At McMaster University, Henry Schwarcz is supervising research on beaver teeth to test seasonal changes in the ratio of ^{18}O to ^{16}O precipitation. Fricke and co-workers traced changes over time in oxygen isotope ratios in the tooth enamel of Inuit and European populations in western Greenland and Denmark (Fricke et al., 1995). The results were consistent with an increasing cool trend in the North Atlantic region from A.D. 1400 to A.D. 1700. This may corroborate the theory that the abandonment of the Viking Greenland settlement was due to environmental stress (Scott et al., 1991; Buckland et al., 1996).

This same process of charting oxygen isotope values can also be used try to understand migration patterns in the past. The idea is that people consume water that is local to the region in which they live. Therefore, if they move into a new area, they will have a different isotopic signature in their bones and teeth than those who grew up in the region. For example, Dupras and Schwarcz (2001) used oxygen isotope values to suggest the presence of foreign individuals in the mortality sample excavated from the site in Dakhleh Oasis, Egypt. Similarly, Prowse and colleagues (2007) compared the ^{18}O ratio in teeth from the Imperial Roman site of Portus, and observed that about one-third of the children had signatures outside the range observed in a modern sample. This, they argued, could be explained by migration into the area at a young age by those individuals.

Reconstructing Settlement Patterns

Settlement archaeology is concerned with two aspects of human occupation: the distribution of sites across a landscape and the relationship of structures within a community.

We can learn a great deal about a past society from the distribution of archaeological sites, and the relationship of these sites to their surrounding physical environments. The size, organization, and location of buildings and other structures within a community reflect the social and political structure of the community. Recognizing this, archaeologists undertake the analysis of settlement patterns to make inferences about past cultures.

Settlement data can tell us about such things as family organization and who performs certain tasks within a household. They can help us to understand the economy of a social group, what resources are important to them, and whether or not people moved during different seasons. They may also reveal clues regarding the different levels of social status, and perhaps even political or religious views within a community. By examining changes over time in the relationship between communities, and structures within communities, a researcher can gain considerable insight about the socio-cultural evolution of a society. For example, Brian Hayden analyzed a series of winter houses at Keatley Creek (about 20 kilometres north of Lillooet on terraces of the Fraser River) in British Columbia. The earliest occupation of the site was around 4800 B.P. (before present era). Hayden's analysis revealed that there was socio-economic variation in wealth

Settlement Archaeology: the study of settlement patterns within the archaeological record.

between houses between 2400 and 1200 B.P. As well, he found possible evidence for long-term regional resource control by key families (Hayden, 1997). In this instance there was one village that contained some huge pit houses that stand out in sharp contrast from other villages in the region. The question is, why do we see these pit houses developing here at this particular time? Hayden argues that powerful families emerged because they were in a position to strategically control important resources. This in turn led to complex social alliances involving many families. As a result, the Keatley Creek sites provide a model for understanding the transition from small kin-based political systems based on family relationships—as we see in hunter-gatherer groups—to larger, more complex political units under the leadership of powerful chiefs.

Settlement archaeology is also interested in the distribution of sites and communities across the landscape as well as human changes to the landscape (for a discussion of landscape archaeology, see Chapter 14). Cultural ecology has become a central concept in settlement archaeology, and it is based on the notion that settlement distribution patterns are strongly related to local and regional changes in economic, environmental, social, subsistence, and technological factors (Fagan, 2000). As an example, annual flooding of river systems might influence the distribution of dwellings or dwelling types within a community situated along a river shore.

A tool that has recently emerged is **Geographic Information Systems (GIS)** analysis (Allen et al., 1990; Wheatley and Gillings, 2002). Stewart and colleagues have recently combined archaeological evidence of seasonal site occupation and oral histories regarding caribou crossings, camps, and other places of cultural significance to interpret recent Inuit land use along the lower Kazan River, Nunavut. These researchers employed Geographic Positioning System (GPS) technology to record individual archaeological features (for example, tent rings, caches) at sites throughout the area. The resulting GIS database showed considerable variation in regional land use including the types of sites observed and season of occupation (Stewart et al., 2000). GIS techniques can also help us to integrate complex data from a variety of sources. Using a GIS analysis of multiple surface and subsurface surveying techniques, Haskel Greenfield demonstrated distinct but complementary patterns of subsurface conditions at the stratigraphically complex Neolithic site of Blagotin in Serbia (Greenfield, 2000).

Archaeological evidence can also shed light on issues of population size and composition (the number of men and women of different ages) in the distant past. Researchers can estimate population size and rates of growth—how fast a population is increasing in size—from settlement data. The size and area of the living site, and how many dwellings are present can help the archaeologist to assess how many people were living in an area. As well, the distribution of artifacts and food remains can also help the archaeologist to refine estimates. For example, the archaeologist can tell the difference between a large dwelling of a single family versus a dwelling housing many families. Finally, ethnohistoric data of population size from recent populations living under similar conditions can serve as models for our estimates from the archaeological record.

However, even when data are available, estimates of population size must often be made through ethnographic analogy. This is a method where the relationship between population size and material remains seen in modern or historic groups is imposed on the archaeological site. One of the major questions that archaeologists have been interested in for many New World (North, South, and Central America) populations is demographic collapse—the drastic decline in population size. What factors led to the demise of entire populations? Can archaeology help us to understand the series of events associated with population collapse, such as that which affected the Maya?

Population collapse has been explored through analyses of *carrying capacity* and *site catchment area.* **Carrying capacity** is the estimated population

Geographic Information Systems (GIS): integrated software package for the input, analysis, and display of spatial information.

Carrying Capacity: the estimated population number and density that a given area of land can support, given the technology used by the people at the time.

Understanding the relationship within and between dwellings is a major component of settlement archaeology.

number and density that a given area of land can support, given the technology used by the people at the time. However, because prehistoric resource patterns are difficult to determine, most studies have focused their efforts on the types and availability of raw resources, and the impact on population structure of changes in resources (Fagan, 2000). **Site catchment analysis** is based on the simple assumption that the more dispersed resources are from habitation sites, the less likely they are to be exploited by a population (Bailey, 1981). Of course, the technology, workforce size, and political organization of a population will have an impact on determining the relative "costs" associated with resource exploitation. For example, the benefits of acquiring labour-intensive resources for a large population may outweigh the costs, relative to a small population that would have to invest a greater proportion of their group's labour to acquire a smaller amount of material.

Site Catchment Analysis: an analysis based on the assumption that the more dispersed resources are from habitation sites, the less likely they are to be exploited by a population.

Alternative approaches to examining the relationship between resource availability and population structure have also been explored. Based on dietary trends from palaeopathological and stable isotope analysis, Lori Wright and Christine White have argued that there is no evidence to link reduced food resources with the demographic collapse of the Maya civilization (Wright and White, 1996). In addition, Katherine Emery and colleagues used stable isotopes to analyze the diet of deer, a common agricultural pest in ancient Mesoamerica, to suggest that ecological decline was not a factor associated with the collapse of the Mayan empire (Emery et al., 2000).

Reconstructing Social Systems

Reconstructing aspects of social systems from the archaeological record is possible by understanding the social context in which material culture accumulates. In addition, the items produced by past peoples can provide information about their social systems. For example, the manufacture of clay pots might include stylistic variations associated with the producer or the producer's family. Jewellery and other items of personal adornment can reflect aspects of self-identity and views of the world. The kinds of foods being consumed may also reflect broad class differences between groups within a society.

One of the major areas of archaeology concerning social status is burials. Human burials and burial practices are an important source of both biological and cultural information for the anthropologist. At the most extravagant, high-status burials like the tombs of Pharaohs from ancient Egypt or a Chinese emperor buried with an army of life-sized ceramic soldiers capture the imagination of the public. Burials can reveal information about social status, as well as trade, religion, and economics. As well, burials and mortuary practices reflect the attitudes, values, symbolism, status, and other beliefs held by prehistoric peoples (Noble, 1968). **Funerary archaeology**—the study of burials—can reveal information regarding social status, trade networks, population structure, and social organization within the society (Gowland and Knusel, 2006). Lewis Binford proposed that increased social complexity resulted in increased variation in burial practices, and that social organization (not necessarily ritual practices or religion) was the primary cause of such variation (Binford, 1972). Based on this notion, the more differences in the manner in which individuals were buried (including the type or number of any goods in the grave), the more socially complex and stratified a society was. By following the changing trends in mortuary customs, archaeologists may better understand the changing relationships between various peoples, as well as the changes associated with the influence of native and foreign cultures through time.

Christine White is a physical anthropologist at the University of Western Ontario who specializes in stable isotope analysis. Much of her research has focused on Mayan sites in Mesoamerica, and includes dietary reconstruction, migration, and social status. Using carbon isotope analyses of human skeletal remains, White has observed differences in the consumption of maize between high-status and low-status individuals. However, these differences are not always consistent. In Belize at the site of Pacbitun, the presence of maize in the diet was associated with high-status individuals, while at the site of Lamanai, maize was associated more with the diet of low-status individuals. White has argued that this difference suggests that high-status individuals from Lamanai may have better diets and greater access to protein than their counterparts at Pacbitun (White and Schwarcz, 1989; White et al., 1993). At other Mayan sites like Copan in present-day Honduras, no differences in stable isotope ratios in bones have been detected between different classes (Reed, 1994).

Funerary Archaeology: the study of burial customs from archaeological evidence.

Trading Patterns

Most prehistoric populations also engaged in some sort of long-distance trade. This can be inferred by the location of raw materials relative to the location of the produced artifact. Trade can also be inferred by observing the physical composition of the material and whether it was made locally or not. Other times more precise chemical techniques are required to determine the precise composition of an item. Regardless, trade is an important part of *cultural diffusion*. Lowie believed that any given cultural trait is derived either from a *cultural antecedent* within the culture or through importing ideas from other foreign populations (Lowie, 1988). The latter process, cultural diffusion (see below), has been and continues to be a major area of investigation in the attempt to explain cultural change.

Cultural Change

The sources of all cultural change are discoveries and inventions, which may originate inside or outside a society. However, they do not necessarily lead to social change. If an invention or discovery is ignored, no change in culture results. It is only when society accepts an invention or discovery and uses it regularly that we can begin to speak of cultural change.

Discovery and Invention

The new thing discovered or invented, the *innovation*, may be an object—the wheel, the plow, the computer—or it may involve behaviour and ideas—buying and selling, democracy, monogamy.

One type of invention can be the consequence of a society's setting itself a specific goal, such as eliminating a specific disease or finding a way to preserve a food. Another type emerges less intentionally. This second process of invention is often referred to as *accidental juxtaposition* or *unconscious invention.* Ralph Linton suggested that some inventions, especially those of prehistoric days, were probably the consequences of literally dozens of tiny initiatives by "unconscious" inventors. These inventors made their small contributions, perhaps over many hundreds of years, without being aware of the part they were playing in bringing one invention, such as the wheel or a better form of hand axe, to completion (Linton, 1936). Consider the example of children playing on a fallen log, which rolls as they walk and balance on it, coupled with the need at a given moment to move a slab of granite from a cave face. The children's play may have suggested the use of logs as rollers and thereby set in motion a series of developments that culminated in the wheel.

Some discoveries and inventions arise out of deliberate attempts to produce a new idea or object. It may seem that such innovations are obvious responses to perceived needs. Nevertheless, perceived needs and the economic rewards that may be given to the innovator do not explain why only some people innovate. We know relatively little about why some people are more innovative than others. The ability to innovate may depend in part on individual characteristics such as high intelligence and creativity. And creativity may be influenced by social conditions.

Types of Cultural Diffusion

The source of new cultural elements in a society may be another society. The process by which cultural elements are borrowed from another society and incorporated into the culture of the recipient group is called **diffusion**. Borrowing sometimes enables a group to bypass stages or mistakes in the development of a process or institution. There are three basic patterns of diffusion: *direct contact*, *intermediate contact*, and *stimulus* diffusion.

Diffusion: the borrowing by one society of a cultural trait belonging to another society as the result of contact between the two societies.

Direct contact occurs when elements of a society's culture are first taken up by neighbouring societies and then gradually spread farther and farther afield. The spread of the use of paper (a sheet of interlaced fibres) is a good example of extensive diffusion by direct contact. The invention of paper is attributed to the Chinese Ts'ai Lun in A.D. 105. Within 50 years, paper was being made in many places in central China. While the art of papermaking was kept secret for about 500 years, paper was distributed as a commodity to much of the Arab world through the markets at Samarkand. But when Samarkand was attacked by the Chinese in A.D. 751, a Chinese prisoner was forced to set up a paper mill. Paper manufacture then spread to the rest of the Arab world; it was first manufactured in Baghdad in A.D. 793, Egypt about A.D. 900, and Morocco about A.D. 1100. Papermaking was introduced as a commodity in Europe by Arab trade through Italian ports in the 12th century. The Moors built the first European paper mill in Spain about 1150. The technical knowledge then spread throughout Europe with paper mills being built in Italy in 1276, France in 1348, Germany in 1390, and England in 1494 (Anonymous, 1980; Anonymous, 1998). In general, the pattern of accepting the borrowed invention was the same in all cases. Paper was first imported as a luxury, then in ever-expanding quantities as a staple product. Finally, and usually within one to three centuries, local manufacture was begun.

Diffusion by *intermediate contact* occurs through the agency of third parties. Frequently, traders carry a cultural trait from the society, where it originated, to another group. As an example of diffusion through intermediaries, Phoenician traders spread the idea of our alphabet, which may have been invented by another Semitic group, to Greece. At times, soldiers serve as intermediaries in spreading a cultural trait. European crusaders, such as the Knights Templar and the Knights of St. John, acted as intermediaries in two ways: they carried Christian culture to Muslim societies of North Africa and brought Arab culture back to Europe. In the 19th century, Western missionaries in all parts of the world encouraged indigenous peoples to wear Western clothing. The result is that in Africa, the Pacific Islands, and elsewhere, all peoples can be found wearing shorts, suit jackets, shirts, ties, and other typically Western articles of clothing.

In *stimulus diffusion*, knowledge of a trait belonging to another culture stimulates the invention or development of a local equivalent. A classic example of stimulus diffusion is the Cherokee syllabic writing system created by Sequoya, a Cherokee, so that his people could write down their language. Sequoya got the idea from his contact with Europeans. Yet he did not adopt the English writing system; indeed, he did not even learn to write English. What he did was use some English alphabetic symbols, alter others, and invent new ones. All the symbols he used represented Cherokee syllables and in no way echoed English alphabetic usage. In other words, Sequoya took English alphabetic ideas and gave them a new, Cherokee form. The stimulus originated with Europeans; the result was peculiarly Cherokee.

The Selective Nature of Diffusion

Although there is a temptation to view the dynamics of diffusion as similar to a stone sending concentric ripples over still water, this view would be an oversimplification of the way diffusion actually occurs. Not all cultural traits are borrowed as readily as the ones we have mentioned, nor do they usually expand in neat, ever-widening circles. Rather, diffusion is a selective process.

We would expect societies to reject items from other societies that are repugnant to them and we would also expect them to reject ideas and technology that do not satisfy some psychological, social, or cultural need. Diffusion is also selective because cultural traits differ in the extent to which they can be communicated. Elements of material culture, such as mechanical processes and techniques, and other traits, such as physical sports and the like, are not especially difficult to demonstrate. Consequently, they are accepted or rejected on their merits. But the moment we move out of the material context into the realm of ideas, we encounter real difficulties. For instance, how do you communicate the complex idea of democracy?

Finally, diffusion is selective because the overt form of a particular trait, rather than its function or meaning, frequently seems to determine how the trait will be received. For example, the enthusiasm for bobbed hair (short haircuts) that swept through much of North America in the 1920s never caught on among the First Nations women of northwestern California. To many women of European ancestry, short hair was a symbolic statement of their freedom. To these First Nations women, who traditionally cut their hair short when in mourning, it was a reminder of death (Foster, 1962).

In the process of diffusion, then, we can identify a number of different patterns. Cultural borrowing is selective rather than automatic, and we can describe how a particular borrowed trait has been modified by the recipient culture. However, current knowledge does not allow us to specify when one or another of these outcomes will occur, under what conditions diffusion will occur, and why it occurs the way it does.

Acculturation

On the surface, the process of change called *acculturation* seems to include much of what we have discussed under the label of diffusion, since acculturation refers to the changes that occur when different cultural groups come into intensive contact. As in diffusion, the source of new cultural items is the other society. More often than not though, the term **acculturation** describes a situation in which one of the societies in contact is much more powerful than the other. Thus, acculturation can be seen as a process of extensive cultural borrowing in the context of an unequal power relationship between societies (Bodley, 1990).

External pressure for cultural change can take various forms. In its most direct form—conquest or colonialization—the dominant group uses force or the threat of force to bring about cultural change in the other group. For example, in the Spanish conquest of Mexico, the conquerors forced many of the native groups to accept Roman Catholicism. Although such direct force is not

Acculturation: the process of extensive borrowing of aspects of culture.

always exerted in conquest situations, dominated peoples often have little choice but to change. Examples of such indirectly forced change abound in the history of Aboriginal peoples in Canada. A strong European missionary movement led to many Aboriginal communities being forced to adopt non-religious aspects of Euro-Canadian culture. After Confederation, the federal government displaced many native populations from their lands, and obliged them to give up many aspects of their traditional ways of life, language, and cultures. Aboriginal children were required to go to residential schools, which taught the dominant society's values. In most cases these attempts at assimilation and acculturation were a misplaced attempt at "improving" the lives of Aboriginal people. In order to survive, they had no choice but to adopt many of the dominant society's traits.

A subordinate society may acculturate to a dominant society even in the absence of direct or indirect force. The dominated people may elect to adopt cultural elements from the dominant society in order to survive in their changed world. Or, perceiving that members of the dominant society enjoy more secure living conditions, the dominated people may identify with the dominant culture in the hope that by doing so they will be able to share some of its benefits. For example, in Arctic areas many Inuit and Lapp groups seemed eager to replace dogsleds with snowmobiles without any coercion (Pelto and Miller-Wille, 1987).

In the following chapters, we will see how the interpretation and reconstruction techniques outlined in this chapter have been applied to tracing the evolution of humans.

Summary

1. Interpretation of the archaeological record is based on a variety of related disciplines that provide data to help reconstruct ecological conditions (environmental archaeology), diet (palaeonutrition), disease load (palaeopathology), settlement patterns, socio-economic status, resource distribution, and allocation (political ecology).
2. Osteology or skeletal biology is the specialized subdiscipline of physical anthropology that deals with the biological remains of humans from past populations.
3. The study of palaeopathology seeks to answer questions about the appearance, prevalence, and spread of diseases in past populations from human skeletal remains.
4. Palaeodemography is the study of demographic structure and population processes in the past.
5. What people ate can be explored from a variety of sources including zooarchaeology (the study of animal remains), experimental archaeology, palaeoethnobotany (the study of plant remains), coprolites, stable isotopes, and trace elements.
6. Environmental archaeology reconstructs ecological and climatic conditions of the past as a means for better understanding people in the past and how environmental conditions affected their lives.
7. Settlement archaeology is concerned with the distribution of sites across a landscape and relationship of structures within a community.
8. Reconstructing the culture of past peoples from the archaeological record is possible by understanding the social context in which material culture accumulates.
9. Culture is always changing. Discoveries and inventions are a major source of cultural change. The process by which cultural elements are borrowed from one society and incorporated into another is called diffusion. However, diffusion is a selective process, and does not occur automatically.

Glossary Terms

acculturation (p. 68)
ancient DNA (aDNA) (p. 53)
carrying capacity (p. 64)
conservation (p. 45)

coprolites (p. 58)
diagenesis (p. 62)
differential diagnosis (p. 51)
diffusion (p. 67)
DNA (deoxyribonucleic acid) (p. 53)
environmental archaeology (p. 62)
ethnographic analogy (p. 54)
experimental archaeology (p. 56)
funerary archaeology (p. 66)
gas chromatography (p. 58)
Geographic Information Systems (GIS) (p. 64)
life table (p. 54)
molecular anthropology (p. 57)
osteology (p. 47)
palaeodemography (p. 53)
palaeoethnobotany (p. 57)
palaeopathology (p. 49)
palynology (p. 62)
polymerase chain reaction (PCR) (p. 53)
remodelling (p. 47)
sedentism (p. 55)
settlement archaeology (p. 63)
sexually dimorphic (p. 48)
site catchment analysis (p. 65)
skeletal age-indicator techniques (p. 47)
stable isotopes (p. 58)
stationary (p. 54)
trace elements (p. 58)
typology (p. 46)
zooarchaeology (p. 55)

Critical Questions

1. How do you think that cultural views of the past affect archaeological research in different societies?
2. Anthropology is a holistic science, yet research is becoming increasingly specialized. How do you think this affects the way in which anthropologists are trained to do research?
3. For various levels of interpretation, different assumptions are made by anthropologists. What are these assumptions, and why do you think they are valid or not valid?

Internet Exercises

1. Go to the Natural Museum's website and view the photo gallery of phytoliths at **www.mnh.si.edu/highlight/phytoliths/index.html.**
2. View the case studies in palaeopathology presented at **www.pathology.vcu.edu/research/paleo/index.html**. Pick one a summarize the basic findings of the case, and the methods used.
3. Review human skeletal anatomy at **http://library.med.utah.edu/kw/osteo/osteology**.

Suggested Reading

Chamberlain AC. 1994. Human Remains: Interpreting the Past. Berkeley: University of California Press. A very brief introduction to the analysis and interpretation of skeletal remains.

Fagan B. 2004. In the Beginning. Upper Saddle River, NJ: Prentice Hall. A very thorough introduction to archaeological methods and interpretation.

Katzenberg MA, Saunders SR, editors. 2000. Biological Anthropology of the Human Skeleton. New York, NY: John Wiley & Sons, Inc. A detailed overview of a variety of specialized areas of skeletal biology, including palaedemography, stable isotopes, trace elements, ancient DNA, and ethics in osteological studies.

Larsen CS. 1999. Bioarchaeology: Interpreting Behavior from the Human Skeleton. Cambridge University Press. A thorough synthesis of the many facets of reconstructing the past from the study of human skeletal remains from archaeological samples.

Roberts C, Manchester K. 2007. Archaeology of Disease, 3rd ed. Cornell University Press. An overview of the field of palaeopathology and how it can contribute to our understanding of health and disease in the past.

EARLY HOMININS

CHAPTER OUTLINE

Early Hominin Cultures

Tool Traditions

Because stone tools found at various sites in East Africa date to about the time of *H. habilis*, some anthropologists surmise that *H. habilis*, rather than the australopithecines, made those tools (see Figure 8-7). After all, *H. habilis* had the greater brain capacity. But the fact is that none of the earliest stone tools are clearly associated with *H. habilis*, so it is impossible as yet to know who made them. All the hominins that lived from at least 2.5 million years ago had a thumb capable of toolmaking, so all of them may have been toolmakers (Susman, 1994). We turn now to those tools and what archaeologists infer about the lifestyles of their makers, the hominins (whoever they were) who lived between about 2.5 million and 1.5 million years ago.

The earliest identifiable stone tools found so far come from various sites in East Africa and date from about 2.5 million years ago (Susman, 1994), and maybe earlier. The oldest tools, some 3000 in number, were discovered recently at Gona, Ethiopia. The tools range from very small flakes (thumb-size) to cobble or core tools that were fist-size (Anonymous, 1997c). These early tools were apparently made by striking a stone with another stone, a technique called **percussion flaking**. Both the sharp-edged flakes and the sharp-edged cores (the pieces of stone left after flakes are removed) were probably used as tools. Archaeologists consider a pattern of behaviour, such as a particular way to make a tool that is shared and learned by a group of individuals, to be a sign of some cultural behaviour. To be sure, toolmaking does not imply that early humans had anything like the complex cultures of humans today, because, as we noted in Chapter 6, chimpanzees have patterns of tool use and toolmaking that appear to be shared and learned, but they do not have that much in the way of cultural behaviour. On the basis of their toolmaking, early hominins had some cultural behaviour, but we cannot tell yet how much culture they had.

What were those earliest stone tools used for? What do they tell us about early hominin culture? Unfortunately, little can be inferred about lifestyles from the earliest tool sites because little else was found with the tools. In contrast, finds of later tool assemblages at Olduvai Gorge in Tanzania have yielded a rich harvest of cultural information. The Olduvai site was uncovered accidentally in 1911, when a German entomologist followed a butterfly into the gorge and found fossil remains. Beginning in the 1930s, Louis and Mary Leakey searched the

Percussion Flaking: a toolmaking technique in which one stone is struck with another to remove a flake.

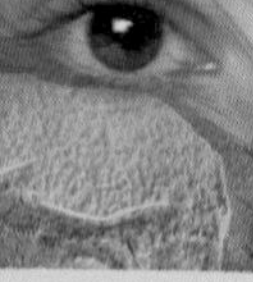

ANTHROPOLOGY IN ACTION

Student Perspectives: Matt Tocheri

I will never forget the first time I became aware of the field of anthropology. When I was around 10 years old my mother had gone back to university and I would often ask her about what she was learning. One time she told me about Dr. Napolean Chagnon and his ethnography of the Yanomamö and I was completely fascinated. Little did I realize that this early introduction to the field of anthropology would later lead to a significant directional change in my adult life.

During my second year at Lakehead University, I came across an "Introduction to Cultural Anthropology" course. I immediately recalled the long-ago conversations I had had with my mom and I registered in the course. I loved it, and after it was over I wanted to take every anthropology course possible. Although I was fascinated with cultural anthropology, I also had a strong interest in biology. After taking three courses in physical anthropology, I was hooked. As I became a more experienced student, Dr. Molto, a physical anthropologist, invited me to participate in bioarchaelogical fieldwork at the Roman-period town of Kellis, as part of the Dakhleh Oasis Project in Egypt.

After I graduated, I began my MA at Arizona State University with Dr. Brenda Baker. During this time I also became involved with the Partnership for Research In Spatial Modeling (PRISM), which was a 3D interdisciplinary research group at ASU, because I was interested in applying 3D techniques to human osteology. This led me to meeting Dr. Mary Marzke, a physical anthropologist who specialized in comparative primate functional morphology. She was already involved in a PRISM project that was developing 3D techniques to study hand and wrist bones and I had been hired as a research assistant to help in the development process. Before long, I became completely captivated with the morphological complexity of the wrist in primates as well as the 3D techniques we were developing to study it. Dr. Marzke became my main PhD advisor and my dissertation focused on using these 3D techniques to answer questions about the evolution and adaptive significance of the wrist in hominids. In particular, my research attempts to provide a more complete picture of how and when the morphology of the wrist changed within the hominin lineage with respect to the evolution of behaviours involving the use and manufacture of stone tools.

My dissertation research led me to the National Museum of Natural History in Washington, DC when I was awarded a one-year Smithsonian Predoctoral Fellowship to work with Dr. Rick Potts, director of the Human Origins Program at the Smithsonian Institution. After this, I continued to work with Dr. Potts on various projects related to human evolution as a postdoctoral fellow. In 2007, in conjunction with a team of American and Indonesian researchers, I am involved in the first description and analysis of the wrist remains of *Homo floresiensis*. Without a doubt, to be involved in such a study is like a dream that has come true. If I think back to all the folks who, over the years, had said to me in a condescending tone, "what are you going to do with a degree in physical anthropology?" I can think of only one adequate response: "You know, I'm not really sure you would believe me if I told you."

Matt Tocheri

Source: Matt Tocheri.

gorge for clues to the evolution of early humans. Of the Olduvai site, Louis Leakey wrote,

> [It] is a fossil hunter's dream, for it shears 300 feet [91.4 metres] through stratum after stratum of earth's history as through a gigantic layer cake. Here, within reach, lie countless fossils and artifacts that but for the faulting and erosion would have remained sealed under thick layers of consolidated rock. (Leakey, 1960)

The oldest cultural materials from Olduvai (Bed I) date from the Lower Pleistocene. The stone artifacts include core tools and sharp-edged flakes, but flake tools predominate. Among the core tools, so-called *choppers* are common. A chopper is a core tool that has been partially flaked and has a side that might have been used for chopping. Other core tools, with flaking along one side and a flat edge, are called *scrapers*.

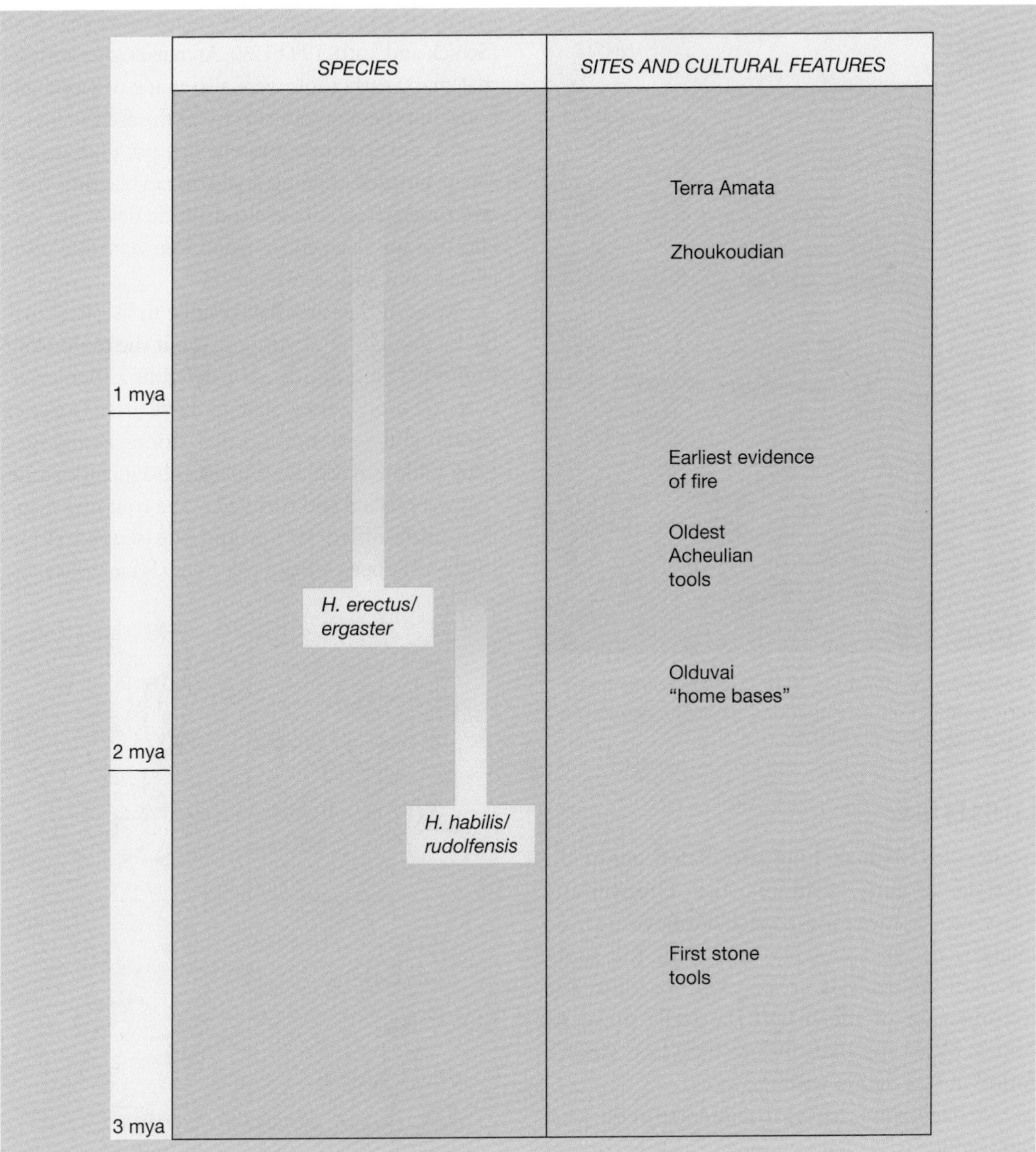

Figure 8–7 Early Evolution of the Genus *Homo*

Whenever a stone has facets removed from only one side of the cutting edge, we call it a **unifacial tool**. If the stone has facets removed from both sides, we call it a **bifacial tool**. Although there are some bifacial tools in the early stone tool assemblages, they are neither as plentiful nor as elaborated as in later tool traditions. The kind of tool assemblage found in Bed I and to some extent in later (higher) layers is referred to as **Oldowan** (see Figure 8–8) (Clark, 1970; Schick and Toth, 1994).

Unifacial Tool: a tool worked or flaked on one side only.
Bifacial Tool: a tool worked or flaked on two sides.
Oldowan: the earliest stone toolmaking tradition, named after the tools found in Bed I at Olduvai Gorge, Tanzania; from about 2.5 million years ago. The stone artifacts include core tools and sharp-edged flakes made by striking one stone against another. Flake tools predominate. Among the core tools, so-called choppers are common.

Olduvai Gorge, Tanzania. Bed I, where evidence of early human culture was found, is at the very bottom of the Gorge.

Lifestyles

Archaeologists have long speculated about the lifestyles of early hominins from Olduvai and other sites. Some of these speculations come from analysis of what can be done with the tools, microscopic analysis of wear on the tools, and examination of the marks the tools make on bones; other speculations are based on what is found in association with the tools.

Archaeologists have experimented with what can be done with Oldowan tools. The flakes appear to be very versatile; they can be used for slitting the hides of animals, dismembering animals, and whittling wood into sharp-pointed sticks (wooden spears or digging sticks). The larger stone tools (choppers and scrapers) can be used to hack off branches or cut and chop tough animal joints (Schick and Toth, 1994). Those who have made and tried to use the stone flake tools for various purposes are so impressed by the sharpness and versatility of flakes that they wonder whether the core tools were really routinely used as tools. The cores could mainly be what remained after flakes were struck off (Schick and Toth, 1994:129). Archaeologists surmise that many early tools were also made of wood and bone, but these do not survive in the archaeological record. For example, present-day populations use sharp-pointed digging sticks for extracting roots and tubers from the ground; stone flakes are very effective for sharpening wood to a very fine point (Schick and Toth, 1994).

None of the early flaked stone tools can plausibly be thought of as weapons. So if the toolmaking hominins were hunting or defending themselves with weapons, they had to have used wooden spears, clubs, or unmodified stones as missiles. Later Oldowan tool assemblages also include stones that were flaked and battered into a rounded shape. The unmodified stones and the shaped stones might have been lethal projectiles (Isaac, 1984).

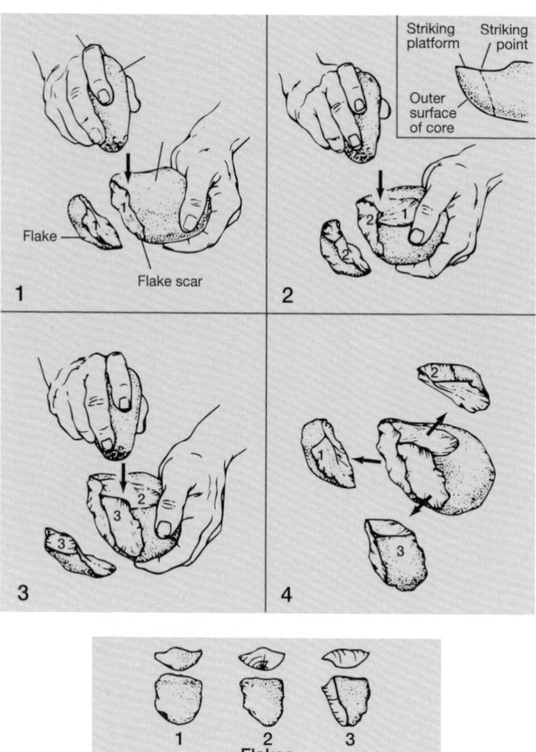

Figure 8–8 The Production of a Simple Oldowan Chopper Core and the Resultant Flakes

Source: Freyman R. The First Technology. Scientific American. © *Scientific American*, Inc. Reprinted by permission of Ed Hanson, artist.

Experiments may tell us what can be done with tools, but they cannot tell us what was actually done with them. Other techniques, such as microscopic analysis of the wear on tools, are more informative. Early studies focused on the microscopic scratches formed when a tool was used in different ways. Scratches parallel to the edge of a tool often occur when a tool is used in a sawing motion; perpendicular scratches suggest whittling or scraping (Whittaker, 1994). Lawrence Keeley used high-powered microscopes in his experimental investigations of tools and found that different kinds of "polish" develop on tools when they are used on different materials. The polish on tools used for cutting meat is different from the polish on tools used for woodworking. On the basis of microscopic investigation of the 1.5-million-year-old tools from the eastern side of Lake Turkana, Keeley and his colleagues concluded that at least some of the early tools were probably used for cutting meat, others for cutting or whittling wood, and others for cutting plant stems (Schick and Toth, 1994).

In the 1950s and 1960s, Olduvai Gorge revealed the presence of both Oldowan tools and the remains of broken bones and teeth from many different animal species. For many years it seemed plausible to assume that hominins were the hunters and the animals their prey. However, archaeologists had to re-examine this assumption with the emergence of the field of *taphonomy*, which is the study of the processes that can alter and distort a sample of bones. So, for example, flowing water can bring bones and artifacts together, which may have happened at Olduvai Gorge about 1.8 million years ago. (The area of what is now the gorge bordered the shores of a shallow lake at that time.) Also other animals such as hyenas could have brought carcasses to some of the same places that hominins frequented. Taphonomy requires archaeologists to consider all the possible reasons that might explain why things may be found together (Speth, 1998).

Regardless, there is little doubt that hominins shortly after 2 million years ago were cutting up animal carcasses for meat. Microscopic analyses show that cut marks on animal bones were unambiguously created by stone flake tools, and microscopic analyses of polish on stone tools show the polish to be consistent with butchering. We still do not know for sure whether the hominins around Olduvai Gorge were just scavenging meat (taking meat from the kills of other animals) or hunting the animals. On the basis of her analysis of cut marks on bone from Bed I in Olduvai Gorge, Pat Shipman suggested that scavenging, not hunting, was the major meat-getting activity of the hominins living there between 2 million and 1.7 million years ago. For example, the fact that cut marks made by stone tools usually (but not always) overlie teeth marks made by carnivores suggests that the hominins were often scavenging the meat of animals killed and partially eaten by non-hominin predators. The fact that the cut marks were sometimes made first, however, suggested to Shipman that the hominins were also sometimes the hunters (Szalay, 1975; Shipman, 1986). On the other hand, prior cut marks may indicate only that the hominins scavenged before carnivores had a chance to.

The artifact and animal remains from Bed I and the lower part of Bed II at Olduvai suggest a few other things about the lifestyles of the hominins there. First, it seems that the hominins moved around during the year; most of the sites in what is now the Olduvai Gorge appear to have been used only in the dry season, as indicated by an analysis of the kinds of animal bones found there (Speth and Davis, 1976). Second, whether the early Olduvai hominins were hunters or scavengers, they apparently exploited a wide range of animals. Although most of the bones are from medium-sized antelopes and wild pigs, even large animals such as elephants and giraffes seem to have been eaten (Isaac, 1971). It is clear, then, that the Olduvai hominins scavenged or hunted for meat, but we cannot tell yet how important meat was in their diet.

There is also no consensus yet about how to characterize the Olduvai sites. In the 1970s, there was a tendency to think of these sites (which contain tools and animal bones) as home bases to which hominins (presumably male) brought meat to share with others (presumably nursing mothers and young children). Indeed, Mary Leakey identified two locations where she thought early hominins had built simple structures (see Figure 8-9). One was a stone circle that she suggested formed the base of a small brush windbreak. The other was a circular area of dense debris surrounded by an area virtually without debris. Leakey suggested that the area lacking debris may represent the location of a ring of thorny brush with which early hominins surrounded their campsite in order to keep out predators—much like pastoralists living in the region do today (Leakey, 1971). But archaeologists today are not so sure that these sites were home bases. For one thing, carnivores also frequented these sites. Places with meaty bones lying around may not have been so safe for hominins to use as home bases. Second, the animal remains at the sites had not been completely dismembered and butchered. If the sites had been hominin home bases, we would expect more complete processing of carcasses (Potts, 1988).

If these sites were not home bases, what were they? Some archaeologists are beginning to think that these early sites with many animal bones and tools may just have been places where hominins processed food but did not live. Why would the hominins return to a particular site? Richard Potts suggests one possible reason—that hominins left caches of stone tools and stones for toolmaking at various locations to facilitate their food-collecting and food-processing activities (Potts, 1988). Future research may tell us more about early hominin life. Did they have home bases, or did they just move from one processing site to another? How did they protect themselves from predators? They apparently did not have fire to keep the predators away. Did they climb trees to get away from predators or to sleep safely?

Regardless of the answers to these questions, the presence of patterned stone tools means that these early hominins had probably developed culture. Archaeologists consider a pattern of behaviour, such as a particular way to make a tool that is shared and learned by a group of individuals, to be a sign of cultural behaviour. To be sure, toolmaking does not imply that early humans had anything like the complex cultures of humans today. Chimpanzees have patterns of tool use and toolmaking that appear to be shared and learned, but they do not have that much in the way of cultural behaviour.

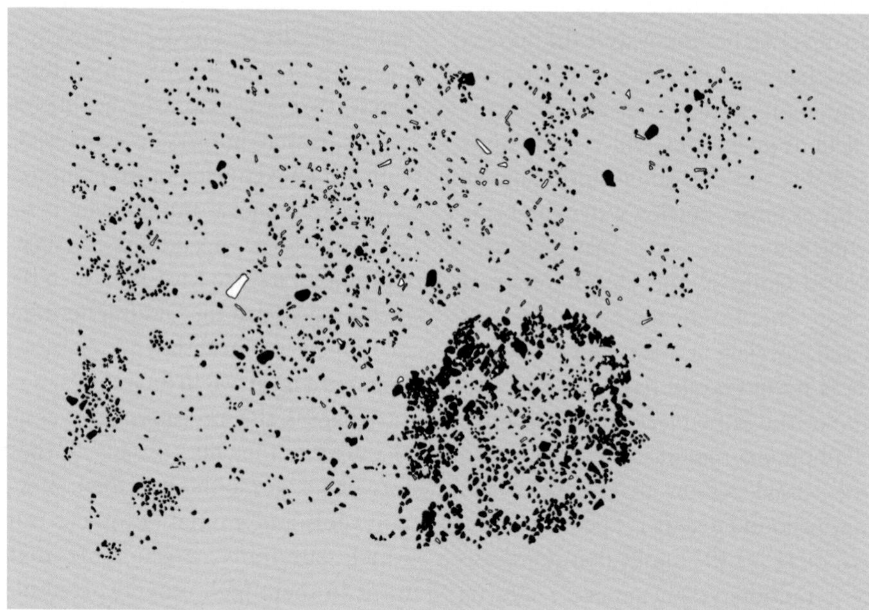

Figure 8–9 Olduvai "Hut"

A ring of stones and bones found in Bed I of Olduvai Gorge that Mary Leakey interpreted as the remains of an ancient hut.

What exactly makes human culture so different from other forms of animal behaviour? Anthropologists have spent more than a century trying to answer this question, and there is still no widely accepted answer. One thing is clear, however. Culture must be understood as a set of interrelated processes, not as a thing (Wolf, 1984). What are the processes that make up culture? Let's consider some of the more important ones.

First, culture is learned and shared. That is the fundamental difference between culture and most other forms of animal behaviour. Culture is not a set of innate behaviours but rather a set of learned ones. Culture is something individuals acquire during their lifetimes as they mature and interact with others. Interaction is key here, because not only are cultural behaviours learned, they are learned through interaction with others and through education and shared experiences. Culture, then, is a social process, not an individual one.

Second, culture is generally adaptive. What this means is that most of the learned and shared behaviours that make up a culture are thought to have developed and spread through a group of people because they help that group of people to survive in a given environment. Thus, cultural behaviour may be favoured by natural selection just as genes are. The extent to which human culture is a product of natural selection is hotly debated, but few anthropologists would argue that culture is not a key aspect of human adaptation. What makes culture quite different from the behavioural systems of other animals is that, because culture is learned and shared rather than innate, humans can develop new behaviours quickly and adapt to diverse and changing conditions with relative ease. Adaptation, therefore, is perhaps the most significant process of culture.

Change is the third major process of culture, for culture is always changing. Culture change regularly occurs as new and beneficial means of adaptation are developed and shared. However, anthropologists also assume that when new behaviours are developed, they tend to become integrated within existing behaviours. That is, new behaviours that conflict with established ones may lead to one or the other changing. For example, a group of early humans could not have both scavenged meat and, at the same time, prohibited eating meat that they themselves did not kill. Such a situation would create a contradiction, and something would have to change. Working out contradictions between new, highly beneficial behaviours and established but less beneficial behaviours may be one of the reasons that cultures are so dynamic.

It seems clear that early hominins, like other primates, were social beings. It also seems clear from the archaeological record that early hominins were making and using stone tools. Tools are frequently found in discrete concentrations, and often in association with animal bones and other debris from activity. As has already been suggested, therefore, these concentrations may reflect campsites or small shelters, implying that home bases may have been a part of early hominin culture.

Whether they reflect home bases or not, these accumulations of tools and other artifacts suggest that the areas were being used by groups of individuals over periods of time. In such a situation, sharing of food is very likely. It seems counterintuitive to think that individuals would have purposely brought food to a common location only to keep it to themselves. While this is only speculation, it does not seem unreasonable to think that closely related individuals, such as families, would be more likely to associate and share food with one another than more distantly related individuals. This speculation is supported by the fact that when food-sharing takes place among chimpanzees it is usually among closely related individuals (Boyd and Silk, 2000). Thus, the ancient locations of early hominin social activity may be evidence for family groups.

Language

As discussed briefly in Chapter 6, the evidence for language capabilities among hominins comes from skeletal evidence like the increased flexion of the basicranium. Other evidence comes from endocasts that can give us clues as to the structure of the brain. Through the reconstruction of the skeletal anatomy associated with language in hominins, australopithecines appear to have had ape-like anatomy and brains that resemble the living apes in both size and external form—thus, there is no apparent evidence for spoken language (Lieberman, 2002). Similarly, there is no strong evidence in support of language capabilities for *H. habilis*, with the exception of a 2-million-year-old endocast that shows a more developed frontal lobe and Broca's area—the area that is responsible for human speech (Tobias, 1987).

However, some have argued that bipedalism, which allowed for the freeing of the hands, may have also provided the ability for increased communication by gestures among the earliest hominins—to a much greater extent than non-human primates (Corballis, 1999). Merlin Donald, a researcher in the Department of Psychology at Queen's University, has suggested that early forms of communication involved the whole body rather than just the hands and arms. There is debate about whether this form of "body language" is distinct from language proper, or whether it is a precursor to the development of spoken language (Corballis, 1999). The earliest hominins appear not to have developed spoken language capabilities, although there may be evidence for selection favouring those features that would be important for spoken language in later hominins.

In the next chapter we will discuss the appearance of *H. erectus*, the first hominin to leave Africa, and early *H. sapiens* populations, including Neandertals.

Summary

1. The drying trend in climate that began about 16 million to 11 million years ago diminished the extent of African rain forests and gave rise to areas of savannah (tropical grasslands) and scattered deciduous woodlands. The more open country probably favoured characteristics adapted to ground living in some primates. In the evolutionary line leading to humans, these adaptations included bipedalism.
2. One of the crucial changes in early hominin evolution was the development of bipedalism. There are several theories for this development. It may have increased the emerging hominin's ability to see predators and potential prey while moving through the tall grasses of the savannah; by freeing the hands for carrying, it may have facilitated transferring food from one place to another; tool use, which requires free hands, may have favoured two-legged walking; and bipedalism may have made long-distance travelling more efficient.
3. Other important physical changes—including the expansion of the brain, modification of the female pelvis to allow bigger-brained babies to be born, and reduction of the face, teeth, and jaws—did not begin until about 2 million years after the emergence of bipedalism. By that time (about 2 million years ago) hominins had come to depend to some extent on scavenging and possibly hunting meat.
4. The remains of undisputed hominins dating back to between 4 million and 3 million years ago have been found in East Africa. These definitely bipedal hominins are now generally classified in the genus *Australopithecus*. Most palaeoanthropologists divide the genus *Australopithecus* into at least four species. Some East African hominins that lived nearly 2 million years ago are classified as an early species of our own genus, *Homo habilis*.
5. The earliest stone tools found so far come from various sites in East Africa and date from about 2.5 million years ago. We do not yet know who made them. These tools were made by striking a stone with another stone to remove sharp-edged flakes. Both the flakes and the sharp-edged cores were used as tools. This early tool tradition is called Oldowan.

Glossary Terms

Ardipithecus ramidus (p. 168)
Australopithecus (p. 159)
Australopithecus aethiopicus (p. 171)

Australopithecus afarensis (p. 169)
Australopithecus africanus (p. 169)
Australopithecus anamensis (p. 169)
Australopithecus bahrelghazali (p. 169)
Australopithecus boisei (p. 171)
Australopithecus garhi (p. 170)
Australopithecus robustus (p. 171)
bifacial tool (p. 183)
foramen magnum (p. 164)
gracile anstralopithecines (p. 169)
Homo (p. 159)
Homo erectus (p. 165)
Homo habilis (p. 165)
Homo rudolfensis (p. 180)
Kenyanthropus platyops (p. 171)
lumbar curve (p. 175)
Oldowan (p. 183)
Orrorin tugenensis (p. 168)
Paranthropus (p. 175)
percussion flaking (p. 181)
Pliocene (p. 172)
robust australopithecines (p. 171)
sagittal crest (p. 171)
Sahelanthropus tchadensis (p. 168)
unifacial tool (p. 183)

Critical Questions

1. How could there have been more than one species of hominin living in East Africa at the same time?
2. What may have enabled australopithecines to survive in the face of many ground predators?
3. What is the evidence for language among the earliest hominins?

Internet Exercises

1. Visit **www.talkorigins.org/faqs/homs/specimen.html** to view some prominent hominin fossils. Write a brief summary of your findings pertaining to *Australopithecus afarensis* and Donald Johanson.
2. Go to **/www.mc.maricopa.edu/dept/d10/asb/anthro2003/origins/hominin_journey/robust3.html** to view information regarding the fossil evidence for robust australopithecines. Create a table of the differences in morphology for each species.
3. Explore a site devoted to stone tool technology at **www.hf.uio.no/iakn/roger/lithic/**. Look in particular for earlier stone tool technologies, and draw a rough progression of technologies.
4. Go to **www.archaeologyinfo.com/homohabilis.htm** and explore the diagnostic features of australopithecines and early *Homo*. What are the major differences? Are there any similarities?
5. Review the classification of early hominin fossils **www.mnh.si.edu/anthro/humanorigins/ha/a_tree.html.**

Suggested Reading

Conroy GC. 1990. Primate Evolution. New York: Norton. Chapter 6 summarizes the fossil record for the australopithecines and early *Homo*, discusses the geography and climate of the early sites, and explains the biomechanical principles of bipedalism.

Ember CR, Ember M, and Peregrine PN, editors. 1998. Research Frontiers in Anthropology. Upper Saddle River, NJ: Prentice Hall. Prentice Hall/Simon & Schuster Custom Publishing. Several chapters in this series deal with the evolution of early hominins and their cultures, for example, Bromage TG, Paleoanthropology and Life History, and Life History of a Paleoanthropologist; Kramer A, The Natural History and Evolutionary Fate of *Homo erectus*; McHenry HM, "Robust" Australopithecines, Our Family Tree, and Homoplasy; Simpson SW, *Australopithecus afarensis* and Human Evolution; Speth JD, Were Our Ancestors Hunters or Scavengers?

Grine FE, editor. 1988. Evolutionary History of the "Robust" Australopithecines. New York: Aldine. A great deal of controversy has surrounded the "robust" australopithecines. In a 1987 workshop, participants from many different fields were asked to summarize recent knowledge of this group of australopithecines.

Phillipson DW. 1993. African Archaeology. Second edition. Cambridge: Cambridge University Press. A summary and interpretation of the archaeological evidence in Africa and what it tells us about human history from its beginnings to historic times. Chapters 2 and 3 are particularly relevant to this chapter.

Schick K, Toth N. 1994. Making Silent Stones Speak. New York: Simon & Schuster. A large part of understanding past tool traditions is making them and using them. The authors describe their experimental work and relate it to the archaeologically recovered tool traditions of the past.

HOMO ERECTUS AND ARCHAIC *HOMO SAPIENS*

CHAPTER OUTLINE

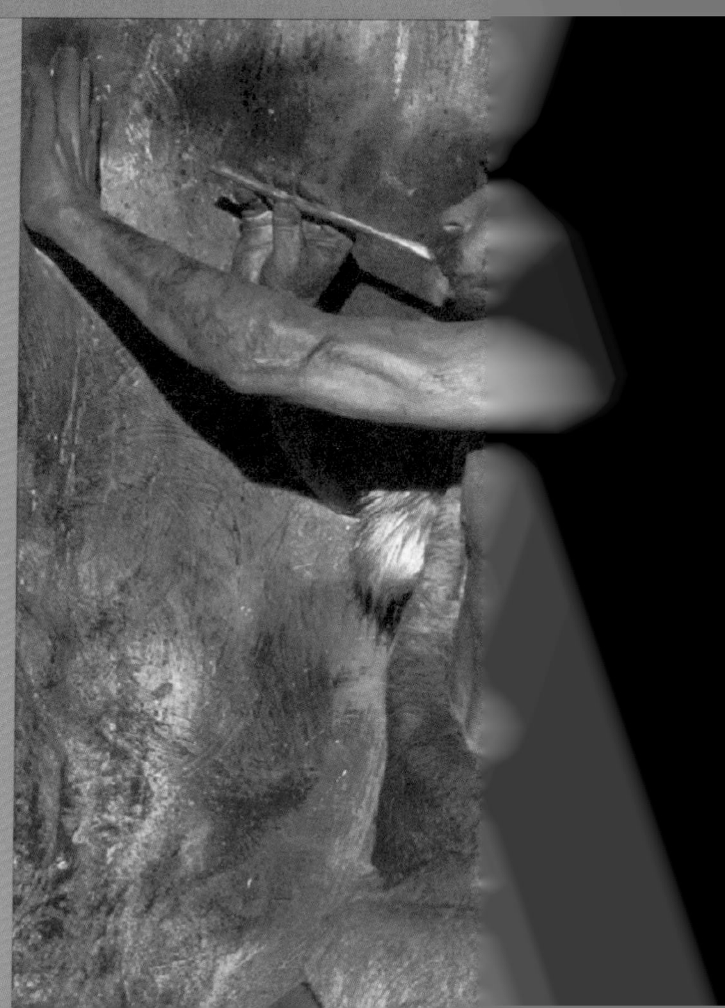

Homo erectus Culture

The archaeological finds of tools and other cultural artifacts dating from 1.8 million years ago to about 200 000 years ago are assumed to have been produced by *H. erectus.* Unfortunately, fossils are not usually associated with these materials. Therefore, it is possible that some of the tools were produced by hominins other than *H. erectus,* such as *H. habilis* earlier and *H. sapiens* later. *Homo erectus* continued to use the Oldowan chopper tool technology, but also developed a more sophisticated tool tradition called Acheulian. The Acheulian tool assemblages dating from 1.5 million years ago to more than a million years later are very similar to each other. *Homo erectus* is the only hominin that spans the entire period, so it is conventionally assumed that *H. erectus* was responsible for most if not all of the Acheulian tool assemblages we describe below (Phillipson, 1993:57).

The Acheulian Tool Tradition

The Acheulian stone toolmaking tradition was named after the site at St. Acheul, France, where the first examples were found. However, the oldest Acheulian tools, dating back about 1.5 million years, have been recovered from East Africa, on the Peninj River, Tanzania (Schick and Toth, 1994). In contrast to Oldowan, the Acheulian tools were larger, with a set of typical designs or shapes. Oldowan tools have sharp edges, made by a few blows. Acheulian toolmakers shaped the stone by knocking more flakes off most of the edges. Many of these tools were made from very large flakes that had been struck from very large cores or boulders. One of the most characteristic and prevalent tools in the Acheulian tool kit is the so-called "hand axe," which is a teardrop-shaped bifacially flaked tool with a thinned sharp tip. Other large tools resemble cleavers and picks. There were also many other kinds of flake tools, such as scrapers with a wide edge. Early Acheulian tools appeared to have been made by blows with a hard stone, but later tools are wider and flatter and may have been made with a soft "hammer" of bone or antler (Schick and Toth, 1994; Whittaker, 1994). This soft hammer technique of making stone tools was an important innovation. Tools made by a hard hammer technique, rock against rock, have limits in terms of their sharpness and form, because only large and thick flakes can be made with a hard hammer technique (unless the flintknapper is very skillful and the stone being used has unique qualities). Flakes created by soft hammer flaking are much thinner and longer than hard hammer flakes, and the flintknapper generally has better control over their size and shape. This means that thinner and sharper tools can be made, as well as tools with complex shapes. Hand axes can be made with either technique, as their shape is simple, but those made using a soft hammer have much thinner and sharper edges (Bordes 1968; Whittaker 1994).

Were hand axes made for chopping trees, as their name suggests? We cannot be sure what they were used for, but experiments with Acheulian hand axes suggest that they are not good for cutting trees; they seem more suited for butchering large animals (Schick and Toth, 1994; Whittaker, 1994). Lawrence Keeley microscopically examined some Acheulian hand axes, and the wear on them is consistent with animal butchery. The picks may have been used for woodworking, particularly hollowing and shaping wood, and they are also good for digging (Schick and Toth, 1994:260).

Acheulian: a stone toolmaking tradition dating from 1.5 million years ago. Compared with the Oldowan tradition, Acheulian assemblages have more large tools created according to standardized designs or shapes. One of the most characteristic and prevalent tools in the Acheulian tool kit is the so-called hand axe, which is a teardrop-shaped bifacially flaked tool with a thinned sharp tip. Other large tools may have been cleavers and picks.

An Acheulian hand axe. Lawrence Keeley examined the edge wear on hand axes to determine how they were used.

Acheulian tools are found widely in Africa, Europe, and western Asia, but bifacial hand axes, cleavers, and picks are not found as commonly in eastern and southeastern Asia. Because *H. erectus* has been found in all areas of the Old World, it is puzzling why the tool traditions seem to differ from west to east. Older arguments suggested differences in technological sophistication between eastern and western populations. However, some archaeologists have suggested that large bifacial tools may be lacking in eastern and southeastern Asia because *H. erectus* there had a better material for making tools—bamboo. Bamboo is used today in Southeast Asia for many purposes, including the making of incredibly sharp arrows and sticks for digging and cutting. Geoffrey Pope showed that bamboo is found in those areas of Asia where hand axes and other large bifacial tools are missing (Pope, 1989; Ciochon et al., 1990). Recent evidence shows the presence of Acheulian hand axes over 800 000 years ago in southern China (Yamei et al., 2000).

Big-Game Eating

Some of the Acheulian sites have produced evidence of big-game eating. F. Clark Howell, who excavated sites at Torralba and Ambrona, Spain, found a substantial number of elephant remains and unmistakable evidence of human presence in the form of tools. These sites are situated strategically on two hilltops flanking a mountain pass. Howell suggests that the humans at those sites used fire to frighten elephants into muddy bogs, from which they would be unable to escape (Howell, 1966). To hunt elephants in this way, the humans would have had to plan and work co-operatively in fairly large groups.

But do these finds of bones of large and medium-sized animals, in association with tools, tell us that the humans definitely were big-game hunters? Some archaeologists who have reanalyzed the evidence from Torralba think that the big game may have been scavenged. Because the Torralba and Ambrona sites are near ancient streams, many of the elephants could have died naturally, their bones accumulating in certain spots because of the flow of water (Binford, 1987; Klein, 1987). It is still unclear whether *H. erectus* deliberately butchered different kinds of game. While different types of tools are found with different types of animal (Freeman, 1994), reanalysis by Pat Shipman and Jennie Rose of the cut marks on the remains has cast new doubt on this evidence. Over 95 percent of the bones present were too poorly preserved to clearly identify stone tool cut marks. Of those that could be clearly identified, only 16 cut marks have been confirmed on four bones (Shipman and Rose, 1983). Thus, whether the humans hunted big game at Torralba and Ambrona is debatable; all we can be sure of, as of now, is that they consumed big game and probably hunted smaller game.

Other sites that may represent evidence of co-operative hunting include BK II in Tanzania, which dates to at least 400 000 years ago. Here there are the remains of wild cattle that may have been driven into the swamp and then killed and butchered by *H. erectus* (Howell, 1966; Butzer, 1982a). At Olorgesailie in Kenya, there is possible evidence of co-operative hunting by *H. erectus.* On the lake edge at this site more than 60 individuals of extinct baboons have been excavated. K/Ar dates for this site suggest it may be as old as 700 000 to 900 000 years (Isaac, 1977). It is worth noting that these are not the savannah baboons with which we are familiar today, but rather an extinct "giant" baboon, *Theropithecus oswaldi,* which could be as big as a female gorilla. Given an animal of this size and power, the argument for some sort of co-operative hunting is strengthened that much more. At both these sites the animal remains have been excavated in association with cobbles and stone tools.

Control of Fire

Because *H. erectus* was the first hominin to be found throughout the Old World and in areas with freezing winters, most anthropologists presume that *H. erectus* had learned to control fire, at least for warmth. There is archaeological evidence of fire in some early sites, but fires can be natural events. Thus, whether fire was under deliberate control by *H. erectus* is difficult to establish.

Suggestive but not conclusive evidence of the deliberate use of fire comes from Kenya in East Africa and is over 1.4 million years old (Isaac, 1984; Brain and Sillen, 1988) and from the Swartkans cave in South Africa dated to between 1.5 and 1 million years ago (Brain and Sillen, 1988). Possible evidence of human control of fire, dating from nearly 500 000 years ago, comes from the cave at Zhoukoudian in China where *H. erectus* fossils have been found (Klein, 1989:171). In that cave are thousands of splintered and charred animal bones, apparently the remains of meals. There are also layers of ash, suggesting human control of fire. But recent analysis raises questions about these finds. The most serious problem is that human remains, tools, and ash rarely occur together in the same layers. In addition, there are no hearths at the Zhoukoudian site. Fires can spontaneously occur with heavy accumulation of organic matter, so clear evidence of human control of fire is still not definitely attested. Even the inference that humans brought the animals to the cave for butchering is only possibly a correct guess. Throughout the cave there is evidence of hyenas and wolves, and they, not the humans, may have brought many of the animal parts to the cave (Binford and Ho, 1985).

More persuasive evidence of human control of fire, dating from nearly 800 000 years ago, comes from the site of Gesher Benot Ya'aqov in Israel. Here researchers found evidence of burned seeds, wood, and stone, as well as concentrations of burned items suggestive of hearths (Goren-Inbar et al., 2004).

Better evidence of the deliberate use of fire comes from Europe somewhat later. Unfortunately, the evidence of control of fire at these European sites is not associated with *H. erectus* fossils either, so the link between deliberate use of fire and *H. erectus* cannot be definitely established yet. The lack of clear evidence does not, of course, mean that *H. erectus* did not use fire. After all, *H. erectus* did move into cold areas of the world, and it is hard to imagine how that could have happened without the deliberate use of fire. Such a move is also hard to imagine if *H. erectus* were relatively hairless and did not get warm skins and furs from hunting.

Clothing, therefore, may have been necessary, but fire might have been even more important, and not only for warmth. Cooking would be possible. The control of fire was a major step in increasing

Homo erectus ate—and probably hunted—large game animals, and probably also learned to control fire.

the energy under human control. Cooking made all kinds of food (not just meat) more safely digestible and therefore more usable. Fires would also have kept predators away, a not inconsiderable advantage given that there were a lot of them around.

Campsites

Acheulian sites were usually located close to water sources, lush vegetation, and large stocks of herbivorous animals. Some camps have been found in caves, but most were in open areas surrounded by rudimentary fortifications or windbreaks. Several African sites are marked by stony rubble brought there by *H. erectus*, possibly for the dual purpose of securing the windbreaks and providing ammunition in case of a sudden attack (Clark, 1970).

The presumed base campsites display a variety of tools, indicating that the camps were the centre of many group functions. More specialized sites away from camp have also been found. These are marked by the predominance of a particular type of tool. For example, a butchering site in Tanzania contained dismembered hippopotamus carcasses and rare heavy-duty smashing and cutting tools. What appear to have been workshops are another kind of specialized site encountered with some regularity. They are characterized by tool debris and are located close to a source of natural stone suitable for toolmaking (Clark, 1970).

A camp has been excavated at the Terra Amata site near Nice, on the French Riviera. The camp appears to have been occupied in late spring or early summer, judging by the pollen found in fossilized human feces. The excavator describes stake holes driven into the sand, associated with parallel lines of stones, presumably marking the spots where the people constructed huts of roughly 4.5 metres by 9 metres (see Figure 9–3). A basic feature of each hut was a central hearth that seems to have been protected from drafts by a small wall built just outside the northeast corner of the hearth. The evidence suggests that the Terra Amata occupants gathered seafood such as oysters and mussels, did some fishing, and hunted in the surrounding area. The animal remains suggest that they obtained both small and large animals, but mostly got the young of larger animals such as stags, elephants, boars, rhinoceroses, and wild oxen. Some of the huts contain recognizable toolmakers' areas, scattered with tool debris; occasionally, the impression of an animal skin shows where the toolmaker actually sat (de Lumley, 1969). The site at Terra Amata, which is geologically dated between 400 000 and 200 000 years ago, has been interpreted as possibly one of the earliest identified hominin shelters (de Lumley, 1969).

Religion and Ritual

Did *H. erectus* take part in rituals? Did *H. erectus* have religion? The data we have to answer these questions are limited, but there are some hints that ritual may have been part of Lower Palaeolithic culture.

Remains of red ochre (oxidized clay) have been found on a number of Lower Palaeolithic sites (Dickson, 1990). This may be significant because in many later cultures, even modern ones, red ochre has been used in rituals of various types to represent blood, or more generally, life. Ochre seems to be particularly important in burial rituals, and human remains sprinkled with red ochre have been found in many parts of the world and dating back as far as the Middle Palaeolithic (about 200 000 years ago). However, there is no evidence to suggest that *H. erectus* buried their dead, nor any evidence that red ochre was used in rituals. It may have been used for body decoration, or simply for protection against insects or sunburn.

More significant, and even more controversial, is the suggestion made by the excavators of Zhoukoudian in northern China that some of the *H. erectus* remains there showed evidence of ritual cannibalism (Dickson, 1990; Tattersall and Schwartz, 2000). The foramen magnum of some specimens had been deliberately enlarged and the facial bones had been deliberately broken away from the cranium on others. A possible reason may have been to remove the brain for ritual consumption. Ritual cannibalism has been widely reported among living peoples, so its presence among ancient peoples is not impossible. But scholars point out that the parts of the skull that seem to have been purposely enlarged to remove the brain are those that are also the weakest points of the skull, and may have broken away

Figure 9–3 A Reconstruction of the Oval Huts Built at Terra Amata
These huts were approximately 4.5 metres by 9 metres.

Source: Copyright © 1969 by Eric Mose.

because of decay or disturbance over time. Therefore, at this time we cannot say with any certainty what role, if any, religion or ritual played in Lower Palaeolithic culture.

Language

We use the same skeletal evidence to determine whether *H. erectus* had developed language that we used to examine language development in earlier hominins. As noted above, while an increased cranial capacity in *H. erectus* could be related to an increase in overall body size, it appears that the skull was proportioned differently than in earlier hominins. This suggests a remodelling of the brain, in particular the differential growth of the frontal and posterior portion of the brain. In other words, the *H. erectus* brain is more similar in form to the modern brain. Analysis of endocasts of *H. erectus* specimens from Ngandong and Sangiran in Java have suggested that hemispheric specialization—the idea that the right and left halves of the brain control different aspects of behaviour, as in modern humans—is present in *H. erectus* (Holloway, 1980; Holloway, 1981). This has been interpreted by some to suggest that by 1.7 million years ago *H. erectus* would have possessed linguistic skills and the ability to manipulate symbols (Holloway, 1980; Holloway, 1981). Other evidence from the basicranial remains of *H. erectus* also supports a modern capability for language. It is suggested that *H. erectus* had the ability for language at the level of a modern 6-year-old (Laitman and Heimbuch, 1984). However, recent studies of the Mojokerto child suggest some differences. Balzeau and colleagues' (2005) study of the Mojokerto endocast suggests that there are differences in development of the frontal lobes. Coqueugniot and co-workers (2004) suggest that the relative brain development of the specimen is more like that of apes than modern humans, and therefore the cognitive abilities of H erectus were not the same as *H. sapiens.*

Archaic *Homo sapiens*

The cultures of early hominins are traditionally classified as Lower Palaeolithic or early Stone Age. In this section we discuss the fossil evidence as well as the controversies about the transition from *H. erectus* to Archaic *Homo sapiens*, which may have begun 500 000 years ago. We also discuss what we know archaeologically about Middle Palaeolithic cultures of the early *H. sapiens* that lived between about 300 000 and 40 000 years ago.

Most palaeoanthropologists agree that *H. erectus* evolved into *H. sapiens*, but they disagree about how and where the transition occurred. There is also disagreement about how to classify some fossils from 400 000 to about 200 000 years ago that have a mix of *H. erectus* and *H. sapiens* traits (Stringer, 1985). A particular fossil might be called *H. erectus* by some anthropologists and "archaic" *Homo sapiens* by others. As we shall see, still other anthropologists see so much continuity between *H. erectus* and *H. sapiens* that they think it is completely arbitrary to call them different species. According to these anthropologists, *H. erectus* and *H. sapiens* may just be earlier and later varieties of the same species and therefore all should be called *H. sapiens.* (*Homo erectus* would then be *H. sapiens erectus.*)

There seems to be a fair degree of homogeneity in *H. erectus* specimens, both geographically and temporally, over the 1 million years or so of their successful existence. While there are regular anatomical changes over time, like a reduction in the size of the rear teeth, an associated decrease in the size of the face and lower jaw, and an increase in incisor size, other features remain relatively constant. Similarly there is also a small increase in cranial capacity over time, but for the most part, even this feature is relatively consistent. Archaeologically, the Acheulian tool kit also seems to remain relatively consistent over time, although later hand axes do appear to be more refined than earlier ones. However, around 400 000 years ago there is a substantial increase in cranial capacity in the fossil hominin record. These new specimens are classed as early *Homo sapiens.* These early *H. sapiens* are not exactly like anatomically modern humans, so they are distinguished as **Archaic *Homo sapiens*.** While modern people are classed in the subspecies *sapiens* (that is, ***Homo sapiens sapiens***), Archaic *H. sapiens* are believed to represent one or several ancient and extinct subspecies.

Archaic *H. sapiens* fossils have been found in Africa, Europe, and Asia. In recent years some scholars have suggested that the "transitional" fossils share common traits and may actually represent a separate species—***Homo heidelbergensis***, named after a jaw found in 1907 in the village of Mauer near Heidelberg, Germany (Rightmire, 1998; Fleagle, 1999). For example, a specimen from the Broken Hill mine in Zambia, Africa, dates from about 200 000 years ago. Its mixed traits include a cranial capacity of over 1200 cc (well within the range of modern *H. sapiens*), together with a low forehead and large brow ridges, which are characteristic of earlier *H. erectus* specimens (Rightmire, 1984:303). The most extensive collection of fossil remains from a single site come from Atapuerca,

Early renditions of Neandertals portrayed them as brutish and very non-human-like.

Archaic *Homo sapiens*: specimens of early *Homo sapiens* that are not exactly like anatomically modern humans are distinguished as Archaic *Homo sapiens.* Neandertals are a specific group of Archaic *Homo sapiens.*
***Homo sapiens sapiens*:** modern-looking humans, undisputed examples of which appeared about 50 000 years ago; may have appeared earlier.
***Homo heidelbergensis*:** classification given by some for *Homo erectus* remains from Europe.

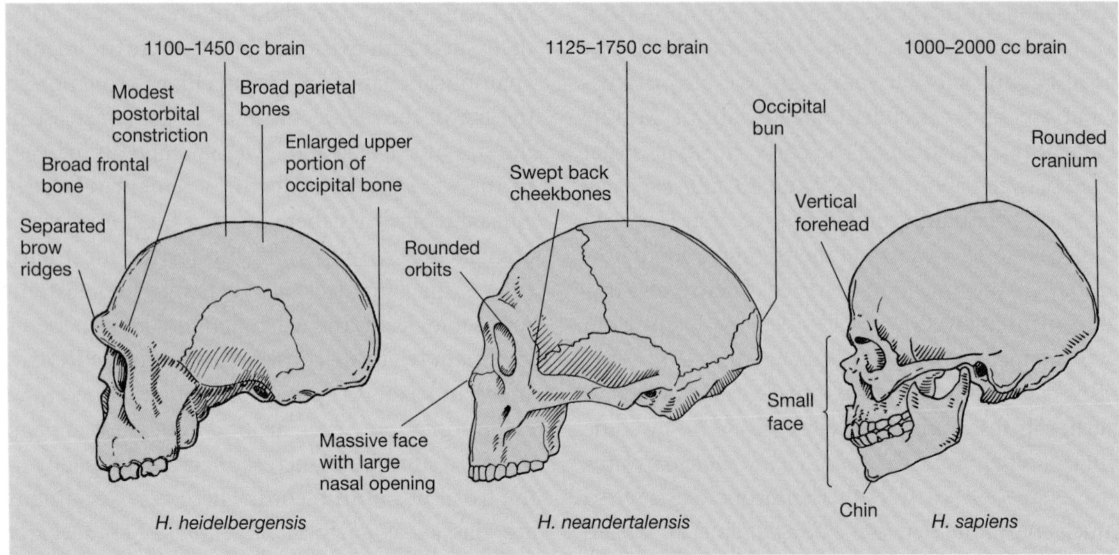

Figure 9–4 Comparison of the Crania of *Homo heidelbergensis*, *Homo neandertalensis*, and *Homo sapiens*, showing important differences

Spain (Arsuaga et al., 1993; Bermudez de Castro and Nicolas, 1997). Other fossils with mixed traits have been found at Bodo, Hopefield, Ndutu, Elandsfontein, and Rabat in Africa; Heidelberg, Bilzingsleben, Petralona, Arago, Steinheim, and Swanscombe in Europe; and Dali and Solo in Asia. New evidence from the site of Atapuerca, dating to over 750 000 years ago, have been used to propose a new species, **Homo antecessor**, that represents the last common ancestor to Neandertals and modern humans (Arsuaga et al., 1999; Bermudez de Castro et al., 1997; Carretero et al., 1999). Somewhat older remains from Ceprano, Italy, have also been suggestive of a transition between *H. erectus* and later *H. heidelbergensis* (Manzi et al., 2001).

H. heidelbergensis differs from *H. erectus* in having smaller teeth and jaws, a much larger brain (on the order of 1300 cc), a skull that lacks a sagittal keel and occipital torus, a brow ridge that divides into separate arches above each eye, and a more robust skeleton. *H. heidelbergensis* differs from *H. sapiens* in retaining a large and prognathic face with relatively large teeth and jaws, a brow ridge, and a long, low cranial vault with a sloping forehead, and in its more robust skeleton (Fleagle, 1999; Rightmire, 1998).

Many scholars question whether *H. heidelbergensis* represents one or several species of Middle Pleistocene hominin, or whether it is indeed a separate species at all. Many would argue that *H. heidelbergensis* should be considered an Archaic *H. sapiens.* As noted, some scholars also argue that *H. erectus* should be included in the *H. sapiens* species (see Figure 9–4).

Neandertals

There may be disagreement about how to classify the mixed-trait fossils from 400 000 to 200 000 years ago, but there is hardly any disagreement about the fossils that are less than 200 000 years old. Nearly all anthropologists agree that they were definitely *H. sapiens.* These early definite *H. sapiens* did not look completely like modern humans, but they were not so different from us either—not even the ones called **Neandertals**, after the valley in Germany where the first

Homo antecessor: a proposed last common ancestor between Neandertals and modern humans.

Neandertal: the common name for the species *Homo neandertalensis.*

evidence of them was found. Somehow through the years the Neandertals have become the victims of their cartoon image, which usually misrepresents them as burly and more ape than human. Actually, they might go unnoticed in a cross-section of the world's population today.

In 1856, three years before Darwin's publication of *The Origin of Species*, a skullcap and other fossilized bones were discovered in a cave in the Neander Valley (*tal* is the German word for "valley"), near Düsseldorf, Germany. The fossils in the Neander Valley were the first that scholars could tentatively consider an early hominin. (The fossils classified as *H. erectus* were not found until later in the 19th century, and the fossils belonging to the genus *Australopithecus* not until the 20th century.) After Darwin's revolutionary work was published, the Neandertal find aroused considerable controversy. A few evolutionist scholars, such as Thomas Huxley, thought that the Neandertal was not that different from modern humans. Others dismissed the Neandertal as irrelevant to human evolution; they saw it as a pathological freak, a peculiar, disease-ridden individual. However, similar fossils turned up later in Belgium, Yugoslavia, France, and elsewhere in Europe, which meant that the original Neandertal find could not be dismissed as an oddity (Spencer, 1984).

The predominant reaction to the original and subsequent Neandertal-like finds was that the Neandertals were too "brutish" and "primitive" to have been ancestral to modern humans. This view prevailed in the scholarly community until well into the 1950s. A major proponent of this view was French anatomist Marcellin Boule, who claimed between 1908 and 1913 that the Neandertals would not have been capable of complete bipedalism. Boule's reconstruction of the La Chapelle-aux-Saints Neandertal remains emphasized the minor differences rather than the remarkable similarities between the Neandertal and modern skeletons. Further, Boule's

Boule's reconstruction of Neandertal (left) as displayed at Chicago's Field Museum in 1929, and a more recent construction (right). The recent reconstruction makes Neandertal seem more like modern humans.

reconstruction was based on an older male, who suffered from severe arthritis. Despite the fact that Boule seemed to have ignored two other healthy skeletons on which to reconstruct the Neandertals, Boule's biased view was maintained in popular culture for a considerable time.

Since the 1950s, however, a number of studies have disputed Boule's claim, and it is now generally agreed that the skeletal traits of the Neandertals are completely consistent with bipedalism. Perhaps more important, when the much more ancient australopithecine and *H. erectus* fossils were accepted as hominins in the 1940s and 1950s, anthropologists realized that the Neandertals did not look that different from modern humans—despite their sloping foreheads, large brow ridges, flattened braincases, large jaws, and nearly absent chins (Trinkaus, 1985). After all, they did have larger brains (averaging more than 1450 cc) than modern humans (slightly more than 1300 cc) (Stringer, 1988b). Some scholars believe that the large brain capacity of Neandertals suggests that they were capable of the full range of behaviour characteristic of modern humans. Their skeletons did, however, attest to one behavioural trait markedly different from that of most modern humans: Neandertals had much more robust and more heavily muscled bodies (Trinkaus and Shipman, 1993).

It took almost 100 years for scholars to accept the idea that Neandertals were not that different from modern humans and therefore should be classified as ***Homo sapiens neandertalensis***. As we shall discuss later though, there is still debate over whether the Neandertals in western Europe were ancestral to modern-looking people who lived later in western Europe, after about 40 000 years ago. In any case, Neandertals lived in other places besides western Europe. A large number of fossils from central Europe strongly resemble those from western Europe, although some features, such as a projecting midface, are less pronounced (Smith, 1984:187). Neandertals have also been found in southwestern Asia (Israel, Iraq) and Central Asia (Uzbekistan). One of the largest collections of Neandertal fossils comes from Shanidar Cave in the mountains of northeastern Iraq, where Ralph Solecki unearthed the skeletons of nine individuals (see site 31 in Figure 9–5) (Trinkaus, 1984).

Homo sapiens neandertalensis: a variety of early *Homo sapiens.*

The Neandertals have received a great deal of scholarly and popular attention, probably because they were the first premodern humans to be found. We now know though, that other premodern *H. sapiens*, some perhaps older than Neandertals, lived elsewhere in the Old World—in East, South, and North Africa, as well as in Java and China (Smith and Spencer, 1984). These other premodern, but definite, *H. sapiens* are sometimes considered Neandertal-like, but more often they are named after the places where they were first found, as indeed the original Neandertal was. For example, the cranium from China called *Homo sapiens daliensis* was named after the Chinese locality, Dali, in which it was found in 1978 (Xinzhi and Maolin, 1985).

What has changed scholars' opinions of the Neandertals so that they are now most commonly seen as not belonging to the *H. sapiens* group?

In 1997, a group of researchers from the United States and Germany published findings that forced a reconsideration of the Neandertals and their relationship to modern humans. These scholars reported that they had been able to extract DNA from the original Neandertal specimen found in 1856 (Krings et al., 1997, 1999). The DNA they extracted was not nuclear DNA—the material that makes up the human genome. Rather, it came from a tiny structure found in all eukaryotic cells (that is, cells with a membrane-bound nucleus and DNA in the chromosomes) called *mitochondria.* Mitochondria produce enzymes needed for energy production, and they have their own DNA, which replicates when a cell replicates but is not thought to be under any pressure from natural selection (Cann, 1988).

The only source of change in mitochondrial DNA (usually referred to as *mt*DNA) is random mutation. Mitochondrial DNA is inherited only from mothers in animals; it is not carried into an egg cell by sperm, but is left with the sperm's tail on the outside of the egg. These unique characteristics make it possible to use mtDNA to measure the degree of relatedness between two species, and even to say how long ago those species diverged

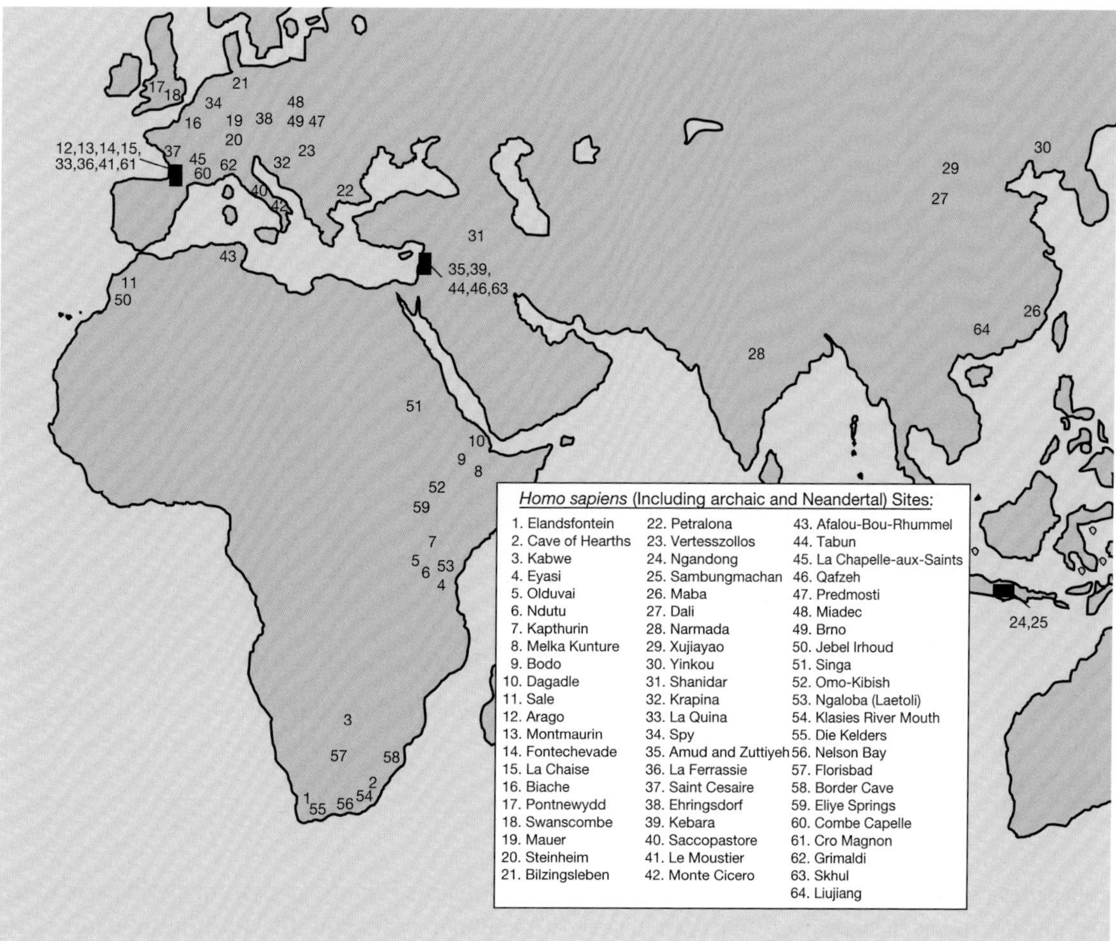

Figure 9–5 *Homo sapiens* Sites

Source: Ciochon RL, Fleagle JG, editors. 1993. The Human Evolution Source Book. Englewood Cliffs, NJ: Prentice Hall. p xi.

(Cann, 1988). The longer two species have been separated, the more differences there will be in their mtDNA, which is thought to mutate at a fairly constant rate of about 2 percent per million years. Thus, the number of differences between the mtDNA of two organisms can be converted into an estimated date in the past when those organisms stopped being part of the same breeding population. While controversy remains over many of the details of how and why mtDNA mutates and about its accuracy for determining absolute dates of divergence, most scholars agree that it is a powerful tool for examining relative degrees of relatedness between species (Vigilant et al., 1991).

How similar is Neandertal mtDNA to modern human DNA? Not as similar as many scholars would have expected. Among individual modern humans, there are usually five to ten differences in the sequence of mtDNA examined by the U.S. and German researchers. Between modern humans and the Neandertal specimen, there tend to be about 25 differences—more than three times that among modern humans (see Figure 9–6). This suggested to the researchers that the ancestors of modern humans and the Neandertal must have diverged about 600 000 years ago (Krings et al., 1997, 1999). If the last common ancestor of ours and the Neandertal lived that long ago, the Neandertal would be a much more distant relative than previously thought. This research has since been replicated with mtDNA from other Neandertal fossils (Ovchinnikov et al., 2000; Scholz et al., 2000), although some have been critical of earlier studies. For example, Gutierrez and

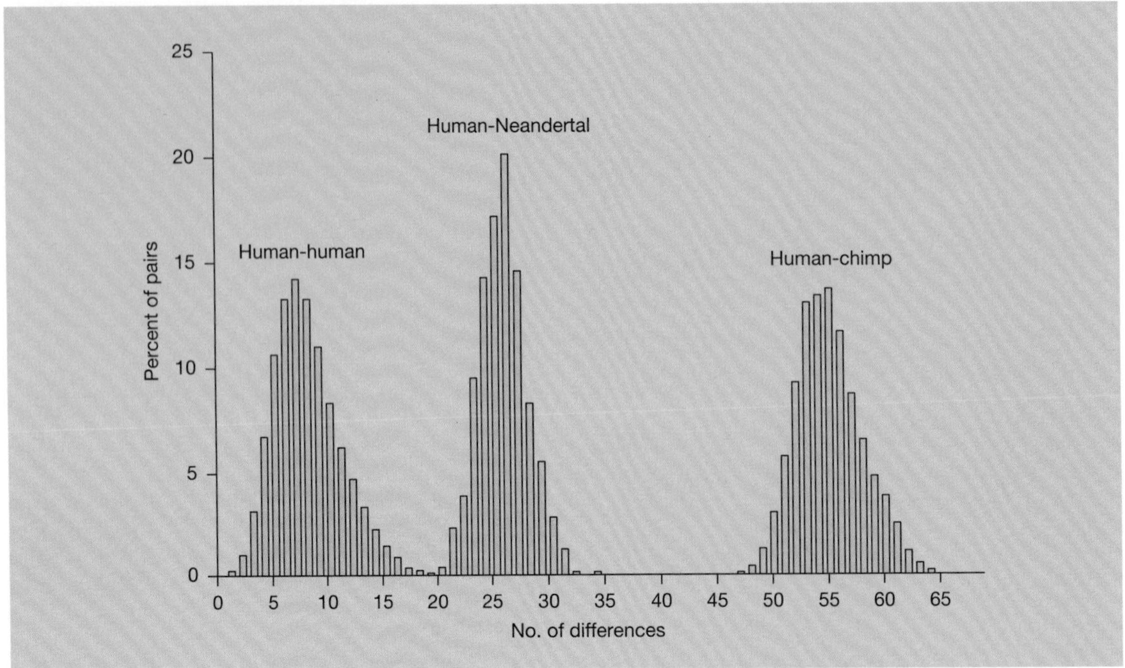

Figure 9–6 Differences in mtDNA Sequences among Humans, the Neandertal, and Chimpanzees

The *x*-axis shows the number of sequence differences; the *y*-axis shows the percent of individuals that share that number of sequence differences.

Source: 1997. Cell (90):25. Reprinted with permission from Elsevier Science.

colleagues (2002) argue that the overlap of modern and Neandertal DNA is greater than earlier studies suggested. More recent analyses have been more conservative in their interpretations, arguing that the lack of Neandertal DNA in modern humans does not rule out some genetic contribution (Cooper et al., 2004; Serre et al., 2004). This is consistent with Trinkaus's (2007) most recent arguments based on morphological variation in the fossil record.

Recent archaeological findings from Europe and the Near East may also indicate that Neandertals and the modern human were different species. It has been known for decades that both modern human and Neandertal fossils are found in the same locations in parts of the Levant, but recent improvements in dating technology and newly discovered fossils have even more clearly demonstrated that the two kinds of hominin coexisted. In fact, several caves in the Mount Carmel region of Israel contain evidence of both modern human and Neandertal occupations. The fact that these two groups of hominins co-inhabited the Near East for perhaps as much as 30 000 years and did not interbreed or share much in the way of tool technology strongly suggests that the two are different species (Tattersall, 1999; Gibbons, 2001). In addition, finds in Europe seem to corroborate that assessment. As early modern humans began moving into Europe, they appear to have displaced populations of Neandertals already living there. Sites with tools thought to be associated with Neandertals become less frequent throughout Europe as sites with tools thought to be associated with modern humans expand their range (Mellars, 1996). Significantly, the area of Europe (Iberia) last colonized by modern humans contains the very latest Neandertal fossils yet found, dating to some 30 000 years ago (Mellars, 1998).

With all this evidence pointing to Neandertals not being part of the modern human species, why is there an ongoing debate? In part, this is because none of the evidence is conclusive, and much of it can be interpreted in alternative ways. There is also evidence suggesting that Neandertals were

CURRENT RESEARCH AND ISSUES

Neandertal Growth and Development

One of the reasons many scholars think the Neandertals did not belong to the *Homo sapiens* species is that their material culture was less sophisticated than that of early modern humans who lived at the same time. Since much of contemporary human behaviour is dependent on learning that takes place during our long period of infant dependency, could it be that Neandertals matured more rapidly than modern humans and thus had a shorter period in which to learn cultural behaviours?

Paleoanthropologist Nancy Minugh-Purvis decided to test this idea by examining growth and development of the skull and face in Neandertals. Minugh-Purvis's study of Neandertal growth and development was feasible largely because Neandertals may have buried their dead. Juvenile and infant skeletons are rare in the archaeological record and often do not preserve well. In juveniles and infants, many of the bones are still growing and thus are relatively delicate. They are also smaller than adult bones, and a wider variety of scavengers can consume them. But because Neandertals may have buried their dead, a number of well-preserved juvenile and infant skeletons are available for study. Indeed, Minugh-Purvis was able to locate more than 100 Neandertal skeletons, ranging in age from newborn to young adult.

To chart the way the skull and face of Neandertals grew from infancy to adulthood, Minugh-Purvis measured the available fossils on a set of standard anthropometric indices—indices that are widely used in physical anthropology to compare the size and shape of bones. She found that newborn Neandertals and modern humans do not differ very much, but that Neandertal infants tend to have thicker cranial bones than modern humans and perhaps heavier musculature. Many of the more striking features of adult Neandertals—a large face with a protruding nose, brow ridges, and a long skull—are not present in infants. These typical Neandertal characteristics begin to appear in children. For example, a 4-year-old Neandertal from the site of Engis, Belgium, already had brow ridges. A 7-year-old from the site of La Quinta in France not only had brow ridges but also a large, protruding nose and face and a long skull. Finally, a 10-year-old from the site of Teshik-Tash in Uzbekistan had all of the typical Neandertal features, and is basically identical to an adult Neandertal except in size. A reanalysis of the Le Moustier 1 by Thompson and Illerhaus suggest that growth in facial height occurred at a faster rate prognathism during the adolescent period.

In short, Neandertals are born similar to modern humans, but by the age of about 10 have developed all of the striking physical features that differentiate Neandertals from modern humans. What does this tell us about Neandertal growth and development? Minugh-Purvis suggests that it was much like our own. Indeed, she argues that many of the physical differences between the Neandertal face and skull and those of modern humans might be due not to genetic differences but rather to behavioural ones. Neandertal teeth show wear patterns that suggest they were used as tools, particularly to hold objects while working on them with the hands. The teeth and jaws were apparently placed under tremendous stress from these uses. Minugh-Purvis suggests that the prognathic face and heavy musculature may be a result of the teeth and jaws being used as tools from a young age, rather than from developmental differences between modern humans and Neandertals.

However, there are other differences between Neandertals and modern humans that cannot be explained by behaviour. The overall picture that appears from Minugh-Purvis's study is that Neandertals did indeed mature slightly faster than modern humans. Thompson and Nelson have also examined several fossils arguing that Neandertals exhibited either slow growth in height or more rapid dental development than modern humans. But was their maturation fast enough to account for the lack of cultural elaboration among the Neandertals? Did Neandertals grow so fast they had no time to learn? Minugh-Purvis suggests the differences are not that significant, and that other factors must be sought to explain the differences in cultural elaboration between Neandertals and modern humans.

Sources: Minugh-Purvis N. 2002. Neandertal Growth: Examining Developmental Adaptations in Earlier *Homo sapiens.* In: Peregrine PN, Ember CR, Ember M, editors. Physical Anthropology: Original Readings in Method and Practice. Upper Saddle River, NJ: Prentice Hall. Also in: Ember CR, Ember M, editors. 2003. New Directions in Anthropology. Upper Saddle River, NJ: Prentice Hall. CD-ROM.

Stringer C, Gamble C. 1993. In Search of the Neanderthals. New York: Thames and Hudson. Journal of Human Evolution 35: 647–665. Journal of Human Evolution 38:475–495.

Trinkaus E. 1987. The Neandertal Face: Evolutionary and Functional Perspectives on a Recent Hominid Face. Journal of Human Evolution 16:429–443.

not all that different physically from modern humans (see Current Research and Issues, "Neandertal Growth and Development"). Perhaps more important, however, Neandertal culture, typically referred to as Middle Paleolithic after the predominant tool technology, has some features that make it seem similar to the culture of early modern humans.

Middle Palaeolithic Cultures

The period of cultural history associated with the Neandertals is traditionally called the **Middle Palaeolithic** in Europe and the Near East and dates from about 300 000 years ago to about 40 000 years ago (Strauss, 1989). For Africa, the term *Middle Stone Age* is used instead of *Middle Palaeolithic.* The tool assemblages from this period are generally referred to as *Mousterian* in Europe and the Near East and as *post-Acheulian* in Africa. (See the timeline in Figure 9–7.)

Tool Assemblages

The Mousterian. The Mousterian type of tool complex is named after the tool assemblage found in a rock shelter at Le Moustier in the Dordogne region of southwestern France. Compared with an Acheulian assemblage, a **Mousterian tool assemblage** has a smaller proportion of large core tools such as hand axes and cleavers and a bigger proportion of small flake tools such as scrapers (Schick and Toth, 1994). Although many flakes struck off from a core were used "as is," the Mousterian is also characterized by flakes that were often altered or "retouched" by striking small flakes or chips from one or more edges (see Figure 9–8) (Klein, 1989). Studies of the wear on scrapers suggest that many were used for scraping hides or working wood. The fact that some of the tools, particularly projectile points, were thinned or shaped on one side suggests that they were hafted or attached to a shaft or handle (Schick and Toth, 1994; Whittaker, 1994).

Toward the end of the Acheulian period, toolmakers developed a technique to produce flake tools of a predetermined size instead of simply chipping flakes away from the core at random. In this **Levalloisian method**, the toolmaker first shaped the core and prepared a "striking platform" at one end. Flakes of predetermined and standard sizes could then be detached by percussion flaking. Although some Levallois flakes date as far back as 400 000 years ago, they are found more frequently in Mousterian tool kits (Klein, 1989).

The tool assemblages in particular sites may be characterized as Mousterian, but one site may have more or fewer scrapers, points, and so forth, than another site. A number of archaeologists have suggested possible reasons for this variation. For example, Sally Binford and Lewis Binford suggested that different activities might have occurred in different sites. Some sites may have been used for butchering and other sites may have been base camps; hence, the kinds of tools found in different sites should vary as a reflection of the range of specialized activities carried out there (Binford and Binford, 1969). And Paul Fish has suggested that some sites may have more tools produced by the Levalloisian technique because larger pieces of flint were available (Fish, 1981).

The Post-Acheulian in Africa. Like Mousterian tools, many of the post-Acheulian tools in Africa during the Middle Stone Age were struck off prepared cores in the Levalloisian way.

Mousterian Tool Assemblage: named after the tool assemblage found in a rock shelter at Le Moustier in the Dordogne region of southwestern France. Compared with an Acheulian assemblage, the Middle Palaeolithic (40 000–300 000 years ago) Mousterian has a smaller proportion of large core tools such as hand axes and cleavers and a bigger proportion of small flake tools such as scrapers. Flakes were often altered or "retouched" by striking small flakes or chips from one or more edges.

Levalloisian Method: a method that allowed flake tools of a predetermined size to be produced from a shaped core. The toolmaker first shaped the core and prepared a "striking platform" at one end. Flakes of predetermined and standard sizes could then be knocked off. Although some Levallois flakes date from as far back as 400 000 years ago, they are found more frequently in Mousterian tool kits.

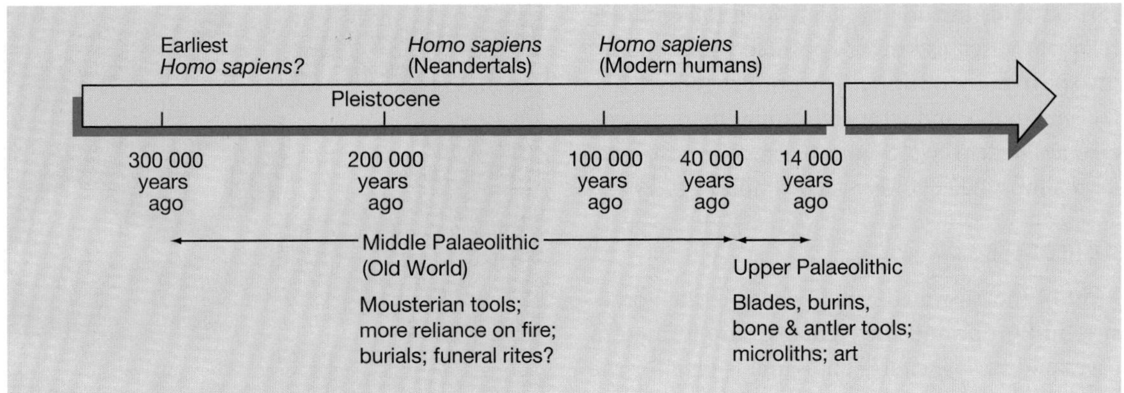

Figure 9–7 An Evolutionary Timeline

The assemblages consist mostly of various types of flake tools. A well-described sequence of such tools comes from the area around the mouth of the Klasies River on the southern coast of South Africa. This area contains rock shelters and small caves in which early and later *H. sapiens* lived. The oldest cultural remains in one of the caves may date back 120 000 years (Butzer, 1982b). These

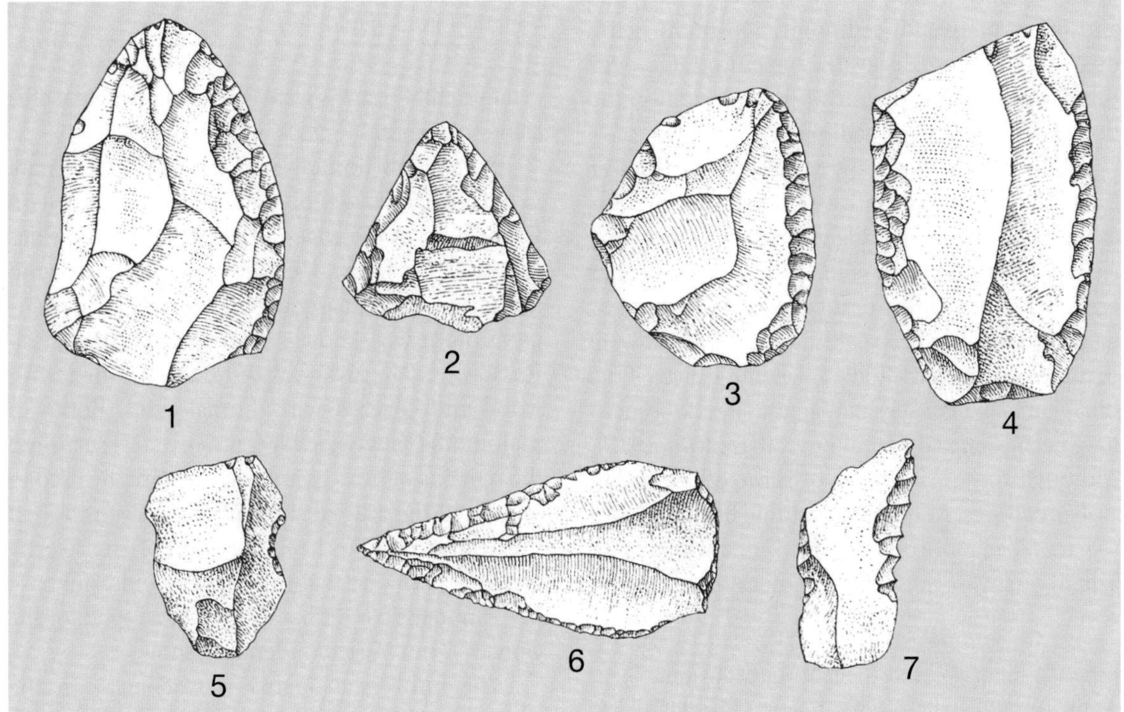

Figure 9–8 A Typical Mousterian Tool Kit

A Mousterian tool kit emphasized sidescrapers (1–4), notches (5), points (6), and sawtoothed denticulates (7). How these stone artifacts were actually used is not known, but the points may have been joined to wood shafts, and denticulates could have been used to work wood. The tools illustrated here are from Mousterian sites in Western Europe.

Source: Klein RG. June 1974. Ice-Age Hunters of the Ukraine. Scientific American 96–105. Reprinted with permission of Nelson H. Prentiss.

earliest tools include parallel-sided flake **blades** (probably used as knives), pointed flakes (possibly spear points), **burins** or gravers (chisel-like incising tools), and scrapers. Similar tools discovered at Border Cave, South Africa, may have been used almost 200 000 years ago (Phillipson, 1993).

Homesites

Most of the excavated Middle Palaeolithic homesites in Europe and the Near East are located in caves and rock shelters. The same is true for the excavated Middle Stone Age homesites in sub-Saharan Africa. We might conclude, therefore, that Neandertals and other early *H. sapiens* lived mostly in caves or rock shelters, although this conclusion could be incorrect. Caves and rock shelters may be overrepresented in the archaeological record because they are more likely to be found than are sites that originally were in the open but now are hidden by thousands of years, and many metres, of sediment. **Sediment** is the dust, debris, and decay that accumulates over time; when we dust the furniture and vacuum the floor, we are removing sediment.

Still, we know that many early *H. sapiens* lived at least part of the year in caves. This was true, for example, along the Dordogne River in France. The river gouged deep valleys in the limestone of that area. Below the cliffs are rock shelters with overhanging roofs and deep caves, many of which were occupied during the Middle Palaeolithic. Even if the inhabitants did not stay all year, the sites do seem to have been occupied year after year (Binford, 1973). Although there is evidence of some use of fire in earlier cultures, Middle Palaeolithic humans seem to have relied more on fire. There are thick layers of ash in many rock shelters and caves, and also evidence that hearths were used to increase the efficiency of the fires (Schick and Toth, 1994).

Archaeologist Hilary Deacon at the mouth of the Klasies River in South Africa, where early modern humans have been found.

Quite a few homesites of early *H. sapiens* were in the open. In Africa, open-air sites were located on floodplains, at the edges of lakes, and near springs (Klein, 1977). Many open-air sites have been found in Europe, particularly eastern Europe. The occupants of the well-known site at Moldova in western Russia lived in river-valley houses framed with wood and covered with animal skins. Bones of mammoths (huge elephants now extinct) surround the remains of hearths and were apparently used to help hold the animal skins in place. Even though the winter climate near the edge of the nearby glacier was cold at that time, there would still have been animals to hunt because the plant food for the game was not buried under deep snow.

The hunters probably moved away in the summer to higher land between the river valleys. In all likelihood, the higher ground was grazing land for the large herds of animals the Moldova hunters depended on for meat. In the winter river-valley sites, archaeologists have found skeletons of wolf, arctic fox, and hare with their paws missing. These animals probably were skinned for pelts that were made into clothing (Klein, 1974).

Blade: a thin flake whose length is usually more than twice its width. In the blade technique of toolmaking, a core is prepared by shaping a piece of flint with hammer stones into a pyramidal or cylindrical form. Blades are then struck off until the core is used up.
Burin: a chisel-like stone tool used for carving and for making such artifacts as bone and antler needles, awls, and projectile points.
Sediment: the dust, debris, and decay that accumulates over time.

Getting Food

How early *H. sapiens* got their food probably varied with their environment. In Africa, they lived in savannah and semi-arid desert. In western and eastern Europe, they had to adapt to cold; during periods of increased glaciation, much of the environment was steppe grassland and tundra.

The European environment during this time was much richer in animal resources than the tundra of northern countries is today. Indeed, the European environment inhabited by Neandertals abounded in game, both big and small. The tundra and alpine animals included reindeer, bison, wild oxen, horses, mammoths, rhinoceroses, and deer, as well as bears, wolves, and foxes (Bordes, 1961). Some European sites have also yielded bird and fish remains. For example, people in a summer camp in northern Germany apparently hunted swans and ducks and fished for perch and pike (Patterson, 1981). Little, however, is known about the particular plant foods the European Neandertals may have consumed; the remains of plants are unlikely to survive thousands of years in a non-arid environment.

In Africa, too, early *H. sapiens* got food in different ways. For example, we know that the people living at the mouth of the Klasies River in South Africa ate shellfish as well as meat from small grazers such as antelopes and large grazers such as eland and buffalo (Phillipson, 1993). But archaeologists disagree about how the Klasies River people got their meat when they began to occupy the caves in the area.

Richard Klein thinks they hunted the large as well as small game. Klein speculates that because the remains of eland of all ages have been found in Cave 1 at this site, the people there probably hunted the eland by driving them into corrals or other traps, where animals of all ages could be killed. Klein thinks that buffalo were hunted differently. Buffalo tend to charge attackers, which would make it difficult to drive them into traps. Klein believes that, because bones from mostly very young and very old buffalo were found in the cave, the hunters were able to stalk and kill only the most vulnerable animals (Klein, 1983).

Lewis Binford thinks the Klasies River people hunted only small grazers and scavenged the eland and buffalo meat from the kills of large carnivores. He argues that sites should contain all or almost all of the bones from animals that were hunted. According to Binford, since more or less complete skeletons were found only from small animals, the Klasies River people were not at first hunting all the animals they used for food (Klein, 1983; Binford, 1984).

But there is new evidence suggesting that people were hunting big game as much as 400 000 years ago. Wooden spears that old were recently found in Germany in association with stone tools and the butchered remains of more than 10 wild horses. The heavy spears resemble modern aerodynamic javelins, which suggests they would have been thrown at large animals such as horses, not at small animals. This new evidence strongly suggests that hunting, not just scavenging, may be older than archaeologists used to think (Wilford, 1997).

The extent and level of hominin hunting during the Middle Palaeolithic has been widely debated. There is a growing realization of the importance of faunal analyses for reconstructing complex behaviour in Middle Palaeolithic hominin populations. Dr. Ariane Burke is an archaeologist at the Université de Montréal. Much of her research has focused on the analysis of faunal remains from Middle Palaeolithic sites in western Crimea in Ukraine. This research has enabled Burke to develop a hypothesis of land use and resource exploitation among Neandertal populations in the Crimea.

One of the issues emerging from this kind of research is that Neandertal resource strategies (getting food and using the land) are far more complicated than have been previously thought. In particular, recent research from a variety of areas in the Old World have emphasized the importance of Neandertal flexibility in their food-gathering activities in response to changes in the seasons and possible different sources of food. For example, studies have implied a mixture of both seasonally focused hunting of specific animals, intermixed with opportunistic hunting of animals that are encountered unintentionally. Further, periods of climatic crisis show a greater variety of foods being utilized by Neandertal populations, which suggests flexibility in hunting strategies during these hard times (Burke. 2000). In contrast, stable isotope analysis of Neadertal remains by Richards and colleagues (2001) have suggested a diet focused primarily on terrestrial sources.

Burke and others (see Burke 2000), through research at a variety of Middle Palaeolithic sites, have begun to challenge the traditional notion of a lack of forethought and planning among Neandertal populations. The capacity for complex planning is abundantly demonstrated by Middle Palaeolithic patterns of land-use and subsistence strategies. This, of course, is important with respect to defining "modern" humans. The idea of a "Neandertal niche"—whereby Neandertals were overspecialized to very specific environmental conditions—implies that Middle Palaeolithic populations were biologically and culturally distinct from anatomically modern Upper Palaeolithic populations. Renewed research in this area brings a greater understanding of what it is to be truly "modern," and helps us to understand both the evolution of modern cultures and why Neandertal populations disappeared.

As this reconstruction illustrates, Neandertals may have been the first humans to purposely bury their dead.

Funeral Rituals?

Some Neandertals were deliberately buried. At Le Moustier, the skeleton of a boy 15 or 16 years old was found with a beautifully fashioned stone axe near his hand. Near Le Moustier, graves of five other children and two adults, apparently interred together in a family plot, were discovered. These finds, along with one at Shanidar Cave in Iraq, have aroused speculation about the possibility of funeral rituals.

The evidence at Shanidar consists of pollen around and on top of a man's body. Pollen analysis suggests that the flowers included ancestral forms of modern grape hyacinths, bachelor's buttons, hollyhocks, and yellow flowering groundsels. John Pfeiffer speculated about this find:

> A man with a badly crushed skull was buried deep in the cave with special ceremony. One spring day about 60 000 years ago, members of his family went out into the hills, picked masses of wild flowers, and made a bed of them on the ground, a resting place for the deceased. Other flowers were probably laid on top of his grave; still others seem to have been woven together with the branches of a pine-like shrub to form a wreath. (Pfeiffer, 1978)

Can we be sure? Not really. All we really know is that there was pollen near and on top of the body. It could have been deposited there because humans put flowers in the grave, or perhaps through other, even accidental, reasons.

Neandertals may have taken part in other rituals as well, but, as with funeral rituals, the evidence is ambiguous. At Drachenloch cave in the Swiss Alps, for example, a stone-lined pit holding the stacked skulls of seven cave bears was found in association with a Neandertal habitation. Why preserve these skulls? One reason might be for rituals intended to placate or control bears. Cave bears were enormous—some nearly 2.7 metres tall—and competed with Neandertals for prime cave-living sites. Perhaps the Neandertals preserved the skulls of bears they killed in the cave as a way of honouring or appeasing either the bears or their spirits. But, as with funeral rituals, the evidence is not completely persuasive. In our own society some may hang a deer or moose head on the wall without any associated ritual. At this point we cannot say for certain whether or not Neandertals engaged in ritual behaviour (Chase and Dibble, 1987).

Altruism

Another aspect associated with Neandertals is the evidence for **altruism**—the concept of caring for and sustaining members of the group who may no longer contribute to the group's survival. The interpretation of altruism among the Neandertals comes from the La Chapelle-aux-Saints and the Shanidar I skeletons that implicitly demonstrate the Neandertals' capacity to care for the sick and aged. For example, the La Chapelle-aux-Saints finds included the remains of a middle-aged male suffering from arthritis. Whether or not this individual could care for himself has been debated, and while it is probable that he was able to interact with the group until his death, it is possible that his survival was in part due to the aid of other members of the group. Better evidence comes from the Shanidar I remains, which include the skeleton of an individual with healed injuries that would have left him blind with a paralyzed right arm (Trinkaus, 1983). In this case it certainly seems likely that the individual's survival, at least during the period of recovery from his injuries, would have been possible only with the support of other members of the group (Trinkaus, 1983).

Cannibalism

Another area of interest for Neandertals that has re-emerged in the news is the possibility of cannibalism. Recent research by Tim White and colleagues suggests that the site of Moula-Guercy—a Neandertal cave site in France dating to 100 000 years ago—contains evidence of cannibalism. The site includes 78 bone fragments representing the remains of at least six individuals including two adults, two adolescents, and two young children. Tim White has suggested that the cut marks on these bones could have been caused by sharp flints, and that the skulls were smashed and long bones broken open, presumably to extract the marrow. Further, there was no evidence of animals gnawing on the bones (Defleur et al., 1999).

Altruism: the concept of caring for and sustaining members of the group who may no longer contribute to the group's survival.

Language

Recall from earlier discussions that the basicranium of the australopithecines is ape-like while that of *H. erectus* is more reminiscent of modern humans. Similarly, the basicrania of Archaic *H. sapiens* appears modern, with specimens from Petralona, Steinheim, Kabwe, and other sites implying a modern ability for language by about 250 000 years ago (Laitman and Heimbuch, 1984). However, there is ongoing debate as to whether Neandertals may have been different. Neandertal specimens do show a greater degree of flexion of the basicranium than those of *H. erectus*, but less so than other Archaic *H. sapiens*. This has led some researchers to suggest that Neandertals had a more constricted range of vocalization than other archaic populations. This notion has been challenged from an analysis of a fully modern-looking hyoid bone from Kebara, Israel (Arensburg et al., 1990).

Evolutionary Relations

One of the primary questions concerning the Neandertals is, what is their evolutionary relationship to modern humans? For a long time it was assumed that modern *H. sapiens* had evolved directly from Archaic populations like Neandertals. However, as we have already discussed, new evidence has emerged with the advent of molecular anthropology, implying that this may not be the case. We also now know from the archaeological record that some Neandertal populations lived at the same time and in some cases in the same place as anatomically modern humans. The question now becomes, what is the evolutionary relation of Neandertals to modern human populations? In the next chapter, we will discuss in further detail the two prevailing models of the origins of modern humans. Regardless of either model, it is clear that the Neandertals disappear from the archaeological record and are replaced, either biologically or culturally, by anatomically modern humans. Whether or not Neandertal genes are incorporated into the modern human genome remains to be debated.

Summary

1. *Homo erectus*, with a larger brain capacity than *H. habilis*, emerged about 1.8 million to 1.6 million years ago. *Homo erectus* was the first hominin species to be widely distributed in the Old World. The tools and other cultural artifacts from about 1.6 million to about 200 000 years ago were probably produced by *H. erectus*; *Acheulian* is the name given to the tool tradition of this period. Acheulian tools include both small flake tools and large tools, but hand axes and other large bifacial tools are characteristic. Although it is presumed that *H. erectus* had learned to use fire to survive in areas with cold winters, there is no definite evidence of the control of fire by *H. erectus*. There is evidence in some sites of big-game eating, but whether *H. erectus* hunted those animals is debated.
2. Most anthropologists agree that *H. erectus* began to evolve into *H. sapiens* after about 500 000 years ago. But there is disagreement about how and where the transition occurred. The mixed traits of the transitional fossils include large cranial capacities (well within the range of modern humans), together with low foreheads and large brow ridges, which are characteristic of *H. erectus* specimens. The earliest definite *H. sapiens*, who did not look completely like modern humans, appeared after about 200 000 years ago.
3. Remains of Archaic *H. sapiens* have been found in many parts of the Old World—in Africa and Asia as well as in Europe. Some of these *H. sapiens* may have lived earlier than the Neandertals of Europe, who were the first premodern humans to be found. There is still debate over whether the Neandertals in western Europe became extinct, or survived and were the ancestors of the modern-looking people who lived in western Europe after about 40 000 years ago.
4. The period associated with the Neandertals is traditionally called the Middle Palaeolithic in Europe and the Near East and dates from about 300 000 to about 40 000 years ago. For Africa, the term *Middle Stone Age* is used. The assemblages of flake tools from this period are generally referred to as *Mousterian* in Europe and the Near East and as *post-Acheulian* in Africa. Compared with an Acheulian assemblage, a Mousterian tool assemblage has a smaller proportion of large hand axes and cleavers and a larger proportion of small flake tools such as scrapers. Some Mousterian sites show signs of intentional burial.

Glossary Terms

Acheulian (p. 200)
altruism (p. 217)
Archaic *Homo sapiens* (p. 205)
blades (p. 214)
burins (p. 214)
Homo antecessor (p. 206)
Homo ergaster (p. 193)
Homo floresiensis (p. 197)
Homo heidelbergensis (p. 205)
Homo sapiens neandertalensis (p. 208)
Homo sapiens sapiens (p. 205)
Levalloisian method (p. 212)
Middle Palaeolithic (p. 212)
Mousterian tool assemblage (p. 212)
Neandertal (p. 206)
occipital torus (p. 195)
prognathic (p. 195)
sagittal keel (p. 195)
sediment (p. 214)
taurodontism (p. 195)

Critical Questions

1. *Homo erectus* lived in many places in the Old World. What enabled them to spread so widely?
2. Why do you think Neandertals became extinct?

3. Archaic *H. sapiens* including Neandertals show evidence of some key cultural differences from earlier hominins. What are they, and how might they have developed?

Internet Exercises

1. Go to **www.modernhumanorigins.com/** and review the important characteristics that are attributed to *H. erectus* specimens. Hyperlinks at the site connect to illustrations of fossil remains. Review the importance of these remains for understanding the evolution of *H. erectus.*
2. Read all about Neandertals at this site: **www.modernhumanorigins.com.** Using the resources that you will find there, pick a global location and season, pretend you are a Neandertal, and list "what I did today, what I ate today, and where I slept last night."
3. Go to **www.dnalc.org/neandertal.html** and explore an interactive overview of the reconstruction of Neandertal fossils.

Suggested Reading

Ciochon RL, Fleagle JG, editors. 1993. The Human Evolution Source Book. Upper Saddle, NJ: Prentice Hall. A collection of original articles about human evolution. Parts VI and VII are particularly relevant to this chapter.

Dibble HL, Mellars P, editors. 1992. The Middle Paleolithic: Adaptation, Behavior, and Variability. Philadelphia: University Museum. A collection of papers that present new data and whose authors rethink the variability in behaviour during the Middle Palaeolithic. The focus is on Europe and the Near East.

Ember CR, Ember M, Peregrine P, editors. 1998. Research Frontiers in Anthropology. Upper Saddle River, NJ: Prentice Hall: Simon & Schuster Custom Publishing. Especially relevant to this chapter are the following: Fryer DW, Testing Theories and Hypotheses about Modern Human Origins; Kramer A, The Natural History and Evolutionary Fate of *Homo erectus;* Minugh-Purvis N, Neandertal Growth: Examining Developmental Adaptations in Earlier *Homo sapiens*; and Tattersall I, Paleoanthropology and Evolutionary Theory.

Fagan BM. 1989. People of the Earth: An Introduction to World Prehistory. Sixth edition. Glenview, IL: Scott, Foresman. Chapters 5 to 8 survey the fossil and archaeological evidence on *H. sapiens* in different parts of the world.

Sigmon BA, Cybulski JS, editors. 1981. *Homo erectus*: Papers in Honour of Davidson Black. Toronto: University of Toronto Press. A series of biographical and historical papers on Davidson Black and his discoveries derived from a symposium at the Canadian Association for Physical Anthropology meetings held in 1976.

Trinkaus E, editor. 1989. The Emergence of Modern Humans: Biocultural Adaptations in the Later Pleistocene. Cambridge: Cambridge University Press. Physical anthropologists and archaeologists review and debate what is known, and not known, about the Neandertals and the transition to modern humans.

Wenke RJ. 1999. Patterns in Prehistory: Humankind's First Three Million Years. Fourth edition. New York: Oxford University Press. A summary of cultural development that focuses on why various crucial changes may have occurred. Chapter 4 is particularly relevant to this chapter.

MODERN *HOMO SAPIENS*

CHAPTER OUTLINE

Until recently, palaeoanthropologists thought that modern-looking people evolved about 50 000 years ago in Europe. Now we know that they appeared earlier. Recent finds in southern Africa and elsewhere indicate the presence of modern-looking people perhaps as much as 100 000 or even 200 000 years ago. In this chapter we examine the major theories regarding the emergence of anatomically modern humans. The two major theories involve the question "Did modern humans evolve from a single population in a single location, or did they evolve from multiple locations throughout the Old World?"

We examine evidence from various sources—fossils, genetics, and archaeological discoveries—to better understand this period. We also discuss the movement of modern human populations into the New World.

The Emergence of Modern Humans

The skeletal resemblances between those humans and recent people are so great that most palaeoanthropologists consider them all to be "anatomically modern humans," *Homo sapiens sapiens.* One palaeoanthropologist, Christopher Stringer, characterizes anatomically modern human, *H. sapiens sapiens,* as having "a domed skull, a chin, small eyebrows, brow ridges, and a rather puny skeleton"(Stringer, 1985). Some of us might not like to be called puny, but except for our larger brain, most modern humans definitely are small compared with *H. erectus* and even with earlier forms of our own species, *H. sapiens.* This smallness is true in many respects including our thinner and lighter bones as well as our smaller teeth and jaws.

Cro-Magnon humans, who appeared in western Europe about 35 000 years ago, were once thought to be the earliest specimens of modern humans, or *H. sapiens sapiens.* The Cro-Magnons are named after the rock shelter in France where their remains were first found in 1868 (Stringer et al., 1984). As of now, the oldest known fossils classified as *H. sapiens sapiens* came from Africa. Some of these fossils, discovered in one of the Klasies River Mouth caves, are possibly as old as 100 000 years (Singer and Wymer, 1982). Other modern-looking fossils of about the same age have been found in Border Cave in South Africa, and a find at Omo in Ethiopia may be an early *H. sapiens sapiens* (Bräuer, 1984; Rightmire, 1984). Remains of anatomically modern humans found at two sites in Israel, at Skhul and Qafzeh, which used to be thought to date back 40 000 to 50 000 years, may be 90 000 years old (Valladas et al., 1988; Schwarcz and Grun, 1992). There are also anatomically modern human finds in Borneo, at Niah, from about 40 000 years ago and in Australia, at Lake Mungo, from about 30 000 years ago (Stringer et al., 1984).

These modern-looking humans differed from the Neandertals and other early *H. sapiens* in that they had higher, more bulging foreheads, thinner and lighter bones, smaller faces and jaws, chins, and slight bone ridges (or no ridges at all) over the eyes and at the back of the head.

Theories about the Origins of Modern Humans

Two hypotheses about the origins of modern humans continue to be debated among anthropologists. We will first consider the **single-origin hypothesis**. This suggests that modern humans emerged in just one part of the Old World (Africa is generally thought to be the place of origin for modern humans) and then spread to other parts, replacing Neandertals and other pre-modern *H. sapiens.*

Single-Origin Hypothesis. According to the single-origin hypothesis, most of the Neandertals and other Archaic *H. sapiens* did not evolve into modern humans. Instead, anatomically modern humans evolved in a limited geographic area.

Single-Origin (or Replacement) Hypothesis: the theory that anatomically modern humans evolved in a single region, Africa, and then replaced all existing Archaic populations in other regions of the world.

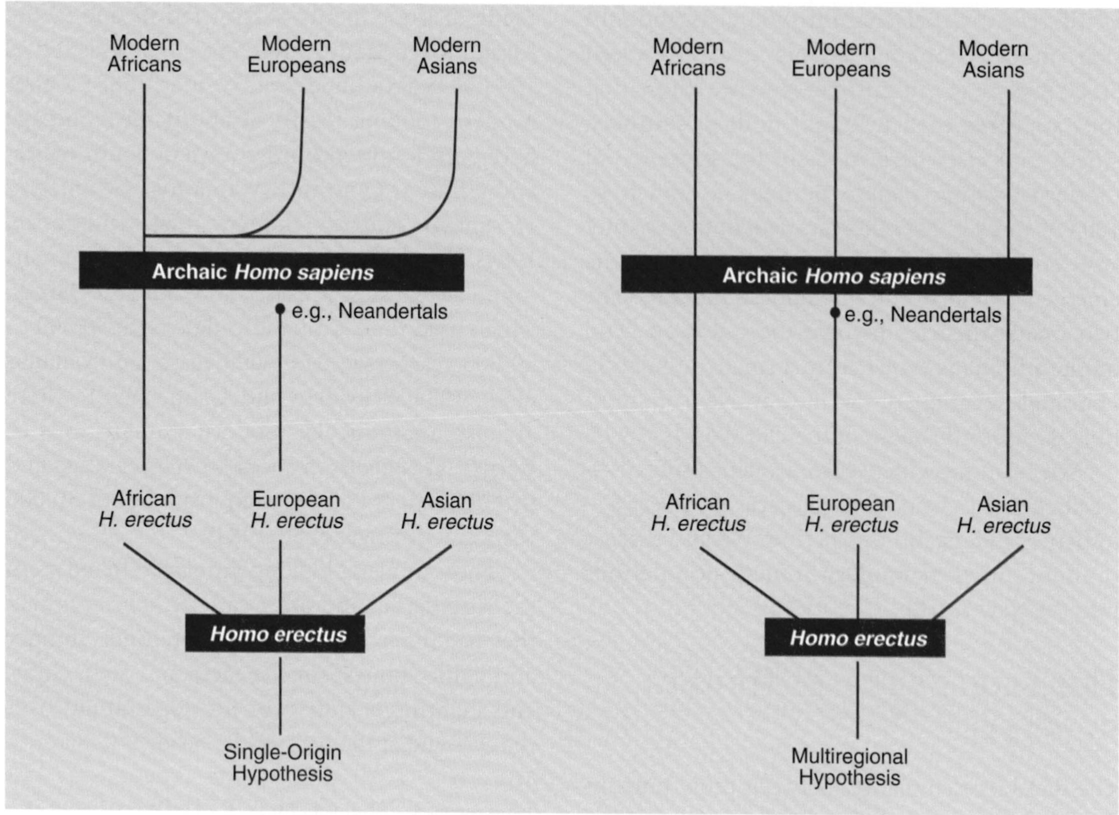

Figure 10–1 Two Possible Evolutionary Models for the Origins of Modern Humans

From there they migrated and either physically replaced the indigenous Archaic populations, or genetically replaced them through interbreeding. So, according to this model, the earliest fossil and cultural evidence for modern humans should have first appeared in a single location and Archaic *H. sapiens* (including Neandertals) and anatomically modern populations should have coexisted in some areas for at least some time. If the single-origin hypothesis is correct, modern genetic diversity should be small, since all modern groups would have descended from a single population relatively recently. Further, genetic diversity should be the greatest in populations from the region where modern humans emerged, because this single population would be the oldest and therefore the most genetically diverse.

The presumed place of origin of the first modern humans for the single-origin hypothesis has varied over the years as new fossils have been discovered. In the 1950s the source population was presumed to be the Neandertals in the Near East, who were referred to as "generalized" or "progressive" Neandertals. Later, when earlier *H. sapiens sapiens* were found in Africa, palaeoanthropologists postulated that modern humans emerged first in Africa and then moved to the Near East and from there to Europe and Asia. Single-origin theorists think that the originally small population of *H. sapiens sapiens* had some biological advantage or cultural advantage, or both, that allowed them to spread and replace Archaic *H. sapiens.*

Multiregional Hypothesis. The second hypothesis has been called the **multiregional hypothesis**. This suggests that modern humans evolved in various parts of the Old World after *H. erectus* spread out of Africa (see Figure 10–1). According to the multiregional hypothesis, *H. erectus* populations in

Multiregional Hypothesis: the theory that anatomically modern humans evolved *in situ* in a variety of different regions around the world.

various parts of the Old World gradually evolved into anatomically modern-looking humans. This hypothesis supports the idea of gradual, "in place" evolution of regional populations of ancient hominins into modern humans. If this hypothesis is correct, we should be able to trace regional morphological traits through the evolutionary record, and we should see the simultaneous evolution toward anatomically modern humans in Europe, Asia, and Africa. It is also assumed that there is sufficient gene flow—movement of genetic material among populations—to maintain a single species.

To explain why human evolution would proceed gradually and in the same direction in various parts of the Old World, multiregional theorists point to cultural improvements in cutting-tool and cooking technology that occurred all over the Old World. These cultural improvements may have relaxed the prior natural selection for heavy bones and musculature in the skull. The argument is that unless many plant and animal foods were cut into small pieces and thoroughly cooked in hearths or pits that were efficient thermally, they would be hard to chew and digest. Thus, people previously would have needed robust jaws and thick skull bones to support the large muscles that enabled them to cut and chew their food. However, robust bone and muscle would no longer be needed after people began to cut and cook more effectively (Trinkaus, 1986).

Alternative Theories. The single-origin and multiregional hypotheses are not the only possible interpretations of the available fossil record. There is also the alternative interpretation that there may have been some replacement of one population by another, some local continuous evolution, and some interbreeding between early modern humans, who spread out of Africa, and populations encountered in North Africa, Europe, and Asia (Trinkaus, 1986). As the biologist Alan Templeton has noted, the debates over a single-origin versus multiregional evolution of *Homo sapiens* "are based on the myth that replacement of one physical feature in a fossil series with another feature can only be created by one population replacing another (either biologically or culturally), but such fossil patterns could be a reflection of one genotype replacing another through gene flow and natural selection. Morphological replacement should not be equated with population replacement when one is dealing with populations that can interbreed" (Templeton, 1996:1363). The next chapter discusses how modern human populations may also vary in physical features because natural selection favours different features in different environments.

Genetic Evidence

The single-origin (sometimes called the "out of Africa" or "replacement") hypothesis first emerged from studies where diversity in mitochondrial DNA (mtDNA) in modern human populations was used for estimating the timing of divergence between various regional populations. The question of modern human relations is based on the notion that mtDNA is inherited from the mother only and that mutation rates remain constant over time. The single-origin hypothesis implies little genetic diversity among modern populations, whereas the multiregional hypothesis implies greater genetic diversity since the genetic makeup of populations in different regions would change relatively independently of one another. Early studies of mtDNA demonstrated that the greatest variation was in African populations, implying that they represented the oldest modern human lineage. Using this information as a "molecular clock" (see Chapter 7), the time of "divergence" for modern humans from their archaic ancestral population was estimated at about 200 000 years ago (Cann et al., 1987). However, a reanalysis of the mtDNA data from the original study that suggested this so-called "Eve hypothesis" is more critical, showing that the computer models could support either model (Excoffier and Langaney, 1989; Stoneking, 1994; Ayala, 1995).

Additional genetic evidence continues to corroborate the mtDNA studies. For example, the analysis of microsatellite segments of nuclear DNA imply an African origin of modern humans from about 150 000 years ago (Seielstad et al., 1999). Like the original mtDNA support for the "Eve" hypothesis, Y-chromosome studies (genetic material passed from males to males only) have implied a common male ancestor to modern living populations who lived about 270 000 years ago (Dorit et al., 1995).

Another issue to keep in mind for these studies, however, is the concept of *genetic bottlenecks* in human evolution. Genetic bottlenecks, which can result from *demographic collapse*, can make human populations appear evolutionarily "younger" than they actually are. The reason is that demographic collapse results in the subsequent populations descending from a reduced gene pool, and therefore showing reduced genetic diversity from a relatively recent period (Harpending et al., 1998). Just as the term *demographic collapse* implies, imagine a wine bottle filled with pebbles of various colours. If you were asked to pick any coloured pebbled from that bottle, you could choose from a wide range. However, if you were asked to choose from only those colours that fall though the neck of the bottle immediately after tipping it over, your current selection, despite the original diversity of the bottle's contents, would be severely limited by the reduced flow of pebbles through the constricted neck of the bottle. Thus, the term *genetic bottleneck* refers to a rapid reduction in gene flow. Genetic bottlenecks among hominoid groups have been implied by various studies, and in some cases may be the result of infectious disease (Harpending et al., 1998). In general though, the molecular anthropological data continues to provide support for the "out of Africa" hypothesis, although the question now remains as to the degree of gene flow and local evolution in other areas. To address this, we must look more closely at the fossil evidence.

Fossil Evidence

As we noted earlier, the oldest known fossils attributed to anatomically modern humans come from Africa. Sites that are dated to around 100 000 years ago include the Klasies River Mouth, the Border Cave in South Africa, and Omo in Ethiopia (Singer and Wymer, 1982; Bräuer, 1984; Rightmire, 1984). Found at the Klasies River Mouth, a modern upper jaw and a lower jaw (mandible) with distinct chin have been dated to 90 000 years ago (Grun et al., 1990). From the Border Cave we have a near complete cranium, a mandible, and partial infant skeleton dating between 60 000 and 80 000 years ago (Grun et al., 1990). The Omo 1 skull dates to 130 000 years ago and the Mumba teeth have been dated as 110 000 years old (Feder and Park, 1997:310). More transitional specimens have been found at the sites of Florisbad, Jebel Irhoud, Omo (Omo 2), and Ngaloba (Laetoli Hominin 18) (Smith et al., 1989). These specimens all have larger, more rounded crania, and smaller brow ridges than do older African archaic populations and are somewhat older than the modern-looking material discussed above.

The Cro-Magnon fossils discovered in 1868 in France remain the oldest evidence of anatomically modern populations in western Europe. They have modern-looking skulls with vertical foreheads, small brow ridges, and a large cranial capacity. Cro-Magnons date to less than 30 000 year ago, and until recently there have been no intermediate forms observed in western Europe. In 1999, a multinational team of anthropologists published the discovery of an early Upper Palaeolithic human burial from Portugal. They argued that this provided evidence of a transitional Neandertal–early modern human, a conclusion that remains debated (Duarte et al., 1999; Tattersall and Schwartz, 1999). The remains are that of a young child (approximately four years old) with an associated date of about 24 500 years ago. The skeleton presents a "mosaic of European early modern human and Neandertal features" (Duarte et al., 1999; Tattersall and Schwartz, 1999). In eastern Europe, however, there is some evidence that has been interpreted as being transitional (Neandertal to modern). Material found in the Czech Republic dates to between 35 000 and 45 000 years ago (Omoto and Tobias, 1998). More recently, radiocarbon dates taken directly on Neandertal remains from the sites of Vindija and Velika Pecina in Croatia have suggested that this group of Archaic *H. sapiens* may have survived until as recently as 28 000 to 29 000 years ago (Smith et al., 1999) although re-dating of these remains places them slightly earlier at 32 000 to 33 000 years ago (Higham et al., 2006).

Based on the range of recent dates noted above, it seems clear that both Neandertals and modern humans (*H. sapiens sapiens*) coexisted in Europe and the Near East for at least 20 000 years, and maybe as long as 60 000 years. But what happened to the Neandertals? Three answers have generally been considered. First, they interbred with modern humans and the unique Neandertal characteristics slowly disappeared from the interbreeding population. Second, they were killed off by modern humans. Third, they were driven to extinction due to competition with modern humans.

The interbreeding scenario seems the most probable, yet evidence supporting it is weak. If modern humans and Neandertals interbred, we should be able to find "hybrid" individuals in the fossil record. In fact, a group of scholars has argued that an Upper Palaeolithic skeleton from Portugal demonstrates a combination of modern human and Neandertal features (Duarte et al., 1999). The finding remains controversial, however, because it is a child's skeleton (approximately four years old) and its Neandertal-like features have not been corroborated by other scholars. More significantly, if the interbreeding hypothesis is correct, then the mtDNA analysis we have discussed several times in this chapter must be wrong.. On the other hand, recent research on Neandertal tools suggests that some Neandertal groups adopted new techniques of tool manufacture that are thought to be uniquely associated with modern humans (Bahn, 1998). If Neandertals were learning from modern humans, then the idea that they could have interbred and perhaps been absorbed within the modern human population gains credibility. Trinkaus (2007) suggests that presence of morphological features seen in early European specimens can best be explained by some level of assimilation of Neandertal populations by modern humans.

The genocide scenario, that modern humans killed off Neandertals, has appeal as a sensational story, but little evidence. Not a single "murdered" Neandertal has ever been found, and one might wonder, in a fight between the powerful Neandertals and the more gracile modern humans, who might get the better of whom.

Finally, it may have been that Neandertals simply could not compete with modern humans. Physical anthropologist Erik Trinkaus has argued, based on both physical characteristics of the Neandertal skeleton and their apparent patterns of behaviour, that Neandertals were less efficient hunters and gatherers than modern humans (Trinkaus, 1986). If this is true, a modern human group would have been able to live and reproduce more easily than a Neandertal group in the same territory, and this would likely drive the Neandertals away. When there were no new territories to run to, the Neandertals would go extinct—precisely what the archaeological record seems to suggest (Klein, 2003). However, as we discussed in the last chapter, archaeological evidence has suggested that Neandertal hunting strategies were more complex than previously demonstrated (Burke, 2000). Thus, it remains that some additional cultural forces were being selected for in anatomically modern humans.

In southwest Asia anatomically modern specimens have been excavated from regions where Neandertals have also been discovered. Modern remains from Skhul and Qafzeh in Israel predate Neandertal remains discovered there (Stringer, 1988a). Similarly, some have argued that fossils from the Levant show Neandertals lived there at the same time as anatomically modern human populations from about 120 000 years ago, although others use the same evidence to suggest a continuum, rather than distinct populations (Corruccini, 1992; Sohn and Wolpoff, 1993). In East Asia there does appear to be some continuity in regional traits from *H. erectus* to Archaic to modern populations. Traits like shovel-shaped incisors, extra cranial sutures, and a mandibular torus that are more common in modern populations from this area seem to imply at least some level of long-term regional continuity.

The fossil evidence does seem to suggest the presence of anatomically modern populations in many areas that would be suggestive of the single-origin model. However, despite many areas having overlap between both Archaic and anatomically modern populations, other regions like eastern Europe show evidence of transitional forms that would seem to support the multiregional hypothesis.

Cultural Evidence

Artifacts found in association with early modern sites do seem to be more sophisticated than other assemblages of the same period from Europe and Asia, including the blade technology. Sites from southern Africa dating to 90 000 years ago have shown worked bone, harpoons, and other tools that are not seen at Archaic sites anywhere (Yellen et al., 1995). Outside of Africa, however, the evidence is problematic. In areas like the Middle East there are few differences in the tool assemblages of Neandertal and Archaic populations from those associated with early modern populations in Africa and southwest Asia (Thorne and Wolpoff, 1992). In Europe, others see a clear increase in sophistication of later Mousterian tools after Neandertals came into contact with modern populations and their more sophisticated tool technology, called Aurignacian. **Aurignacian tools**—a stone tool technology that began in Europe around 35 000 years ago—included the production of long, narrow blade tools.

Upper Palaeolithic Cultures

The period of cultural history in Europe, the Near East, and Asia known as the **Upper Palaeolithic** dates from about 40 000 years ago to the period known as the **Mesolithic** (about 14 000 to about 10 000 years ago, depending on the area). In Africa, the cultural period comparable to the Upper Palaeolithic is known as the Later Stone Age and may have begun much earlier. To simplify terminology, we use the term *Upper Palaeolithic* in referring to cultural developments in all areas of the Old World during this period.

In many respects, lifestyles during the Upper Palaeolithic were similar to lifestyles before. People were still mainly hunters and gatherers and fishers who probably lived in highly mobile bands. They made their camps out in the open in skin-covered huts and in caves and rock shelters, and continued to produce smaller and smaller stone tools.

The Upper Palaeolithic is also characterized by a variety of new developments. One of the most striking is the emergence of art—painting on cave walls and stone slabs and carving tools, decorative objects, and personal ornaments out of bone, antler, shell, and stone. (Perhaps for this, as well as other purposes, people began to obtain materials from distant sources.) Because more archaeological sites date from the Upper Palaeolithic than from any previous period and some Upper Palaeolithic sites seem larger than any before, many archaeologists think that the human population increased considerably during the Upper Palaeolithic (White, 1982). At the same time, new inventions, such as the bow and arrow, the spear-thrower, and tiny replaceable blades that could be fitted into handles, appear for the first time (Strauss, 1982).

The Last Ice Age

The Upper Palaeolithic world had an environment very different from today's. The earth was gripped by the last ice age, with glaciers covering Europe as far south as Berlin and Warsaw, and North America as far south as Chicago. To the south of these glacial fronts was a tundra zone extending in Europe to the Alps and in North America to the Ozarks, Appalachians, and well out onto the Great

Aurignacian Tools: a stone tool technology associated with modern humans that began in Europe around 35 000 years ago. It includes the production of long, narrow blade tools.

Upper Palaeolithic: the period associated with the emergence of modern humans and their spread around the world.

Mesolithic: the archaeological period in the Old World beginning about 12 000 B.C. Humans were starting to settle down in semipermanent camps and villages as people began to depend less on big game (which they used to have to follow over long distances) and more on relatively stationary food resources such as fish, shellfish, small game, and wild plants rich in carbohydrates, proteins, and oils.

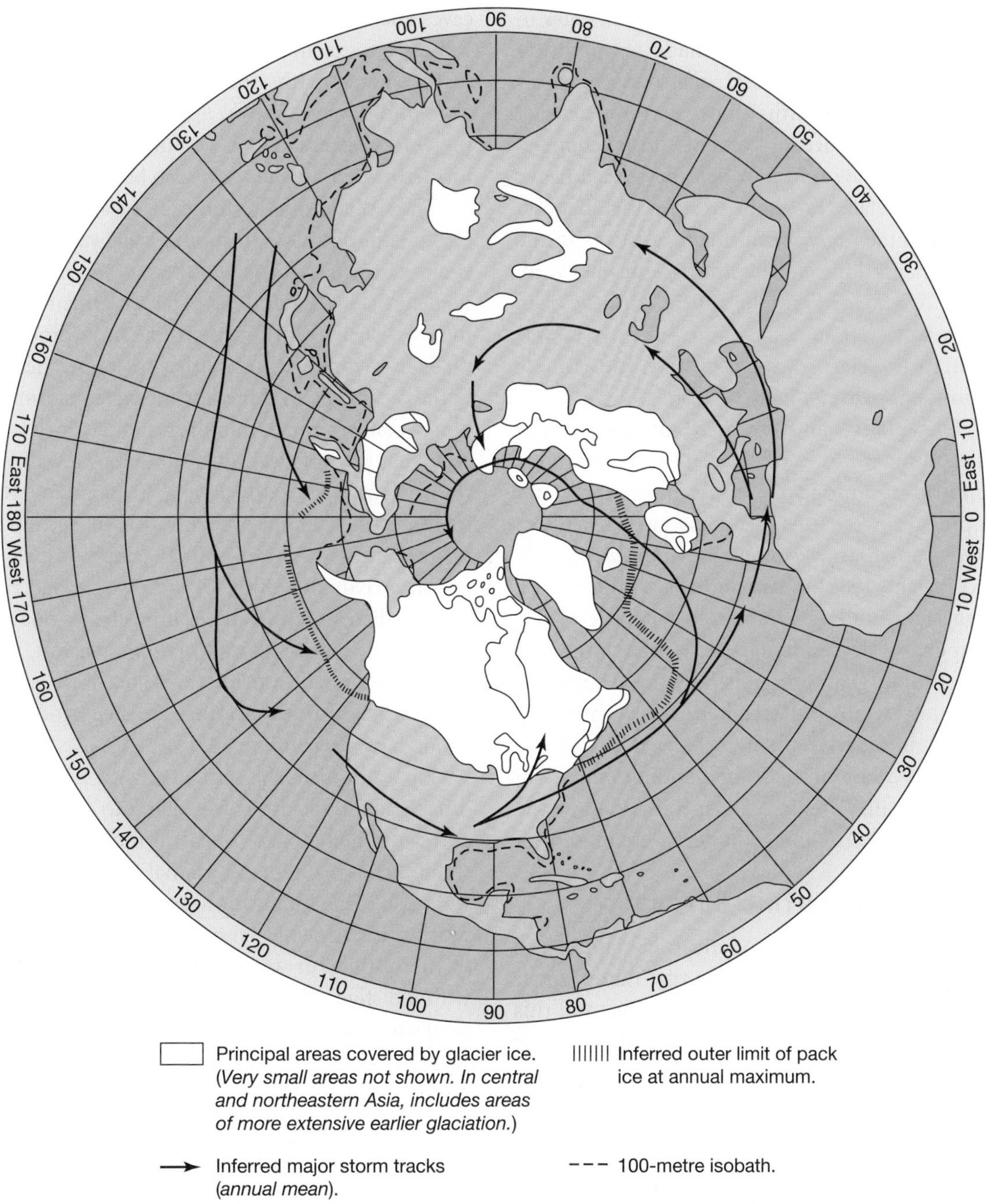

Figure 10–2 The Extent of Glaciation during the Upper Palaeolithic

Source: Stein P, Rowe B. 2000. Physical Anthropology. Seventh edition. Boston: McGraw-Hill. Copyright © 2000. Reprinted by permission of The McGraw-Hill Book Company.

Plains (see Figure 10–2). Environmentally, both Europe and North America probably resembled contemporary Siberia and northern Canada. Elsewhere in the world conditions were not as extreme, but were still different from conditions today (Dawson, 1992).

For one thing, the climate was different. Average annual temperatures were as much as

10 degrees Celsius below today's, and changes in ocean currents would have made temperature contrasts (that is, the differences between summer and winter months) more extreme as well. The changing ocean currents also changed weather patterns, and Europe experienced heavy annual snowfall. Not all the world was cold, however; still, the presence of huge ice sheets in the north changed the climate throughout the world. North Africa, for example, appears to have been much wetter than today, and South Asia was apparently drier. And everywhere the climate seems to have been highly variable.

The plants and animals of the Upper Palaeolithic world were adapted to these extreme conditions. Among the most important, and impressive, were the large game animals collectively known as *Pleistocene megafauna* (Martin and Wright, 1967). These animals, as their name suggests, were huge compared with their contemporary descendants. In North America, for example, giant ground sloths stood some 2.5 to 3 metres tall and weighed a few thousand kilograms. Siberian mammoths were the largest elephants ever to live—some standing more than 4 metres tall. In East Asia, species such as the woolly rhinoceros and giant deer were present.

Upper Palaeolithic Europe

With the vast supplies of meat available from *megafauna*, it is not surprising that many Upper Palaeolithic cultures relied on hunting, and this was particularly true of the Upper Palaeolithic peoples of Europe, on whom we focus here. Their way of life represents a common pattern throughout the Old World. But as people began to use more diverse resources in their environments, the use of local resources allowed Upper Palaeolithic groups in much of the Old World to become more sedentary than their predecessors. They also began to trade with neighbouring groups in order to obtain resources not available in their local territories (Mellars, 1994).

As was the case in the known Middle Palaeolithic sites, most of the Upper Palaeolithic remains that have been excavated were situated in caves and rock shelters. In southwestern France, some groups seem to have paved parts of the floor of the shelter with stones. Tent-like structures were built in some caves, apparently to keep out the cold (Patterson, 1981). Some of what were formerly open-air sites have also been excavated.

The site at Dolni Vestonice in what is now the Czech Republic dates to about 25 000 years ago. It is one of the first for which there is an entire settlement plan (Klima, 1962). The settlement seems to have consisted of four tent-like huts, probably made from animal skins, with a great open hearth in the centre. Around the outside were mammoth bones, some rammed into the ground, which suggests that the huts were surrounded by a wall. All told, there were bone heaps from about 100 mammoths. Each hut probably housed a group of related families—about 20 to 25 people. (One hut was approximately 8 by 14 metres and had five hearths distributed inside it, presumably one for each family.) With 20 to 25 people per hut, and assuming that all four huts were occupied at the same time, the population of the settlement would have been 100 to 125.

Up a hill from the settlement was a fifth and different kind of hut. It was dug into the ground and contained a bake oven and more than 2300 small, fired fragments of animal figurines. There were also some hollow bones that may have been musical instruments. Another interesting feature of the settlement was a burial find of a woman with a disfigured face. She may have been a particularly important personage, because her face was found engraved on an ivory plaque near the central hearth of the settlement.

Upper Palaeolithic Tools

Upper Palaeolithic toolmaking appears to have had its roots in the Mousterian and post-Acheulian traditions, because flake tools are found in many Upper Palaeolithic sites. The Upper Palaeolithic, however, is characterized by a preponderance of blades; there were also burins, bone and antler tools, and *microliths* (see Figure 10–3).

In addition, two new techniques of toolmaking appeared—*indirect percussion* and *pressure*

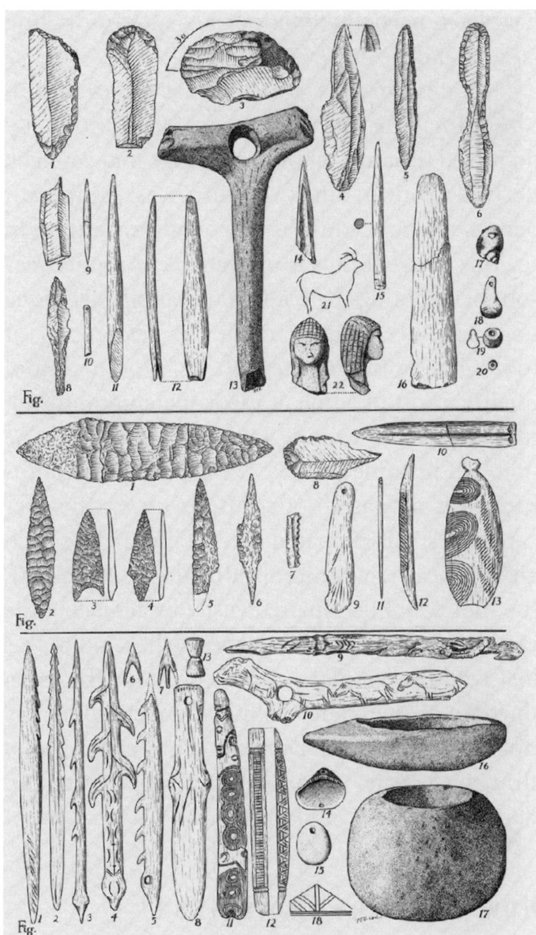

Figure 10–3 Upper Palaeolithic tools

Upper Palaeolithic peoples made a much wider variety of tools than their predecessors.

Source: American Museum of Natural History.

flaking. Blades were found in Middle Palaeolithic assemblages, but they were not widely used until the Upper Palaeolithic. Although blades can be made in a variety of ways, **indirect percussion** using a hammer-struck punch was commonly used in the Upper Palaeolithic. After shaping a core into a pyramidal or cylindrical form, the toolmaker put a punch of antler or wood or another hard material into position and struck it with a hammer. Because the force is directed, the toolmaker was able to strike off consistently shaped blades, which are more than twice as long as they are wide (Schick and Toth, 1994; Whittaker, 1994) (see Figure 10–4).

The Upper Palaeolithic is also noted for the production of large numbers of bone, antler, and ivory tools; needles, awls, and harpoons made of bone appear for the first time (Whittaker, 1994). The manufacture of these implements may have been made easier by the development of many varieties of burins. Burins are chisel-like stone tools used for carving (see Figure 10–3); bone and

Indirect Percussion: a toolmaking technique common in the Upper Paleolithic. After shaping a core into a pyramidal or cylindrical form, the toolmaker could put a punch of antler or wood or another hard material into position and strike it with a hammer. Using a hammer-struck punch enabled the toolmaker to strike off consistently shaped blades.

Figure 10–4 Percussion Flaking

One way to remove blades from a core is to hit them with a punch using indirect percussion. The object being struck is the punch, which is made of bone or horn.

Source: Fagan BM. 1972. In the Beginning. Boston: Little, Brown. p 195.

antler needles, awls, and projectile points could be produced with them (Bordaz, 1970). Burins have been found in Middle and Lower Palaeolithic sites but are present in great number and variety only in the Upper Palaeolithic.

Pressure flaking also appeared during the Upper Palaeolithic. Rather than using percussion to strike off flakes as in previous technologies, pressure flaking works by employing pressure with a bone, wood, or antler tool at the edge of the tool to remove small flakes. Pressure flaking would usually be used in the final stages of retouching a tool (Whittaker, 1994).

As time went on, all over the Old World smaller and smaller blade tools were produced. The very tiny ones, called **microliths**, were often hafted or fitted into handles, one blade at a time or several blades together, to serve as spears, adzes, knives, and sickles. The hafting required inventing a way to trim the blade's back edge so that it would be blunt rather than sharp. In this way the blades would not split the handles into which they might be inserted; the blunting would also prevent the users of an unhafted blade from cutting themselves (Phillipson, 1993).

Some archaeologists think that the blade technique was adopted because it made for more economical use of flint. André Leroi-Gourhan of the Musée de l'Homme in Paris calculated that with the old Acheulian technique, a 1-kilogram lump of flint yielded 40 centimetres of working edge and produced only two hand axes. If the more advanced Mousterian technique were used, a lump of equal size would yield 1.8 metres of working edge. The indirect percussion method of the Upper Palaeolithic would yield as much as 22.8 metres of working edge (Bordaz, 1970). With the same amount of material, a significantly greater number of tools could be produced. Getting the most out of a valuable resource may have been particularly important in areas lacking large flint deposits.

Jacques Bordaz suggested that the evolution of toolmaking techniques, which continually increased the amount of usable edge that could be derived from a lump of flint, was significant because people could then spend more time in regions where flint was unavailable. Another reason for adopting the blade toolmaking technique may have been that it made for easy repair of tools. For example, the cutting edge of a tool might consist of a line of razor-like microliths set into a piece of wood. The tool would not be usable if just one of the cutting edge's microliths broke off or was chipped. If, however, the user carried a small, prepared core of flint from which an identical-sized microlith could be struck off, the tool could be repaired easily by replacing the lost or broken microlith. A spear whose point was lost could be similarly repaired. Thus, the main purpose of the blade toolmaking technique may not have been to make more economical use of flint, but rather to allow easy replacement of damaged blades (Clark, 1977).

How Were the Tools Used?

The tools made by Upper Palaeolithic people suggest that they were much more effective hunters and fishers than their predecessors (Klein, 1994). During the Upper Palaeolithic, and probably for the first time, spears were launched with a spear-thrower rather than thrown with the arm. We know this because bone and antler **atlatls** (the Aztec word for "spear-thrower") have been found in some sites. A spear propelled off a grooved board could be sent through the air with increased force, causing it to travel farther and hit harder, and with less effort by the thrower. The bow and arrow was also used in various places during the Upper Palaeolithic; and

Pressure Flaking: toolmaking technique whereby small flakes are struck off by pressing against the core with a bone, antler, or wood tool.

Microlith: a small, razor-like blade fragment that was probably attached in a series to a wooden or bone handle to form a cutting edge.

Atlatl: Aztec word for "spear-thrower."

harpoons, used for fishing and perhaps for hunting reindeer, were invented at this time.

These new tools and weapons for more effective hunting and fishing do not rule out the possibility that Upper Palaeolithic people were still scavenging animal remains. Olga Soffer suggests that Upper Palaeolithic people may have located their settlements near places where many mammoths died naturally in order to use the bones for building (see Figure 10–5). For example, in Moravia the mammoths may have come to lick deposits of calcite and other sources of magnesium and calcium, particularly during the late spring and early summer when food resources were short and mortality was high. Consistent with the idea that humans may not have killed all the enormous mammoths found there is the fact that in some places there are few human-made cut marks on mammoth bones. For example, at Dolni Vestonice, where bones of 100 mammoths were found, few bones show cut marks from butchering and few bones were found inside the huts. In contrast, the living floors are littered with bison, horse, and reindeer bones, suggesting that these other animals were deliberately killed and eaten by humans. If the people had actually killed all the mammoths that we find the remains of, why would they have hunted so many other animals (Soffer, 1993)?

Art

The earliest discovered traces of art are beads and carvings, and then paintings, from Upper Palaeolithic sites. We might expect that early artistic efforts were crude, but the cave paintings of Spain and southern France show a marked degree of skill. So do the naturalistic paintings on slabs of stone excavated in southern Africa. Some of those slabs appear to have been painted as much as 28 000 years ago, which suggests that painting in Africa is as old as painting in Europe (Phillipson, 1993). In fact, painting may be even older than that. The early Australians may have painted on the walls of rock shelters and cliff faces at least 30 000 years ago and maybe as much as 60 000 years ago (Morell, 1995).

Peter Ucko and André Rosenfeld identified three principal locations of paintings in the caves of western Europe: (1) in obviously inhabited rock shelters and cave entrances—art as decoration or

Figure 10–5 Mammoth Shelters

Here we see the type of mammoth-bone shelters constructed about 15 000 years ago on the East European Plain. Often mammoth skulls formed part of the foundation for the tusk, long bone, and wooden frame, covered with hide. As many as 95 mammoth mandibles were arranged around the outside in a herringbone pattern. Ten men and women could have constructed this elaborate shelter of 24 square metres in six days, using 20 800 kilograms of bone.

"art for art's sake"; (2) in "galleries" immediately off the inhabited areas of caves; and (3) in the inner reaches of caves, whose difficulty of access has been interpreted by some as a sign that magical-religious activities were performed there (Ucko and Rosenfield, 1967).

The subjects of the paintings are mostly animals. The paintings rest on bare walls, with no backdrops or environmental trappings. Perhaps, like many contemporary peoples, Upper Palaeolithic men and women believed that the drawing of a human image could cause death or injury. If that were indeed their belief, it might explain why human figures are rarely depicted in cave art. Another explanation for the focus on animals might be that these people sought to improve their luck at hunting. This hypothesis is suggested by evidence of chips in the painted figures, perhaps made by spears thrown at the drawings. However, if hunting magic was the chief motivation for the paintings, it is difficult to explain why only a few show signs of having been speared. Perhaps the paintings were inspired by the need to increase the supply of animals. Cave art seems to have reached a peak toward the end of the Upper Palaeolithic period, when the herds of game were decreasing.

The particular symbolic significance of the cave paintings in southwestern France is more explicitly revealed, perhaps, by the results of Patricia Rice and Ann Paterson's statistical study (Rice and Paterson, 1985; Rice and Paterson, 1986). The data suggest that the animals portrayed in the cave paintings were mostly the ones that the painters preferred for meat and for materials such as hides. For example, wild cattle (bovines) and horses are portrayed more often than we would expect by chance, probably because they were larger and heavier (meatier) than the other animals in the environment. In addition, the paintings mostly portray animals that the painters may have feared the most because of their size, speed, natural weapons such as tusks and horns, and unpredictability of behaviour. That is, mammoths, bovines, and horses are portrayed more often than deer and reindeer. Thus, the paintings are consistent with the idea that "the art is related to the importance of hunting in the economy of Upper Palaeolithic people" (Rice and Paterson, 1985:98). Consistent with this idea, according to the investigators, is the fact that the art of the cultural period that followed the Upper Palaeolithic also seems to reflect

A piece of three-dimensional Upper Palaeolithic art from France. This depiction of a bison licking itself is both accurate and beautifully executed, clearly showing the skill of Upper Palaeolithic artists.

The Venus of Willendorf, one of the most famous Venus figurines.

how people got their food. However, in that period, when getting food no longer depended on hunting large game (because they were becoming extinct), the art ceased to focus on portrayals of animals.

Upper Palaeolithic art was not confined to cave paintings. Many shafts of spears and similar objects were decorated with figures of animals. Alexander Marshack has an interesting interpretation of some of the engravings made during the Upper Palaeolithic. He believes that as far back as 30 000 B.C., hunters may have used a system of notation, engraved on bone and stone, to mark the phases of the moon. If this is true, it would mean that Upper Palaeolithic people were capable of complex thought and were consciously aware of their environment. In addition, figurines representing the human female in exaggerated form have been found at Upper Palaeolithic sites. Called *Venuses*, these figurines portray women with broad hips and large breasts and abdomens. It has been suggested that the figurines were an ideal type or an expression of a desire for fertility. Most of these figurines were made during the Gravettian period from about 25 000 to 23 000 years ago. Clive Gamble argues that the Venus figurines were religious in nature. As such, their presence in the archaeological record implies a widespread belief system shared between geographically isolated groups. From her analysis of the shape, size, and form of almost 200 figurines, Patricia Rice concluded that the figurines reflect a distribution of ages similar to the demographic profiles seen in contemporary foraging groups. A number of questions remain unanswered, however, particularly regarding the general featureless style of the figures. LeRoy McDermott suggests they are a reflection of how a woman represents herself through self-observation, including the absence of anatomical features and distortions in the bodily proportions. However, more recent exploration of these artifacts by Soffer and colleagues suggests that a variety of aspects of these figurines have been missed or misinterpreted by past investigations. In particular, these researchers have argued that a number of the figurines are depicted wearing clothing that demonstrates considerable craftsmanship and knowledge of woven fabric (Marshack, 1972). In addition to the Venus figurines, there are other depictions of women in Upper Palaeolithic art (see New Perspectives on Gender, "Depictions of Women in Upper Palaeolithic Art").

What the Venus figurines symbolized remains controversial. As is usually the case in current scholarly controversies, there is little or no evidence available now that might allow us to accept or reject a particular interpretation. But not all controversies in anthropology continue because of lack of evidence. Sometimes a controversy continues because there is some, usually disputed evidence on all sides. This was the case until recently with the controversy to which we now turn—whether there were people in the Americas before about 11 500 years ago.

Upper Paleolithic Cultures in Africa and Asia

Europe was not the only region where Upper Palaeolithic peoples thrived. In North Africa, for example, Upper Palaeolithic peoples hunted large animals on the grasslands that covered the region during that period. They lived in small communities located within easy access to water and other resources, and moved regularly, probably to follow the animal herds. Trade took place between local groups, particularly for high-quality stone used in making tools (Hawkins and Kleindienst, 2001). In eastern and southern Africa, a way of life known as the Later Stone Age developed that persisted in some areas until very recently. People lived in small, mobile groups, hunting large animals and collecting a wide variety of plant foods. Interaction was common among these bands. Among their ethnographically known descendants, individuals would regularly switch their membership from one band to another (Peregrine, 2001).

In South Asia the Upper Palaeolithic saw an increasingly sedentary lifestyle developing along the banks of freshwater streams. The Upper Palaeolithic peoples in South Asia combined hunting, fishing, and gathering with seasonal

NEW PERSPECTIVES ON GENDER

Depictions of Women in Upper Palaeolithic Art

Image of four women from Gönnersdorf cave.

Source: Duhard J-P. 1993. Upper Paleolithic Figures as a Reflection of Human Morphology and Social Organization. Antiquity 67:86.

It is a common misperception that depictions of the human form in Upper Palaeolithic art are restricted to Venus figurines. To the contrary, there are many other depictions of humans, both female and male, running the whole range of ages from infants to old people. For women, figures of obese or pregnant women, like those sometimes depicted in Venus figurines, appear to be only one type in a wide range of images, many of which offer accurate rather than stylized representations.

In a survey of Upper Palaeolithic art, Jean-Pierre Duhard found that all shapes and sizes of women, as well as all age ranges, were present. Indeed, he argued that a range of female body types can be seen. One engraved figure from Gönnersdorf cave on the Rhine River, for example, depicts four women. Three are the same size, but one is smaller and has small breasts—she may be an adolescent. Of the three larger figures, one appears to have a child tied to her back, and she also has large, rounded breasts, as opposed to the flat and pointed breasts of the other two. Duhard argued that this is an accurate depiction of four women, one with a child she is breast-feeding.

Duhard suggested that women's roles as mothers may have given them a privileged status in Upper Palaeolithic life, which may be why that status is the most frequently depicted subject in Upper Palaeolithic art. In a similar way, Patricia Rice has argued that Venus figurines accurately reflect the social importance of women in Upper Palaeolithic society. She demonstrated that a range of body types and ages are represented in Venus figurines, and argued that, since the Venuses depict real women of all ages, not just pregnant women, they should be seen as symbols of "womanhood" rather than "motherhood." The wide distribution of Venus figurines and their apparent importance to Upper Palaeolithic peoples reflect, according to Rice, the recognized importance of women in Upper Palaeolithic society.

Arguing along similar lines, Olga Soffer examined the clothing worn by some Venus figures. Soffer and her colleagues show that woven items are the most frequently depicted, and argue that, since these woven items would have been highly valued in Upper Palaeolithic society, their presence on some Venus figurines suggests that some women held positions of high status in Upper Palaeolithic society.

Duhard also argued that while depictions of women are common in Upper Palaeolithic art, similar depictions of men and children are comparatively rare. He suggested this disparity may reflect women's status in Upper Palaeolithic societies. Most depictions of women show them in some motherhood role—pregnant, in childbirth, or carrying an infant (and perhaps walking with older children).

Sources: Duhard J-P. 1993. Upper Palaeolithic Figures as a Reflection of Human Morphology and Social Organization. Antiquity 67:83–91.

Rice P. 1981. Prehistoric Venuses: Symbols of Motherhood or Womanhood? Journal of Anthropological Research 37:402–414.

Soffer O, Adovasio JM, Hyland DC. 2000. The "Venus" Figurines: Textiles, Basketry, Gender, and Status in the Upper Palaeolithic. Current Anthropology 41:511–537.

movements to exploit seasonally abundant resources (Jayaswal, 2002). In East and Southeast Asia ocean resources became vital to coastal-dwelling peoples, while those inland lived primarily in caves, hunting and collecting broadly in the local environment. Many of these sites appear to have been occupied for long periods of time, suggesting some degree of sedentism. During the Upper Palaeolithic, peoples from Asia also populated Australia, New Guinea, and some of the islands of western Melanesia, clearly demonstrating the ability of these peoples to navigate on the sea and to use its resources (Peregrine and Bellwood, 2001).

Paintings in the "Hall of Bulls" at Lascaux in France. Cave paintings like this demonstrate the remarkable skill of Upper Paleotlithic artists.

The Earliest Humans in the New World

So far in this chapter we have dealt only with the Old World—Africa, Europe, and Asia. What about the New World—North and South America? How long have humans lived there, and what were their earliest cultures like?

Because only *H. sapiens sapiens* fossils have been found in North and South America, migrations of humans to the New World had to have taken place sometime after the emergence of *H. sapiens sapiens.* When exactly these migrations occurred is subject to debate, particularly about when people got to areas south of Alaska. At the Old Crow site on the Porcupine River in the Yukon Territory, a possible early human occupation site has been dated to between 12 000 and 27 000 years ago (Morlan et al., 1990). If the site is indeed that old, it represents the oldest known human habitation site in the New World. Nearby, the Bluefish Caves site in the Yukon Territory revealed the faunal remains of mammoth, horse, bison, and caribou. Stone tools, including some microblades, were discovered at the site. Radiocarbon dating on bone collagen from the faunal remains suggests a date of between 15 000 and 12 000 years ago (Harington and Cinq-mars, 1995; Burke and Cinq-mars, 1998). Because of a lack of archaeological evidence in the northwest Arctic, the prevailing view has been that humans were not present south of Alaska until after 15 000 years ago. However, evidence from an archaeological site called Monte Verde in Chile suggests that modern humans might have been living in southern South America at least 12 500 years ago, and maybe as much as 33 000 years ago. (See Current Research and Issues, "When and How Did Humans Populate the New World?" on page 238.) The Monte Verde site contains more than 700 stone tools, the remains of hide-covered huts, and a child's footprint next to a hearth (McDonald, 1998).

The people there may or may not have hunted big game, but just a little while later there were people living in the tropical rain forest of the Amazon basin in what is now Brazil who were definitely not hunters of mammoths and other big game, as their contemporaneous North American counterparts were. In other words, it looks like the earliest inhabitants of the New World—in what is now Chile and Brazil, and in North America—varied in culture. The people in the Amazon lived by collecting fruits and nuts, fishing, and hunting small game. They lived in caves with painted art on the walls and left 30 000 stone chips from making tips of spears, darts, or harpoons (Gibbons, 1995; Roosevelt et al., 1995).

According to the comparative linguists Joseph Greenberg and Merritt Ruhlen, there were three waves of migration into the New World (Greenberg and Ruhlen, 1992). They compared hundreds of languages in North and South America, grouping them into three different language families. Because each of these language families has a closer relationship to an Asian language family than to the other New World language families, it would appear that three different migrations came out of Asia. The first arrivals spoke a language that diverged over time into most of the languages found in the New World—the Amerind family of languages; the speakers of these related languages came to occupy all of South and Central America as well as most of North America. Next came the ancestors of the people who speak languages belonging to the Na-Dené family, which today includes Haida on the northwest coast of Canada, Navaho and Apache in the southwestern United States, and various Athapaskan languages. Finally, perhaps 4000 years ago, came the ancestors of the Inuit and Aleut (the latter came to occupy the islands southwest of Alaska and the adjacent mainland), who speak languages belonging to the Inuit-Aleut family.

Christy Turner's study of New World teeth supports the Greenberg and Ruhlen proposal of three separate migrations. Turner looked at the proportions of shovel-shaped incisors, a common Asian trait, in New World populations. The varying proportions fall into three distinct groupings, the same three suggested by the linguists (Turner II, 1989) (see Figure 10–6). In contrast, genetic analysis suggests that Inuit-Aleut may have split from Na-Dené in the New World (Szathmáry, 1993). In their study of mtDNA, Rubicz and colleagues (2004) also suggest that the Aleut represent a distinct wave of migration across Beringia. Schurr and Sherry's (2004) analysis of mtDNA and Y chromosome data suggest a migration from Siberia into the New World around 15 000 to 20 000 years ago. The peopling of the New World may have been even more complicated. There could have been four separate migrations from the Old World, from different regions of Asia (McDonald, 1998).

A jury of visiting archaeologists at the Monte Verde site in Chile confirmed that modern humans arrived in southern South America at least 12 500 years ago.

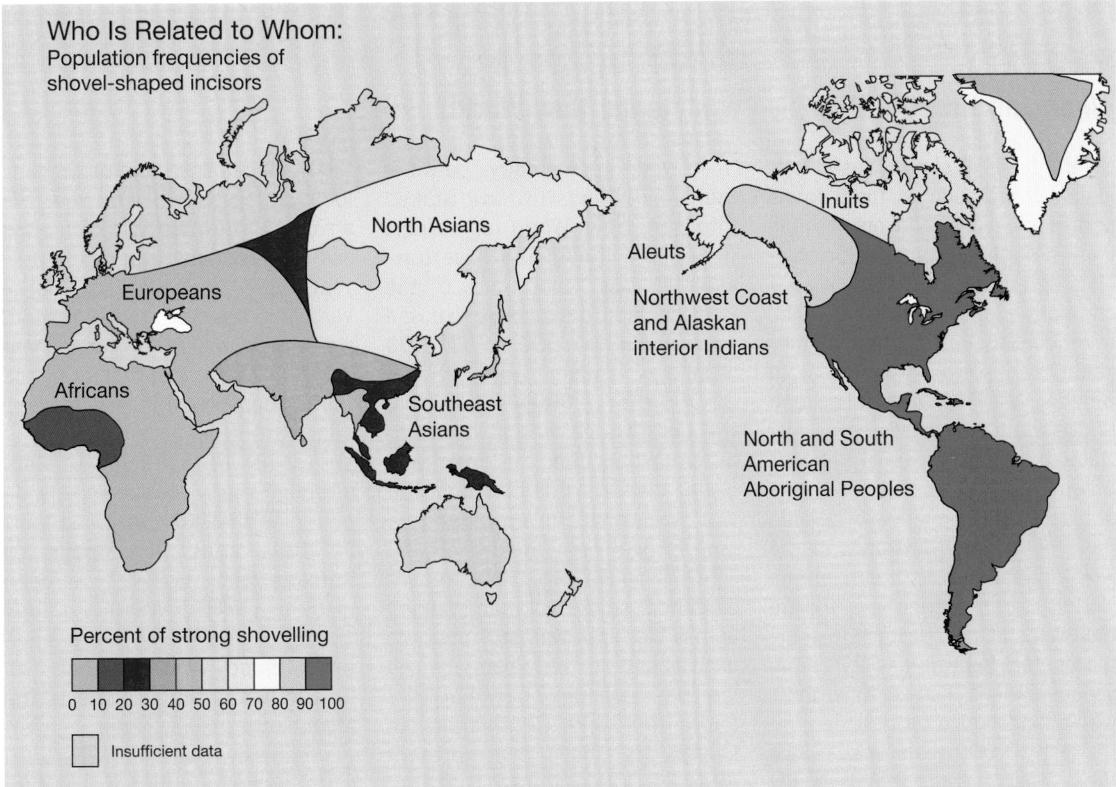

Figure 10–6 Who is Related to Whom?: Population Frequencies of Shovel-Shaped Incisors

Inuit and Aleuts, speakers of Na-Dené languages, and other Native American language groups differ in the frequency of shovel-shaped incisors. These genetic differences seem to reflect three waves of migration into the New World.

Source: Turner II CG. January 1987. Telltale Teeth. Natural History 8. Courtesy of *Natural History* magazine.

The Paleo-Indians

Archaeological remains of early New World hunters, called *Paleo-Indians,* have been found in the United States, Mexico, and Canada. Just south of the farthest reaches of the last glaciation, the area east of the Rockies known as the High Plains abounded with mammoths, bison, wild camels, and wild horses. The tools found with mammoth kills are known as the *Clovis complex,* which includes the Clovis projectile point as well as stone scrapers and knives and bone tools. The Clovis projectile point is large and leaf-shaped, flaked on both sides. It has a broad groove in the middle, presumably so that the point could be attached to a wooden spear shaft (Wheat 1967). Because one mammoth was found with eight Clovis points in it, there is little dispute that Clovis people hunted large game (Fagan 1991:79). Recent dating places most Clovis sites between 11 200 and 10 900 years ago (Hoffecker et al 1993).

Clovis points.

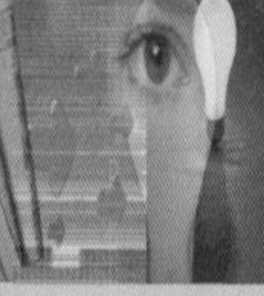

CURRENT RESEARCH AND ISSUES

When and How Did Humans Populate the New World?

On the basis of similarities in biological traits such as tooth forms and blood types, and on possible linguistic relationships, anthropologists agree that Native Americans originally came from Asia. The traditional assumption is that they came to North America from Siberia, walking across a land bridge (Beringia) that is now under water (the Bering Strait) between Siberia and Alaska. The ice sheets or glaciers that periodically covered most of the high latitudes of the world contained so much of the world's water (the ice sheets were thousands of metres thick in some places) that **Beringia** was dry land in various periods. For example, there was a land bridge for a while until the last 10 000 years or so. Since then, the glaciers have mostly melted, and the Bering "bridge" has been completely covered by a higher sea level. We now know that the Monte Verde site in Chile was occupied at least 12 500 years ago, so it would seem that there was at least one wave of human migration into the New World before then, by walking and/or perhaps in boats. Even when the last glaciers were at their fullest extent, there was still a small ice-free corridor through which people could have walked (see the diagram in this box).

It was geologically possible then for humans to have walked into the New World at various times, and they could have travelled by boat, too. Parts of the Beringia land bridge were exposed from about 60 000 to 25 000 years ago. It wasn't until between 20 000 and 18 000 years ago that the land bridge was at its maximum. When did the last land bridge disappear? Until recently, it was widely believed that the land bridge was flooded around 14 000 years ago, but recent evidence suggests that walking across Beringia was still possible until about 10 000 years ago. An ice-free corridor between the Laurentide and Cordilleran ice sheets may have been present after 25 000 years ago, but that corridor is not likely to have supported big game, and permitted humans to hunt enough, until after about 14 000 years ago. So some investigators suggest that moving through the ice-free corridor to what is now south of Canada was not likely until after that time.

There is no disagreement that humans were living south of Canada around 11 000 years ago. The Clovis people, as they are called (after an archaeological site near Clovis, New Mexico), left finely shaped spear points in many locations in North America. We also have the presence of human skeletal remains after 11 000 years ago. Now that the Monte Verde site has been reliably dated, we know that there were people south of Canada earlier than the Clovis people were in New Mexico. There are other possible sites of pre-Clovis occupation as well, although many archaeologists do not agree that the presumed tools at these sites were made by humans (they could have been made by rockfalls or other natural forces) or that the sites are accurately dated. One site that may be another pre-Clovis site is the Meadowcroft Rockshelter in western Pennsylvania.

In the bottom third of a stratum that seems to date from 19 600 to 8000 years ago, the Meadowcroft site shows clear signs of human occupation—a small fragment of human bone, a spear point, and chipped knives and scrapers. If the dating is accurate, the tools would be about 12 800 years old. William Parry suggests we need to date the human bone found in the site. If the bone turns out to date from before 12 000 years ago, few anthropologists would question the conclusion that humans occupied

The mammoth disappeared in North America about 10 000 years ago (for possible reasons, see Chapter 11), and the now-extinct large, straight-horned bison became the largest prey species of humans. The hunters of that bison used a projectile point called the Folsom point, which was much smaller than the Clovis point. Tools are also found with many other kinds of animal remains, including wolf, turtle, rabbit, horse, fox, deer, and camel, so the bison hunters obviously depended on other animals as well (Jennings, 1968). In the Rio Grande valley, the Folsom toolmakers characteristically established a base camp on low dune ridges overlooking both a large pond and broad, open grazing

Beringia: the land mass that is now under water (the Bering Strait) between Siberia and Alaska.

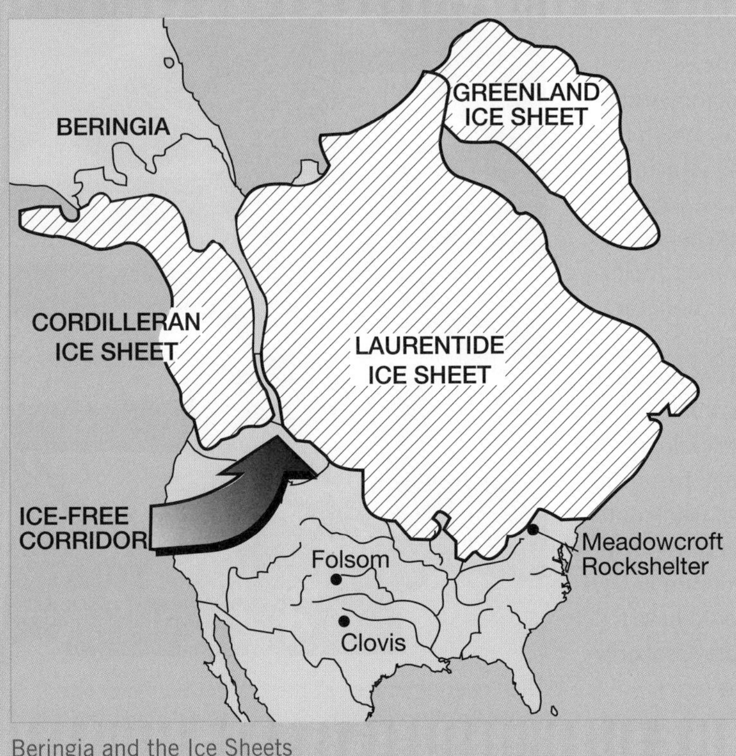

Beringia and the Ice Sheets

Source: Meltzer DK. 1993. Pleistocene Peopling of the Americas. Evolutionary Anthropology. Vol. 1. Copyright © 1993. Reprinted by permission of Wiley-Liss, Inc. a subsidiary of John Wiley and Sons, Inc.

the Meadowcroft site before the time of the Clovis people.

People now cross the Bering Strait by water. Could earlier humans have come to the New World the same way, before a land bridge existed? If they had come by water, instead of by walking over a land bridge and down through an ice-free corridor, there would be coastal sites with evidence of humans who travelled by water. Such sites would now be covered by water because the sea level is higher. It is conceivable then that humans came very early to the New World by water, but there is as yet no evidence of that under water along the coast. Even if people did come early to the New World by water, they might not have survived long enough and spread widely enough to give archaeologists a chance to find their remains. There might be some remains somewhere, but that has not yet been definitely established.

Exactly when humans first came into the New World, how many migrations there were, and how they spread south of Canada are questions to which we still have only tentative answers. New evidence continues to surface regularly, so we should have firmer answers to these questions before too long. That is part of what makes research exciting. There is always something new to look for.

Sources: Hoffecker JF, Powers WG, Goebel T. 1 January 1993. The Colonization of Beringia and the Peopling of the New World. Science 46–53.

McDonald KA. 13 March 1998. New Evidence Challenges Traditional Model of How the New World Was Settled. Chronicle of Higher Education A22ff.

Parry WJ. 1998. When and How Did Humans Populate the New World? In: Ember CR, Ember M, Peregrine PN, editors. Research Frontiers in Anthropology. Upper Saddle River, NJ: Prentice Hall. Prentice Hall/Simon & Schuster Custom Publishing.

areas. If we assume that the pond provided water for the grazing herds, the people in the camp would have been in an excellent position to watch the herds (Judge and Dawson, 1972).

As the climate of what is now the American Southwest became drier, the animals and the cultural adaptations changed somewhat. About 9000 years ago the earlier straight-horned bison variety became extinct and were replaced by smaller modern forms (Wheat, 1967). Base camps began to be located farther from ponds and grazing areas and closer to streams. If the ponds were no longer reliable sources of water during these drier times, the animals probably no longer frequented them, which would explain why the hunters had to change the sites of their base camps. Not that much is known about the plant foods these people may have exploited, but on the desert fringes plant gathering may have been vital. In Nevada and Utah, archaeologists have found milling stones and other artifacts for processing plant food (Fagan, 1989).

The Olsen-Chubbuck site, a kill site excavated in Colorado, shows the organization that may have been involved in hunting bison (Wheat, 1967). In a dry gulch dated to 6500 B.C. were the remains of 200 bison. At the bottom were complete skeletons and at the top, those of completely butchered animals. This find clearly suggests that hunters deliberately stampeded the animals into a natural *trapùan arroyo*, or steep-sided dry gully. The animals in front were probably pushed by the ones behind into the arroyo. Joe Wheat estimated that the hunters might have obtained 25 000 kilograms of meat from this one kill. If we judge from the habits of 19th-century Plains Indians, who could prepare bison meat to last a month, and estimate that each person would eat half a kilogram a day, the kill at the Olsen-Chubbuck site could have fed more than 1800 people for a month (they probably did not all live together throughout the year).

The "river of bones" at the Olsen-Chubbuck site. These are the remains of bison that Palaeo-Indian hunters stampeded into an arroyo.

The hunters must have been highly organized, not only for the stampede itself, but also for butchering. It seems that the enormous carcasses had to be dragged to flat ground for that job. In addition, the 25 000 kilograms of meat and hides had to be carried back to camp (Wheat, 1967). Since a dead bison is too bulky and heavy to move whole, the kill site is usually the scene of primary butchering. This involves cutting manageable portions off the carcass and removing them for secondary butchering and processing elsewhere. The low-value portions of the skeleton are abandoned in the "kill floor," perhaps to be exposed later by the archaeologist. In this case they are overlying the unbutchered animals that got trampled under by the stampede into the trap. There are important social implications associated with all the processes required for an undertaking of this magnitude. In particular it requires large groups and thorough political integration to organize these kills and subsequently distribute the meat and hides among participants.

Although big game may have been most important on the High Plains, other areas show different adaptations. For example, Paleo-Indian people in woodland regions of what is now the United States seem to have depended more heavily on plant food and smaller game. In some woodland areas, fish and shellfish may have been a vital part of the diet (Fagan, 1989). On the Pacific coast, some Paleo-Indian people developed food-getting strategies more dependent on fish (Fagan, 1991). And in other areas, the lower Illinois River valley being one example, Palaeo-Indian people who depended on game and wild vegetable foods managed to get enough food to live in permanent villages of perhaps 100 to 150 people (Fagan, 1989).

As the climate became warmer and drier, the flora and fauna of North America changed. Megafauna, as elsewhere in the world, went extinct, and were replaced by smaller mammals, particularly deer. The availability of meat was greatly reduced—hunters could count on coming home with kilograms, not tonnes, of meat. Warmer adapted plants replaced cold adapted plants, and were used for food to replace the meat that was no longer available. Warmer adapted plants had advantages as food resources for humans over cold adapted ones because edible seeds, fruits, and nuts were more common, and often more plentiful and accessible, on the warmer adapted plants. Thus a much greater diversity of plants and animals came to be used by the Archaic peoples (Daniel, 2001).

The Archaic peoples of North America began to follow a more sedentary lifestyle. Two forms of Archaic settlement appear to have been typical. One was a residential base camp, which would have been inhabited seasonally by several, probably related families. The other was a special-purpose camp, which would have been a short-term habitation near a particular resource or perhaps used by a group of hunters for a short period (Sassaman, 1996). On the Atlantic coast, for example, individual groups apparently moved seasonally along major river valleys, establishing summer base camps in the piedmont and winter camps near the coast. Special-purpose camps were created year-round as groups went out from the base camp to hunt and collect particular resources, such as stone for making tools (Sassaman, 1996).

One of the innovations of the Archaic peoples was the development of ground stone woodworking tools. Axes, adzes, and tools for grinding seeds and nuts become more and more common in the tool kit (Brown, 1983). This probably reflects the emergence of greater areas of forest following the retreat of the glaciers from North America, but it also demonstrates a greater reliance on forest products and, most likely, a greater use of wood and wood products. Fish and shellfish also came to be relied upon in some areas, and this too reflects the adjustment made by the Archaic peoples to the changing conditions they faced at the end of the last ice age.

Early Arctic Populations

The **Palaeo-Arctic tradition** represents the first undisputed cultural development in the Arctic, after the more tentative early occupation sites associated with the peopling of the New World. The earliest well-documented Palaeo-Arctic sites are dated from 8000 B.C. to 5000 B.C., and are identified by stone tools, including microblades and small bifaces—no bone artifacts have been found (McGhee, 1996). The Palaeo-Arctic tradition is present throughout Alaska, east into the southwestern Yukon and south to the Queen Charlotte Islands in British Columbia. Following the Palaeo-Arctic tradition comes the **Arctic Small Tool tradition**, representing the first humans to move into the eastern Canadian Arctic and Greenland. In Alaska the Arctic Small Tool tradition evolved into the *Norton tradition,* while in the eastern Arctic it became the *Dorset culture.* The later Thule tradition developed from the Norton tradition in the area around Bering Strait and subsequently spread throughout the entire Arctic region with the exception of the Aleutian Islands (see Figure 10–7).

Arctic Small Tool Tradition

The Arctic Small Tool tradition represents a widespread phenomenon in the North American Arctic that occurred between approximately 2000 B.C. and 800 B.C. It is characterized by finely made microblades, burins, scrapers, and blades, and, more important, the bow and arrow. The Arctic Small Tool tradition does not appear to be related to the preceding Palaeo-Arctic tradition, but is most likely the product of a rapid migration of people from eastern Siberia.

Dorset. The Dorset culture was an incredibly stable Arctic culture, surviving longest in the eastern Arctic regions (Maxwell, 1985; McGhee, 1996). The Dorset subsistence pattern depended mostly on seal, caribou, muskox, and fish, but bones of walrus, polar bear, and some bird species have also been found (Maxwell, 1985; McGhee, 1996). Seal was probably primarily hunted on the sea ice or by hunting along the edge of ice floes; the Dorset do not appear to have had the equipment necessary for open-water

Palaeo-Arctic Tradition: the first undisputed cultural development in the Arctic, after the more tentative early occupation sites associated with the peopling of the New World. The earliest well-documented Palaeo-Arctic sites occur from 8000 B.C. to 5000 B.C.

Arctic Small Tool Tradition: culture that follows the Palaeo-Arctic tradition, representing the first humans to move into the eastern Canadian Arctic and Greenland. In Alaska the Arctic Small Tool tradition evolved into the Norton tradition, while in the eastern Arctic it became the Dorset culture.

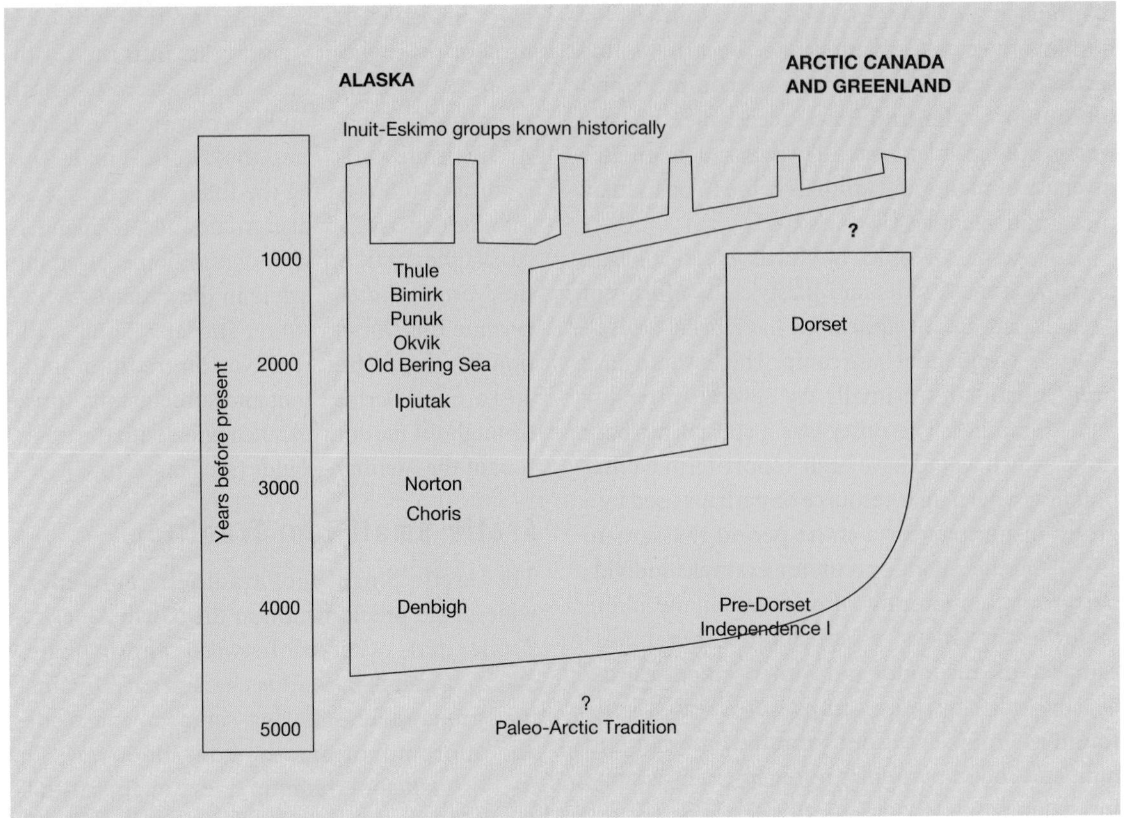

Figure 10–7 A Model of the Cultural Relationships between Early Arctic Peoples in North America

This model, proposed by Robert Park, shows the relationship between modern Inuit populations and a variety of archaeologically defined Arctic populations over the past 5000 years. In particular note that it is the Thule rather than the Dorset tradition that is the precursor to modern Arctic populations.

Source: Robert Park's webpage (**http://anthropology.uwaterloo.ca/park.html**). Reprinted with permission of Robert Park.

hunting, as they probably made only small kayaks. Caribou hunting was a group effort as the herds were channelled into a small area bounded by previously constructed rows of rock piles.

Dorset technology was somewhat limited when compared with the later Thule culture. Although the Dorset possessed the kayak, they lacked the larger seagoing umiak and flotation gear of the Thule. This gear included the toggling harpoon head (that would fix the removable head into the flesh of the animal) and the bladder balloons, which enabled the Thule to hunt sea mammals on open water and to prevent the loss of their prey underwater once it had been killed. The general lack of dog bones found on Dorset sites implies that the Dorset did have sleds but that they were pulled by hand rather than by dogs like the later Thule sleds. There are snow knives found on Dorset sites that would indicate that they did make winter snow houses like the later Thule. Other Dorset winter dwellings were probably structures built of sod blocks and roofed with skins.

Thule. The Thule represent a population migration from Alaska that brought with it a whole new technology. These included the use of metals including iron (the Dorset had made use of some cold-worked copper), which came through contact with Siberia in their Alaskan homeland (Maxwell, 1985; McGhee, 1996). In the west, some Thule groups also made use of crude ceramics, but in the eastern Arctic soapstone was utilized for bowls and cooking pots. It is from the Thule population that the modern Inuit peoples derive (Park, 1993; Park, 2000). (See Anthropology in Action, "Reconstructing Thule Life: Bob Park.")

ANTHROPOLOGY IN ACTION

Anthropologist at Work: Bob Park

Robert W. Park is an anthropological archaeologist at the University of Waterloo interested in the past cultures of the Far North (including the Canadian Northwest Territories, Nunavut, Greenland, and Alaska). Archaeological research in the Arctic presents a number of unique challenges, including short field seasons and excavation into permafrost (permanently frozen ground). These difficulties are compensated for by the richness of the Inuit ethnographic record, the complexity of their material culture, and the marvellous preservation of evidence sometimes provided by permafrost. The Arctic is also an incredibly vast region. Due to the large area involved and the small number of researchers working there, Arctic archaeology was until very recently mostly exploratory, trying to fill in gaps in the region's cultural history. Archaeologists rarely had the luxury of completely excavating sites, or of testing more than a very few sites within a region. When archaeologists were able to begin asking more complex questions concerning the ancient peoples of the Arctic, they had to adopt new, very different research strategies for reconstructing Arctic life.

Early in his career, Park became interested in the social and demographic characteristics of the Thule people, the immediate ancestors of the Inuit. From historic records we know that when Europeans arrived in the Arctic, large groups of Inuit would spend the winter together in a series of mobile snow-house (igloo) camps out on the sea ice. From archaeological evidence, we know that their Thule ancestors spent the winter in a quite different fashion, passing the entire winter in semi-subterranean houses on the Arctic coasts. Thule winter house sites are the most prominent archaeological remains in the Canadian Arctic, and can contain from two to more than 50 houses. However, over one-third of all known sites have three or fewer houses, and thus would have had no more than a very small population. Some archaeologists are convinced that at the larger sites the Thule wintered in comparably larger groups but, by coming up with a way of demonstrating that the Thule recycled building materials from abandoned houses into newly constructed ones, Park was able to show that only a few of the 14 houses at a site he was investigating would have been occupied during any given winter. Thus, the site was never the winter home to more than a few families. He hopes to explore further the reasons for this pronounced difference between Thule and historic Inuit settlement patterns.

In an attempt to go beyond cultural history in Arctic archaeology, Park compared the abundance of Thule toys—miniature versions of specific tools, such as hunting implements, with the proportion of full-sized, functional versions of the same types. He found that the miniature and full-sized versions of several classes of artifacts occurred in strikingly similar proportions, but with a few significant exceptions. Studying these patterns allowed him to explore differences in gender roles between children and

adults in Thule culture. He was able to demonstrate that the historic Inuit practice of treating children as "miniature adults" was practised by the Thule people as well. Intriguingly, there are hints that children in the Dorset culture did not have the same types of toys, suggesting that the experience of childhood may have been different in that earlier culture.

Sources: Park RW. 1997. Thule Winter Site Demography in the High Arctic. American Antiquity 62:2:273–284.

Park RW. 1998. Current Research and the History of Thule Archaeology in Arctic Canada. In: Smith PJ, Mitchell D, editors. Bringing Back the Past: Historical Perspectives on Canadian Archaeology. Mercury Series Paper 158. Hull: Canadian Museum of Civilization, Archaeological Survey of Canada. pp 191–201.

Park RW. 1998. Size Counts: The Miniature Archaeology of Childhood in Inuit Societies. Antiquity 72:269–281.

Summary

1. Fossil remains of fully modern-looking humans have been found in Africa, the Near East, Asia, and Australia, as well as in Europe. The oldest of these fossils have been found in South Africa and may be 100 000 years old.
2. Two theories about the origins of modern humans continue to be debated among anthropologists. One, the *single-origin* hypothesis (among other names), suggests that modern humans emerged in just one part of the Old World—the Near East and, more recently, Africa have been the postulated places of origin—and spread to other parts of the Old World, superseding Neandertals and other premodern *H. sapiens*. The second hypothesis, the *multiregional* hypothesis, suggests that modern humans emerged in various parts of the Old World, becoming the varieties of humans we see today.
3. The period of cultural history known as the Upper Palaeolithic in Europe, the Near East, and Asia, or the Later Stone Age in Africa, dates from about 40 000 years ago to about 14 000 to 10 000 years ago. The Upper Palaeolithic is characterized by the preponderance of blades; there were also burins, bone and antler tools, and (later) microliths. In many respects, lifestyles were similar to lifestyles before. People were still mainly hunters and gatherers and fishers who probably lived in highly mobile bands. They made their camps in the open and in caves and rock shelters.
4. The Upper Palaeolithic is also characterized by a variety of new developments: new techniques of toolmaking, the emergence of art, population growth, and new inventions such as the bow and arrow, the spear-thrower (atlatl), and the harpoon.
5. Only *H. sapiens* remains have been found in the New World. The prevailing opinion is that humans migrated to the New World over a land bridge between Siberia and Alaska in the area of what is now the Bering Strait. The prevailing view until recently was that humans were not present south of Alaska until after 15 000 years ago. Now it appears from an archaeological site called Monte Verde in Chile that modern humans got to southern South America by at least 12 500 years ago, and perhaps as many as 33 000 years ago.
6. The Palaeo-Arctic tradition represents the first undisputed cultural development in the Arctic. The earliest well-documented Palaeo-Arctic sites occur throughout Alaska, east into the southwestern Yukon and south to the Queen Charlotte Islands in British Columbia from 8000 B.C. to 5000 B.C. Following this comes the Arctic Small Tool tradition, representing the first humans to migrate into the eastern Canadian Arctic and Greenland. In Alaska, the Arctic Small Tool tradition evolved into the Norton tradition, while in the eastern Arctic it becomes the Dorset culture. The Thule tradition developed from the Norton tradition in the area around Bering Strait and later spread throughout most of the Arctic.

Glossary Terms

Critical Questions

1. If the single-origin or "out of Africa" hypothesis is correct, by what mechanisms could one group of *H. sapiens* have been able to replace another?
2. If modern human traits emerged in *H. erectus* populations in different areas more or less at the same time, what mechanisms would account for similar traits emerging in different regions?
3. Upper Palaeolithic cave paintings arouse our imaginations. We have described some research that tested ideas about what these paintings might mean. Can you think of other ways to understand the significance of cave art?
4. The peopling of the New World continues to be debated by archaeologists. A variety of different kinds of evidence can be used to understand how various populations are related to one another in the New World. Given the different kinds of evidence available, why is there so much debate regarding this issue?

Internet Exercises

1. Out of Africa ... or elsewhere ... or everywhere? Read the essay by the discoverer of "Lucy" at **www.actionbioscience.org/evolution/johanson.html** and compare the out-of-Africa model with the multiregional model also presented. To what extent could there be truth to both theories, or must they conflict?
2. Take a virtual tour through the cave of Lascaux at **www.culture.gouv.fr/culture/arcnat/lascaux/en/**. View the remarkable paintings made by Upper Palaeolithic peoples and learn how they were made. When you are done, test your knowledge with the site's questionnaire.
3. A team of experts has endorsed the findings from a site in Chile named Monte Verde suggesting that humans were in the New World earlier than traditionally thought. Look at the press release at **www.nationalgeographic.com/society/ngo/events/97/monteverde/dallas.html**. Then visit **www.civilization.ca/archeo/ hnpc/npvol21e.html** to view a presentation on the Paleo-Eskimos. Compare the information, particularly the dates, found at the two sites.

Suggested Reading

A special edition of Scientific American, "A New Look at Human Evolution" (August 2003), presents a variety of papers by various experts on the latest controversies in human evolution.

Lahr MM. 1996. The Evolution of Modern Human Diversity. Cambridge: Cambridge University Press. This book looks at the evolution of anatomically modern humans and how earlier Archaic populations differ from modern *H. sapiens* populations. The multiregional and single-origin models are discussed in light of the current evidence.

Maxwell MS. 1985. Prehistory of the Eastern Arctic. Orlando, FL: Academic Press. A classic examination of the archaeological evidence for the distribution and development of populations in the eastern Arctic.

McGhee R. 1996. Ancient People of the Arctic. Vancouver: University of British Columbia Press. This book examines the life of the first peoples to enter and inhabit the North American Arctic. It uses an analysis of hundreds of artifacts, including art and tools, to paint a picture of Palaeo-Eskimo life.

Schledermann P. 1996. Voices in Stone: A Personal Journey into the Arctic Past. Komatik Series, No. 5. Calgary: The Arctic Institute of North America of the University of Calgary. A personal account of the discovery of archaeological materials in the High Arctic, examining not only the archaeology of Arctic populations but also recounting life in the field with constant threats of sudden, violent storms or curious polar bears.

ORIGINS OF FOOD PRODUCTION AND SETTLED LIFE

12

CHAPTER OUTLINE

- Food Collection and Production
- Pre-Agricultural Developments
- The Domestication of Plants and Animals
- Why Did Food Production Develop?
- Consequences of the Rise of Food Production

Toward the end of the Upper Palaeolithic, people seem to have obtained most of their food from hunting migratory herds of large animals, such as wild cattle, antelope, bison, and mammoths. These hunter-gatherers were probably highly mobile in order to follow the migrations of the animals. Beginning about 14 000 years ago, people in some regions began to depend less on big-game hunting and more on relatively stationary food resources, such as fish, shellfish, small game, and wild plants (see Figure 12–1). In some areas, particularly Europe and the Near East, the exploitation of local, relatively permanent resources may account for an increasingly settled way of life. The cultural period in Europe and the Near East during which these developments took place is called the *Mesolithic.* Other areas of the world show a similar switch to what is called *broad- spectrum* food collecting, but they do not always show an increasingly settled lifestyle.

We see the first clear evidence of a changeover to food production—the cultivation and domestication of plants and animals—in the Near East, about 8000 B.C. (Miller, 1992). This shift, called the "Neolithic revolution," occurred, probably independently, in other areas of the Old and New Worlds within the next few thousand years. In the Old World there were independent centres of domestication in China, Southeast Asia (what is now Malaysia, Thailand, Cambodia, and Vietnam), and Africa around 6000 B.C. (MacNeish, 1991; Crawford, 1992; Phillipson,

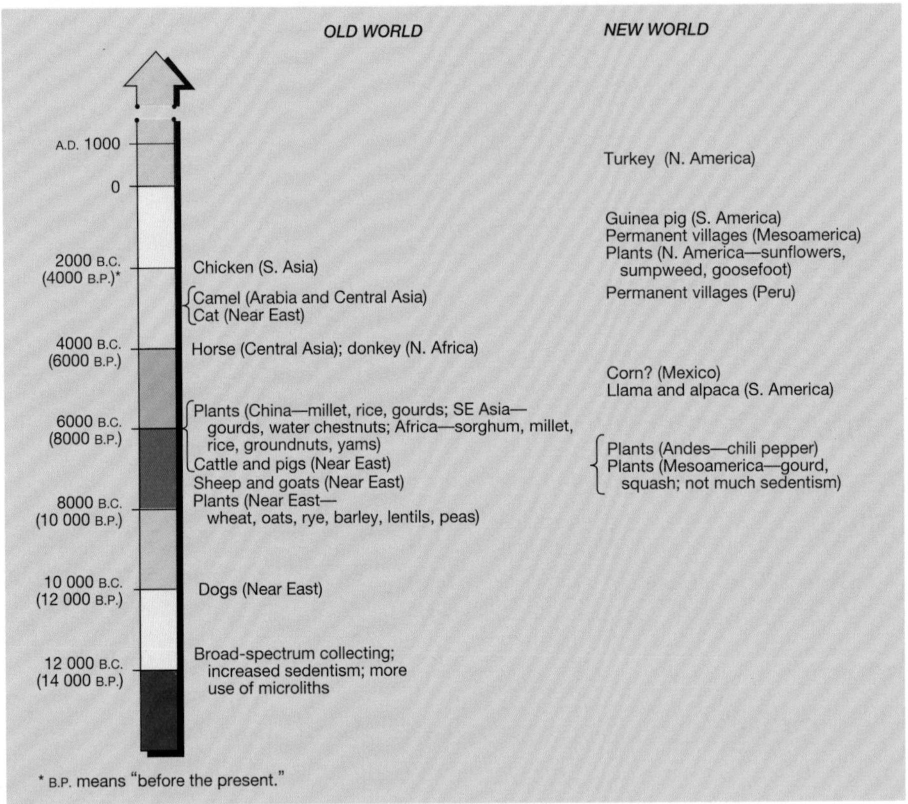

Figure 12–1 The Evolution of Domestication

Source: Dates for animal domestication are from Clutton-Brock J. 1992. Domestication of Animals. In: Jones J, Martin R, Pilbeam D, editors. The Cambridge Encyclopedia of Human Evolution. New York: Cambridge University Press. p 384.

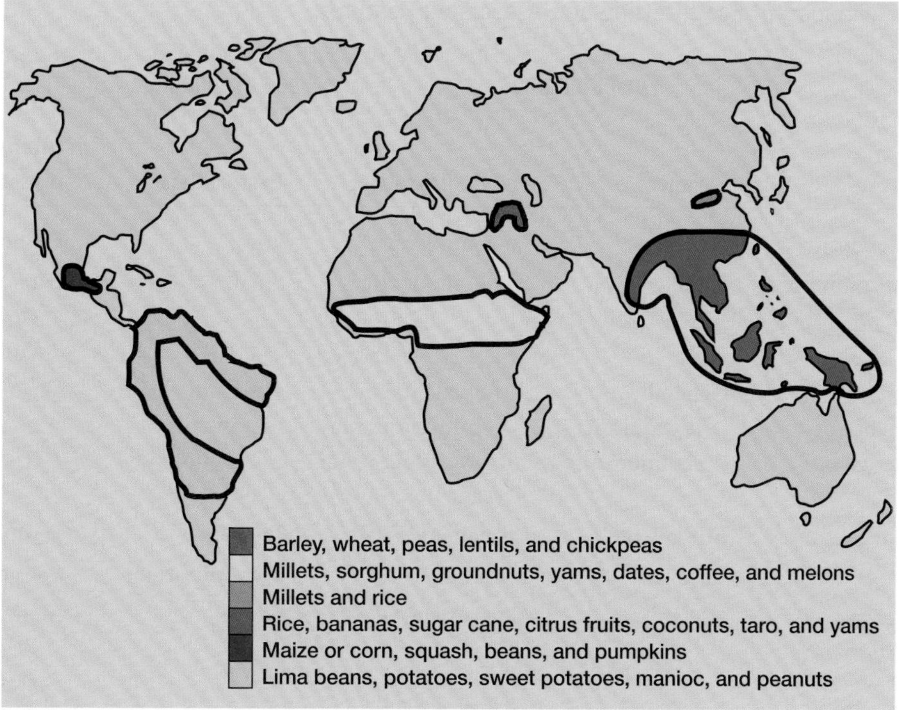

Figure 12–2 Original Locations of the World's Main Food Crops

The world's main food crops were originally domesticated in different regions.

Source: Hole F. 1992. Origins of Agriculture. In: Jones S, Martin R, Pilbeam D, editors. The Cambridge Encyclopedia of Human Evolution. New York: Cambridge University Press. p 376. Reprinted with permission of Cambridge University Press.

1993). In the New World there were centres of cultivation and domestication in the highlands of Mesoamerica (about 7000 B.C.), the central Andes around Peru (about 7000 B.C.), and the Eastern Woodlands of North America (about 2000 B.C.) (Flannery, 1986; Pearsall, 1992; Smith, 1992a). Most of the world's major food plants and animals were domesticated well before 2000 B.C. Also developed by that time were techniques of plowing, fertilizing, fallowing, and irrigation (Hole, 1992). Figure 12–2 shows the regions of the world that domesticated today's main food crops.

In this chapter we discuss what is believed about the origins of food production and settled life, called sedentism—how and why people in different places may have come to cultivate and domesticate plants and animals and to live in permanent villages. Agriculture and a sedentary life did not necessarily go together. In some regions of the world, people began to live in permanent villages before they cultivated and domesticated plants and animals, whereas in other places people planted crops without settling down permanently. Much of our discussion focuses on the Near East and Europe, the areas we know best archaeologically for the developments leading to food production and settled life. As much as we can, however, we try to indicate how data from other areas appear to suggest patterns different from, or similar to, those in Europe and the Near East.

Sedentism: settling in a single, permanent location.

Table 12–1 Variation in Food-Getting and Associated Features

	Food Collectors		Food Producers	
	Foragers	**Horticulturalists**	**Pastoralists**	**Intensive Agriculturalists**
Population density	Lowest	Low–moderate	Low	Highest
Maximum community size	Small	Small–moderate	Small	Large (towns and cities)
Nomadism/permanence of settlements	Generally nomadic or seminomadic	More sedentary: communities may move after several years	Generally nomadic or seminomadic	Permanent communities
Food shortages	Infrequent	Infrequent	Frequent	Frequent
Trade	Minimal	Minimal	Very important	Very important
Full-time craft specialists	None	None or few	Some	Many (high degree of craft specialization)
Individual differences in wealth	Generally none	Generally minimal	Moderate	Considerable
Political leadership	Informal	Some part-time political officials	Part- and full-time political officials	Many full-time political officials

Food Collection and Production

Food collection may be generally defined as all forms of **subsistence technology** in which food-getting is dependent on naturally occurring resources, that is, wild plants and animals. Although this was the way humans got their food for most of human history, the few remaining food collectors in the world today, also referred to as **foragers**, live in what have been called the *marginal areas* of the earth—deserts, the Arctic, and dense tropical forests—habitats that do not allow easy exploitation by modern agricultural technologies.

Anthropologists are interested in studying the relatively few food-collecting societies still available for observation because these groups may help us understand some aspects of human life in the past when all people were foragers (see Table 12-1). Ethnographic analogy from contemporary or recent

Food Collection: all forms of subsistence technology in which food-getting is dependent on naturally occurring resources—wild plants and animals.
Subsistence Technology: the methods humans use to procure food.

Foragers: people who subsist on the collection of naturally occurring plants and animals. Also referred to as hunter-gatherers.

historic hunter-gatherer and foraging populations can also provide us with models for prehistoric populations (Fix, 1977; Howell, 1979; Ray and Roth, 1984; Bogerhoff Mulder, 1992; Early and Peters, 1992). The basic premise underlying ethnographic data is that recent foragers and hunter-gatherers are like prehistoric populations in the same kinds of environments in terms of the ways in which they get food and therefore similar in terms of demographic structure, mobility patterns, social networks, etc. However, the range of fertility (the number of births per mother) and mortality among different hunter-gatherer, forager, and sedentary populations is so diverse that ethnographic analogy from subsistence base and mobility is extremely problematic (Harpending and Pennington, 1991; Pennington and Harpending, 1991; Pennington, 1992).

We must be cautious in drawing inferences about the past from our observations of contemporary food collectors for three reasons. First, early foragers lived in almost all types of environments, including some very bountiful ones. Therefore, what we observe among recent and contemporary food collectors may not be comparable to what would have been observable in more favourable environments in the past (Ember, 1978). Second, contemporary foragers are not relics of the past. Like all contemporary societies, they have evolved and are still evolving. Indeed, recent research suggests considerable variation in economic behaviour as well as in social structure in foraging groups that share common ancestry. This implies that recent foragers have responded to differences in local environmental conditions (Kent, 1996). Third, recent and contemporary foragers have been interacting with kinds of societies that did not exist until after 10 000 years ago—agriculturalists, pastoralists (groups who maintain and/or follow grazing herd animals), and intrusive powerful state societies (Schrire, 1984; Myers, 1988). So what we see in intersociety relations recently may be different from intersociety relations in the past. As a result, we must be careful not to automatically assume that similar subsistence strategies necessarily reflect social or cultural similarities between past and present societies.

Is there a typical pattern of food-getting among food collectors? Many anthropologists have assumed that foragers typically get their food more from gathering than from hunting, and that women contribute more than men to subsistence, because women generally do the gathering (Lee and DeVore, 1968). (See New Perspectives on Gender, "From Man the Hunter, to Woman the Gatherer, to . . . ?")

Beginning about 10 000 years ago, certain peoples in widely separated geographic locations made the revolutionary changeover to **food production**. That is, they began to cultivate and then domesticate plants and animals. (Domesticated plants and animals are different from the ancestral wild forms.) With domestication of these food sources, people acquired control over certain natural processes, such as animal breeding and plant seeding. Today, most peoples in the world depend for their food on some combination of domesticated plants and animals.

Horticulture

The word **horticulture** may conjure up visions of people with "green thumbs" growing orchids and other flowers in greenhouses. To anthropologists though, the word means the growing of crops of all kinds with relatively simple tools and methods, in the absence of permanently cultivated fields. The tools are usually hand tools, such as the digging stick or hoe, not plows or other equipment pulled by animals or tractors. Nor do the methods used include fertilization, irrigation, or other ways to restore soil fertility after a growing season.

There are two kinds of horticulture. The more common one involves a dependence on **shifting cultivation**. The land is worked for short periods

Food Production: the form of subsistence technology in which food-getting is dependent on the cultivation and domestication of plants and animals.
Horticulture: plant cultivation carried out with relatively simple tools and methods; nature replaces nutrients in the soil, in the absence of permanently cultivated fields.
Shifting Cultivation: a type of horticulture in which the land is worked for short periods and then left to regenerate for some years before being used again.

NEW PERSPECTIVES ON GENDER

From Man the Hunter, to Woman the Gatherer, to . . . ?

Anthropologists know it is important to understand the food-collecting way of life, for all humans were food collectors until 10 000 years ago. An important conference was held in 1966 to bring together anthropologists of all types to discuss what was known about food collectors. Organized by Richard B. Lee and Irven DeVore, the conference and the resulting book were called *Man the Hunter.* At the time, the word *man* was used widely in anthropology as a way of referring to humans in general. But referring to "man the hunter" appeared to ignore women, since women rarely do the hunting among recent foragers. It was not that women's contribution was entirely ignored by the participants in the conference. Indeed, Richard Lee pointed out that some food collectors such as the !Kung of southwest Africa depended mostly on gathering, which was mainly women's work. Even so, the title of the conference and of the resulting book conveyed that hunting and the work of men were most important among food collectors.

With the growing women's movement in North America, thinking in anthropology subsequently began to change. New questions began to be asked. What were women doing? How much did they contribute to subsistence and to other essential economic activities? How much time did they work? What were their views of the world? What kinds of mate choices do women have? What kinds of decisions did they make? How much influence did women have?

In 1981, a book edited by Frances Dahlberg appeared. It was titled *Woman the Gatherer.* The editor was well aware that gathering is not usually the most important subsistence activity among food collectors. It may be more important among contemporary foragers such as the !Kung and Australian aborigines, who live in warmer climates, but gathering is less important in colder climates, where most recent foragers have lived. Indeed, if we look at a large sample of recent foragers, we discover that fishing is more often the most important subsistence activity, more important (providing more calories) than either gathering or hunting. Why the title *Woman the Gatherer* then? Although the editor did not say so explicitly, we suggest that the title was intended to raise consciousness about the importance of women. We now know that food-collecting societies show considerable variability in how they get their food, so neither "Man the Hunter" nor "Woman the Gatherer" describe most foragers accurately.

Sources: Dahlberg F, editor. 1981. Woman the Gatherer. New Haven, CT: Yale University Press.

Ember CR. 1978. Myths about Hunter-Gatherers. Ethnology 18:439–448. Reprinted in: Ember M, Ember CR. 1983. Marriage, Family, and Kinship: Comparative Studies of Social Organization. New Haven, CT: HRAF Press. pp 313–331.

Lee RB, DeVore I, editors. 1968. Man the Hunter. Chicago: Aldine.

and then left idle for some years. During the years when the land is not cultivated, wild plants and brush grow up; when the fields are later cleared by **slash-and-burn techniques**, nutrients are returned to the soil. The other kind of horticulture involves a dependence on long-growing tree crops. The two kinds of horticulture may be practised in the same society, but in neither case is there permanent cultivation of field crops.

Slash-and-Burn Techniques: a form of shifting cultivation in which the natural vegetation is cut down and burned off. The cleared ground is used for a short time and then left to regenerate.

Most horticultural societies do not rely on crops alone for food. Many also hunt or fish; a few are nomadic for part of the year. For example, the northern Kayapo of the Brazilian Amazon leave their villages for as long as three months at a time to trek through the forest in search of game. The entire village participates in a trek, carrying large quantities of garden produce and moving their camp every day (Werner, 1978). Other horticulturalists raise domestic animals, but these are usually not large animals, such as cattle and camels (Anonymous, 1967). More often than not, the animals raised by horticulturalists are smaller ones, such as pigs, chickens, goats, and sheep.

In most horticultural societies, simple farming techniques have tended to yield more food from a given area than is generally available to food collectors. Consequently, horticulture is able to support larger, more densely populated communities. The way of life of horticulturalists is more sedentary than that of food collectors, although communities may move after some years to farm a new series of plots. (Some horticulturalists have permanent villages because they depend mostly on food from trees that keep producing for a long time.) In contrast with most recent food-collecting groups, horticultural societies exhibit the beginnings of *social differentiation*. For example, some individuals may be part-time craft workers or part-time political officials, and certain members of a kin group may have more status than other individuals in the society.

Intensive Agriculture

People engaged in **intensive agriculture** use techniques that enable them to cultivate fields permanently. Essential nutrients may be put back in the soil through the addition of fertilizers, which may be organic material (most commonly dung from humans or other animals) or inorganic (chemical) fertilizers. There are, however, other ways to restore nutrients. The Luo of western Kenya plant beans around corn plants. Bacteria growing around the roots of the bean plant replace lost nitrogen, and the corn plant conveniently provides a pole for the bean plant to wind around as it grows. Some intensive agriculturalists use irrigation from streams and rivers to ensure an adequate supply of waterborne nutrients. Crop rotation—using different fields from year to year—and plant stubble that has been plowed under also restore nutrients to the soil.

Intensive Agriculture: food production characterized by the permanent cultivation of fields and made possible by the use of the plow, draft animals or machines, fertilizers, irrigation, water-storage techniques, and other complex agricultural techniques.

Pre-Agricultural Developments

Europe

After about 10 000 years ago in Europe, the glaciers began to disappear. With their disappearance came other environmental changes. The melting of the glacial ice caused the oceans to rise, and, as the seas moved inland, the waters inundated some of the richest fodder-producing coastal plains, creating islands, inlets, and bays. Other areas, particularly in Scandinavia, were opened up for human occupation as the glaciers retreated and the temperatures rose (Collins, 1976). The cold, treeless plains, tundra, and grasslands eventually gave way to dense mixed forests, mostly birch, oak, and pine, and the mammoths became extinct. The warming waterways gradually cleared of glacial sediment, and began to be filled with fish and other aquatic resources (Chard, 1969).

Archaeologists believe that these environmental changes induced some populations in Europe to alter their food-getting strategies. When the tundra and grasslands disappeared, hunters could no longer obtain large quantities of meat simply by remaining close to large migratory herds of animals, as they probably did during Upper Palaeolithic times. Even though deer and other game were available, the number of animals per square kilometre (density) had decreased, and it became more difficult to stalk and kill animals sheltered in the thick woods. Thus, in many areas of Mesolithic Europe people seem to have turned from a reliance on big-game hunting to the intensive collecting of wild plants, molluscs, fish, and small game to make up for the extinction of the mammoths and the northward migration of the reindeer.

The Maglemosian Culture of Northern Europe. Some adaptations to the changing environment can be seen in the cultural remains of the settlers in northern Europe who are called Maglemosians by archaeologists. Their name derives from the peat bogs (*magle mose* in Danish means "great bog") where their remains have been found.

To deal with the new, more forested environment, the Maglemosians made stone axes and adzes to chop down trees and form them into various objects. Large timber appears to have been split for houses; trees were hollowed out for canoes; and smaller pieces of wood were made into paddles. The canoes presumably were built for travel and perhaps for fishing on the lakes and rivers that abounded in the postglacial environment.

We do not know to what extent the Maglemosians relied on wild plant foods, but there were a lot of different kinds available, such as hazelnuts. However, we do know many other things about the Maglemosians' way of life. Although fishing was fairly important, as suggested by the recovery of fish hooks, and the frequent occurrence of bones from pike and other fish, these people apparently depended mainly on hunting for food. Game included elk, wild ox, deer, and wild pig. In addition to many fishing implements and the adzes and axes, the Maglemosians' tool kit included the bow and arrow. Some of their tools were ornamented with finely engraved designs. Ornamentation independent of tools also appears in amber and stone pendants and small figurines such as the head of an elk (Clark, 1975).

Like the Maglemosian finds, many of the European Mesolithic sites are along lakes, rivers, and marine shorelines. But these sites probably were not inhabited year-round; there is evidence that at least some groups moved seasonally from one place of settlement to another, perhaps between the coast and inland areas (Petersen, 1973). Finds such as kitchen middens with piles of shells that centuries of Mesolithic seafood-eaters had discarded and remains of fishing equipment, canoes, and boats indicate that Mesolithic people depended much more heavily on fishing than had their ancestors in Upper Palaeolithic times. The very fact that this domestic waste accumulated in middens is indicative of the growing degree of sedentism associated with the Mesolithic.

The Near East

Cultural developments in the Near East seem to have paralleled those in Europe (Binford, 1971). Here, too, there seems to have been a shift from

With the disappearance of mammoths in the northern hemisphere, hunter-gatherers had to change how they got their food. They began to rely more on smaller game and marine resources.

mobile big-game hunting to the utilization of a broad spectrum of natural resources. There is evidence that people subsisted on a variety of resources, including fish, molluscs, and other water life; wild deer, sheep, and goats; and wild grains, nuts, and legumes (Flannery, 1973a). The increased utilization of stationary food sources such as wild grain may partly explain why some people in the Near East began to lead more sedentary lives during the Mesolithic.

Even today, a traveller passing through the Anatolian highlands of Turkey and other mountainous regions in the Near East may see thick stands of wild wheat and barley growing as densely as if they had been cultivated. Wielding flint sickles, Mesolithic people could easily have harvested a bountiful crop from such wild stands. Just how productive these resources can be was demonstrated in a field experiment duplicating prehistoric conditions. Using the same kind of flint-blade sickle that a Mesolithic worker would have used, researchers were able to harvest a little over 1 kilogram of wild grain in an hour. A Mesolithic family of four, working only during the few weeks of the harvest season, probably could have reaped more wheat and barley than they needed for the entire year (Harlan, 1967).

The amount of wild wheat harvested in the experiment prompted Kent Flannery to conclude, "Such a harvest would almost necessitate some degree of sedentism—after all, where could they go with an estimated metric ton of clean wheat?" (Flannery, 1971). Moreover, the stone equipment used for grinding would have been a clumsy burden to carry. Part of the harvest would probably have been set aside for immediate consumption, ground, and then cooked either by roasting or boiling. The rest of the harvest would have been stored to supply food for the remainder of the year. A grain diet, then, could have been the impetus for the construction of roasters, grinders, and storage pits by some Mesolithic people, as well as for the construction of solid, fairly permanent housing. Once a village was built, people may have been reluctant to abandon it. We can visualize the earliest pre-agricultural settlements clustered around such naturally rich regions, as archaeological evidence indeed suggests they were.

The Natufians of the Near East. Eleven thousand years ago the Natufians, a people living in the area that is now Israel and Jordan, inhabited caves and rock shelters and built villages on the slopes of Mount Carmel in Israel. At the front of their rock shelters they hollowed out basin-shaped depressions in the rock, possibly for storage pits. Examples of Natufian villages are also found at the Eynan site in Israel.

Eynan is a stratified site containing the remains of three villages in sequence, one atop another. Each village consisted of about 50 circular pit houses. The floor of each house was sunk a few metres into the ground, so that the walls of the house consisted partly of earth, below ground level, and partly of stone, above ground level. Pit houses had the advantage of retaining heat longer than houses built above the ground. The villages appear to have had stone-paved walks; circular stone pavements ringed what seem to be permanent hearths; and the dead were interred in village cemeteries.

The tools suggest that the Natufians harvested wild grain intensively. Sickles recovered from their villages have a specific sheen, which experiments have shown to be the effect of flint striking grass stems, as the sickles would have been used in the cutting of grain. The Natufians are the earliest Mesolithic people known to have stored surplus crops. Beneath the floors of their stone-walled houses, they constructed plastered storage pits. In addition to wild grains, the Natufians exploited a range of other resources (Mellaart, 1961). The remains of many wild animals are found in Natufian sites; Natufians appear to have concentrated on hunting gazelle, which they would take by surrounding whole herds (Henry, 1989).

The Natufians, as well as food collectors in other areas at the time, show many differences as compared with food collectors in earlier periods (Brown and Price, 1985). Not only was Natufian food collection based on a more intensive use of stationary resources, such as wild grain, but the archaeological evidence suggests increasing social complexity. Natufian sites were, on average, five times larger than those of their predecessors. Communities were now occupied for most of the year, if not year-round. Burial patterns suggest

Hayonim, one of the many caves in which the Natufians built relatively permanent settlements. Archaeologists are at work at the site.

more social differences between people. Although wild cereal resources appear to have enabled the Natufians to live in relatively permanent villages, their diet seems to have suffered. Their tooth enamel shows signs of nutritional deficiency, and their stature declined over time (Henry, 1989; Henry, 1991; Olszewski, 1991).

Mesoamerica

A similar shift toward more broad-spectrum hunting and gathering occurred in the New World at the end of the Palaeo-Indian period, about 10 000 years ago. Climate change seems to have been vital here, too, as it was in the Old World. The retreat of glacial ice from North America and overall warmer and wetter climate brought dramatic changes to plant and animal communities throughout North America and Mesoamerica. Pleistocene megafauna, such as mammoths, mastodon, rhinoceros, giant ground sloth, and others, as well as a variety of smaller game animals, such as the horse, all went extinct in a relatively short period of time (Martin and Wright, 1967). Hunting strategies shifted toward a broader range of game species, particularly deer, antelope, bison, and small mammals. At the same time, deciduous woodlands and grasslands expanded, providing a range of new plants to exploit. Ground-stone woodworking tools such as axes and adzes first appeared, as did nut-processing tools such as mortars and pestles. Shellfish began to be exploited in some areas. Throughout North America and Mesoamerica people began to expand the range of plants and animals they relied upon (Brown, 1985; Keuhn, 1998).

The Archaic Peoples of Highland Mesoamerica. In Highland Mesoamerica, that is, the mountainous regions of central and southern Mexico, we also see a shift from big-game hunting to a broader use of resources, in part due to a change in climate more like today's. Altitude became an important factor in the hunting and collecting regime, as different altitudes have different plant and animal resources. Valleys tend to have scrubby, grassland vegetation, whereas foothills and mountains have "thorn forests" of cactuses and succulents giving way to oak and pine forests at higher altitudes, where there is more moisture. This vertical zonation means that a wide range of plants and animals were available in relatively close proximity—different environments were close by—and the Archaic peoples took advantage of these varied conditions to hunt and collect a range of resources (Marcus and Flannery, 1996).

About 8000 years ago the Archaic peoples in Mesoamerica appear to have moved seasonally between communities of two different sizes: camps with 15 to 30 residents (*macrobands*) and camps with only 2 to 5 residents (*microbands*). Macroband camps were located near seasonally abundant resources, such as acorns or mesquite pods. Several families would have come together when these resources were in season, both to take advantage of them and to work together to harvest them while they were plentiful, to perform rituals, and simply to socialize. Microband camps were also inhabited seasonally, probably by a single family, when groups were not assembled into macroband camps. Remains of these microband camps are often found in caves or rock shelters from which a variety of environments could be exploited by moving either upslope or downslope from the campsite (Marcus and Flannery, 1996).

Unlike the Natufians of the Near East, there is no evidence of social differences among the Archaic peoples of Highland Mesoamerica. The largest social unit, the macroband camp, was probably composed of related family groups, and leadership in these groups was probably informal. There is little evidence of ritual behaviour beyond the presence of what may have been a ceremonial dance floor at Gheo-Shih, a macroband campsite in the Valley of Oaxaca. In short, lifestyles remained much like the simple and egalitarian ones of the Palaeo-Indians, despite the transition to a much broader strategy of food collection.

Other Areas

People in other areas in the world also shifted from hunting big game to collecting many types of food before they apparently began to practise agriculture. The still-sparse archaeological record suggests that such a change occurred in Southeast Asia, which may have been one of the important centres of original plant and animal domestication. The faunal remains recovered from inland sites in the region indicate that many different sources of food were being exploited from the same base camps. For example, these base camps yield the remains of animals from high mountain ridges as well as lowland river valleys, birds and primates from nearby forests, bats from caves, and fish from streams. The few coastal sites indicate that many kinds of fish and shellfish were collected and that animals such as deer, wild cattle, and rhinoceros were hunted (Gorman, 1970). As in Europe, the pre-agricultural developments in Southeast Asia probably were responses to changes in the climate and environment, including a warming trend, more moisture, and a higher sea level (Chang, 1970; Gorman, 1970).

In Africa, too, the pre-agricultural period was marked by a warmer, wetter environment. The now-numerous lakes, rivers, and other bodies of water provided fish, shellfish, and other resources that apparently allowed people to settle more permanently than they had before. For example, there were lakes in what is now the southern and central Sahara desert, where people fished and hunted hippopotamuses and crocodiles. This pattern of broad-spectrum food-collecting seems also to have been characteristic of the areas both south and north of the Sahara (Clark, 1970). One area showing increased sedentism is the Dakhleh Oasis in the Western Desert of Egypt. Between 9000 and 8500 years ago, the inhabitants lived in circular stone huts on the shores of rivers and lakes. Bone harpoons and pottery are found there and in other areas from the Nile Valley through the central and southern Sahara westward to what is now Mali. Fishing seems to have allowed people to remain along the rivers and lakes for much of the year (Phillipson, 1993).

At about the same time in the Americas, people were beginning to exploit a wide variety of wild food resources. For example, evidence from present-day Alabama and Kentucky shows that, by about 5000 B.C., people had begun to collect freshwater mussels as well as wild plants and small game. In the Great Basin of what is now the United States, people were beginning to spend longer and longer periods each year collecting the wild resources around and in the rivers and glacial lakes (Patterson, 1973).

Why Did Broad-Spectrum Collecting Develop?

It is apparent that the pre-agricultural switch to broad-spectrum collecting was fairly common throughout the world. Climate change was probably at least partly responsible for the exploitation of new sources of food. For example, the worldwide rise in sea level may have increased the availability of fish and shellfish. Changes in climate may have also been partly responsible for the decline in the availability of big game, particularly the large herd animals. In addition, it has been suggested that another possible cause of that decline was human activity, specifically overkilling of some of these animals. The evidence suggesting overkill is that the extinction in the New World of many of the large Pleistocene animals, such as the mammoth, coincided with the movement of humans from the Bering Strait region to the southern tip of South America (Martin, 1973).

The overkill hypothesis has been largely discredited on the basis of the breadth of extinctions that includes bird as well as mammal species in the Americas. An enormous number of bird species also became extinct during the last few thousand years of the North American Pleistocene, and it is difficult to argue that human hunters caused all of those extinctions. Because the bird and mammal extinctions occurred simultaneously, it is likely that most or nearly all the extinctions were due to climatic and other environmental changes (Grayson, 1977, 1989; Guthrie, 1984; Marshall, 1984).

The decreasing availability of big game may have stimulated people to exploit new food resources, but they may have turned to a broader spectrum of resources for another reason—population growth (see Figure 12–3). As Mark Cohen has noted, hunter-gatherers were "filling up" the world, and they may have had to seek new, possibly less desirable sources of food (Cohen, 1977a). (We might think of shellfish as more desirable than mammoths, but only because we don't have to do the work to get such food. A lot of shellfish have to be collected, shelled, and cooked to obtain about the same amount of protein obtainable from one large animal.) Consistent with the idea that the

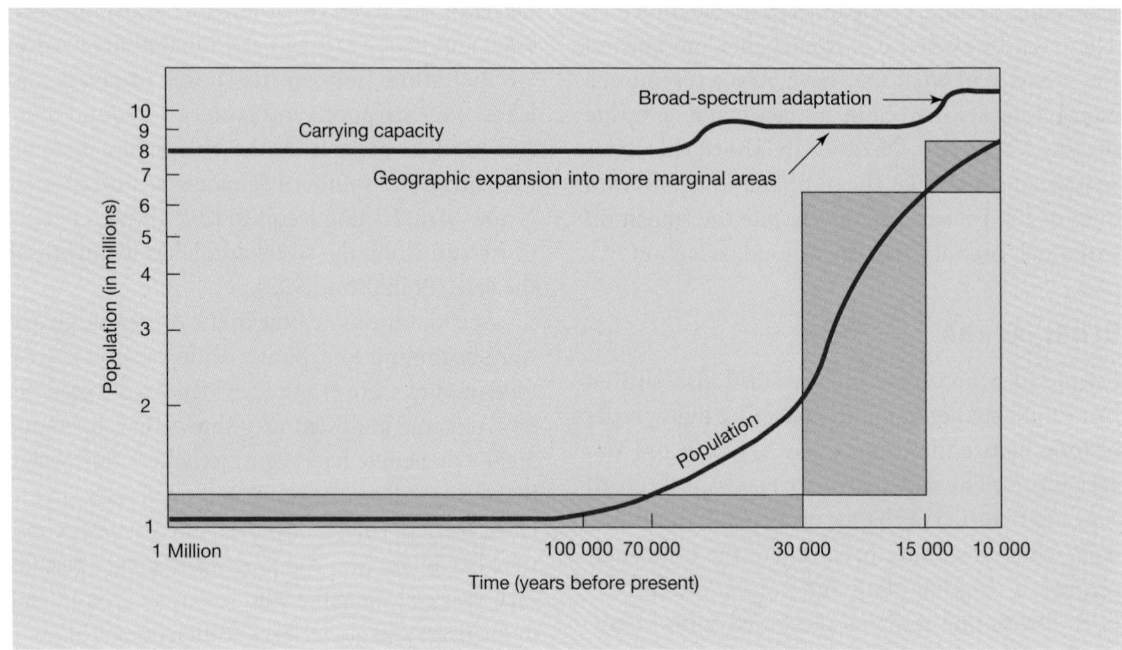

Figure 12–3 Reconstructed Increases in World Population and Carrying Capacity for Humans during the Pleistocene

Estimates of human population suggest that substantial increases preceded the movement of humans into more marginal areas. Further population increase preceded the emergence of broad-spectrum collecting.

Source: Adapted from Hassan FA. 1981. Demographic Archaeology. New York: Academic Press. p 207.

world was filling up around this time is the fact that not until after 30 000 years ago did hunter-gatherers begin to move into previously uninhabited parts of the world, such as Australia and the New World (Cohen, 1977a; Hassan, 1981; Bailey et al., 1989).

Broad-spectrum collecting may have involved exploitation of new sources of food, but that does not necessarily mean that people were eating better. A decline in stature often indicates a poorer diet. During the Mesolithic, height apparently declined by as much as 5 centimetres in many parts of the Old World (Greece, Israel, India, and northern and western Europe) (Cohen, 1989). This decline may have been a result of decreasing nutrition, but it could also be that natural selection for greater height was relaxed because leverage for throwing projectiles such as spears was not so favoured after the decline of big-game hunting. (Greater limb-bone length, and therefore greater height, would enable you to throw a spear with more force and farther [Frayer, 1981].) In other areas of the world, such as Australia and what is now the midwestern United States, skeletal evidence also suggests a decline in the general level of health with the rise of broad-spectrum collecting (Cohen, 1989).

Broad-Spectrum Collecting and Sedentism

Does the switch to broad-spectrum collecting explain the increasingly sedentary way of life we see in various parts of the world in pre-agricultural times? The answer seems to be both yes and no. In some areas of the world—some sites in Europe, the Near East, Africa, and Peru—settlements became more permanent. In other areas, such as the semi-arid highlands of Mesoamerica, the switch to broad-spectrum collecting was not associated with increasing sedentism. Even after the highland Mesoamericans began to cultivate plants, they still did not live in permanent villages (Flannery, 1973b). The question is why.

It would seem that it is not simply the switch to broad-spectrum collecting that accounts for increasing sedentism in many areas. Rather, a comparison of settlements on the Peruvian coast

The !Kung of the Kalahari Desert on the move. Spacing births an average of four years apart helps to ensure that a woman will not have to carry more than two children at a time. The woman in front is carrying both a large and a small child.

suggests that the more permanent settlements were located nearer (within 6 kilometres) than were temporary settlements to most, if not all, of the diverse food resources exploited during the year. The community that did not have a year-round settlement seems to have depended on more widely distributed resources. What accounts for sedentism may thus be the nearness (Patterson, 1971) or the high reliability and yield (Harris, 1977; Johnson, 1977) of the broad-spectrum resources, rather than the broad spectrum itself.

Sedentism and Population Growth

Although some population growth undoubtedly occurred throughout the hunting and gathering phase of world history, some anthropologists have suggested that populations would have increased dramatically when people began to settle down. The evidence for this suggestion comes largely from a comparison of recent nomadic and sedentary !Kung populations.

The settling down of a nomadic group may reduce the typical spacing between births (Lee, 1972; Sussman, 1972). Nomadic !Kung have children about every four years; in contrast, recently settled !Kung have children about every three years. Why might birth spacing change with settling down? There are several possibilities.

Regulating the spacing of childbirths can occur in a number of ways. One way, if effective contraceptives are not available, is prolonged sexual abstinence after the birth of a child—the postpartum sex taboo—that is common in recent human societies. Another way is abortion or infanticide (Harris, 1977). Nomadic groups may be motivated to have children farther apart because of the problem of carrying small children. Carrying one small child is difficult enough; carrying two might be too burdensome. Thus, sedentary populations could have children spaced more closely because carrying children would not always be necessary.

It is possible that intensive collectors and early horticulturalists may have seen advantages to having larger families (more individuals could contribute to labour). It may be that women, who were likely doing much of the plant foraging and early horticulture, saw an advantage from having more children as a means of improving the efficiency of the group.

Although some nomadic groups may have deliberately spaced births by abstinence or infanticide, there is no evidence that such practices explain why there is typically four years between births among nomadic !Kung. There may be another explanation, involving an unintended effect of how babies are fed. Nancy Howell and Richard Lee have suggested that the presence of baby foods other than mother's milk may be responsible for the decreased birth spacing in sedentary agricultural !Kung groups (Howell, 1979; Lee, 1979). It is now well established that the longer a mother nurses her baby without supplementary foods, the longer it is likely to be before she starts ovulating again. Nomadic !Kung women have little to give their babies in the way of soft, digestible food, and the babies depend largely on mother's milk for two to three years. Sedentary !Kung mothers can, however, give their babies soft foods such as cereal (made from cultivated grain) and milk from domesticated animals. Such changes in feeding practices may shorten birth spacing by shortening the interval between birth and the resumption of ovulation. In pre-agricultural sedentary communities, it is possible that baby foods made from wild grains might have had the same effect. For this reason alone, therefore, populations may have grown even before people started to farm or herd.

Another reason sedentary !Kung women may have more babies than nomadic !Kung women has to do with the ratio of body fat to body weight. Some investigators suspect that a critical minimum of fat in the body may be necessary for ovulation. A sedentary !Kung woman may have more fatty tissue than a nomadic !Kung woman, who walks many kilometres daily to gather wild plant foods, often carrying a child around with her. Thus, sedentary !Kung women might resume ovulating sooner after the birth of a baby and so may be likely for that reason alone to have more closely spaced children. If some critical amount of fat is necessary for ovulation, that would explain why in our own society many women who have little body fat—long-distance runners, gymnasts, and ballet dancers are examples—do not ovulate regularly (Howell, 1979; Frisch, 1980).

Mesolithic Technology

Technologically, Mesolithic cultures did not differ radically from Upper Palaeolithic cultures (Phillipson, 1993). (*Mesolithic*, like the term *Upper Palaeolithic*, properly applies only to cultural developments in the Old World. However, we use the term *Mesolithic* here to represent some general pre-agricultural trends.) The trend toward smaller and lighter tools continued. Microliths, small blades 1.2 centimetres to 5 centimetres long, which were made in late Upper Palaeolithic times, were now used in quantity. In place of the one-piece flint implement, Mesolithic peoples in Europe, Asia, and Africa equipped themselves with composite tools—that is, tools made of more than one material.

Microliths, too small to be used one at a time, could be fitted into grooves in bone or wood to form arrows, harpoons, daggers, and sickles. A sickle, for example, was made by inserting several microliths into a groove in a wooden or bone handle. The blades were held in place by resin. A broken microlith could be replaced like a blade in a modern razor. Besides being adaptable for many uses, microliths could be made from many varieties of available stone; Mesolithic people were no longer limited to flint. Since they did not need the large flint nodules to make large core and flake tools, they could use small pebbles of flint to make the small blades (Semenov, 1970; Whittaker, 1994).

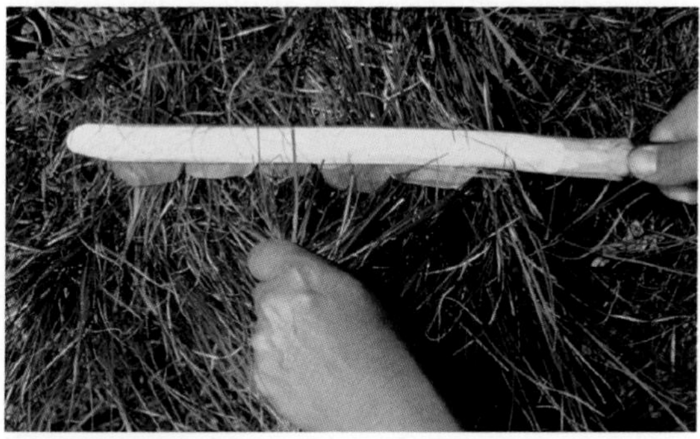

A sickle made with microliths.

The Domestication of Plants and Animals

Neolithic means "of the new stone age"; the term originally signified the cultural stage in which humans invented pottery and stone tools with ground edges. We now know, however, that both were present in earlier times, so we cannot define a Neolithic state of culture on the basis of the presence of pottery and ground-stone tools. At present, archaeologists generally define the Neolithic in terms of the presence of domesticated plants and animals. In this type of culture, people began to produce food rather than merely collect it.

The line between food-collecting and food-producing occurs when people begin to plant crops and to keep and breed animals. How do we know when this transition occurred? In fact, archaeologically we do not see the beginning of food production; we can see signs of it only after plants and animals show differences from their wild varieties. When people plant crops, we refer to the process as *cultivation.* It is only when the crops cultivated and the animals raised are modified—and become different from wild varieties—that we speak of plant and animal domestication. A domesticated plant or animal is one that depends upon human intervention for its continued survival.

We know, in a particular site, that domestication occurred if plant remains have characteristics different from those of wild plants of the same types. For example, wild grains of barley and wheat have a fragile rachis—the seed-bearing part of the

Neolithic: originally meaning "the new Stone Age," now meaning the presence of domesticated plants and animals. The earliest evidence of domestication comes from the Near East about 8000 B.C.

Domestication: modification or adaptation of plants and animals for use by humans. When people plant crops, we refer to the process as cultivation. It is only when the crops cultivated and the animals raised have been modified—are different from wild varieties—that we speak of plant and animal domestication.

Rachis: the seed-bearing part of a plant. In the wild variety the rachis shatters easily, releasing the seeds. Domesticated grains have a tough rachis, which does not shatter easily.

stem—which shatters easily, releasing the seeds. Domesticated grains have a tough rachis, which does not shatter easily. Similarly, domesticated plants tend to have larger seeds than their wild ancestors. In addition, plants found in areas for which there is no naturally growing ancestral form are assumed to have been brought there by humans, and are therefore, by definition, domesticates.

How did the domesticated plants get to be different from the wild varieties? Artificial or human selection, deliberate or accidental, obviously was required. Consider how the rachis of wheat and barley may have changed. As we said, when wild grain ripens in the field, the rachis shatters easily, scattering the seed. This trait is selectively advantageous under wild conditions; it is nature's method of propagating the species. Plants with a tough rachis, therefore, have only a slight chance of reproducing themselves under natural conditions, but they are more desirable for maximizing yield during harvesting. When humans arrived with sickles and flails to collect the wild stands of grain, the seeds harvested probably contained a high proportion of tough-rachis mutants, because these could best withstand the rough treatment of harvest processing. If planted, the harvested seeds would be likely to produce tough-rachis plants (see Figure 12–4). If in each successive harvest seeds from these plants were the least likely to be lost, tough-rachis plants would come to predominate (Zohary, 1969).

Domesticated species of animals also differ from the wild varieties. For example, the horns of wild goats in the Near East are shaped differently from those of domesticated goats (Flannery, 1965). Differences in physical characteristics may not be the only indicators of domestication. Some archaeologists believe that imbalances in the sex and age ratios of animal remains at particular sites also suggest that domestication had occurred. For example, at Zawi Chemi Shanidar in Iraq, the proportion of young to mature sheep remains was much higher than the ratio of young to mature sheep in wild herds. One possible inference to be drawn is that the animals were domesticated, the adult sheep being saved for breeding purposes while the young were eaten. (If mostly young animals were eaten, and only a few animals were allowed to grow old, most of the bones found in a site would be from the young animals that were killed regularly for food [Flannery, 1965; Collier and White, 1976].)

Figure 12–4 Seed Heads of Wild and Domesticated Wheat

Note the larger and more numerous seeds on domesticated wheat.

Source: Feder K. 2000. Past in Perspective. Second edition. Mountain View, CA: Mayfield. Copyright © 2000 by Mayfield Publishing Company. Reprinted by permission of The McGraw-Hill Book Company.

Domestication in the Near East

For some time most archaeologists have thought that the arc of land stretching up from Israel and the Jordan Valley through southern Turkey and then downward to the western slopes of the Zagros Mountains in Iran (see Figure 12–5) was one of the earliest centres of plant and animal domestication. We know that several varieties of domesticated wheat were grown there after about 8000 B.C., as were oats, rye, barley, lentils, peas, and various fruits and nuts (apricots, pears, pomegranates, dates, figs, olives, almonds, and pistachios) (MacNeish, 1991; Hole, 1992). It appears that the first animals were domesticated in the Near East. Dogs were first domesticated before the rise of agriculture, around 10 000 B.C. (see Current Research and Issues, "Did Dogs [and Cats] Domesticate Themselves?" on page 292), goats and sheep around 7000 B.C., and cattle and pigs around 6000 B.C. (Clutton-Brock, 1988).

Let us look at two early Neolithic sites in the Near East to see what life there may have been like after people began to depend on domesticated plants and animals for food.

Ali Kosh. At the stratified site of Ali Kosh in what is now southwestern Iran (see Figure 12–5), we see the remains of a community that started out about 7500 B.C. living mostly on wild plants and animals. Over the next 2000 years, until about 5500 B.C., agriculture and herding became increasingly important. After 5500 B.C. we see the appearance of two innovations—irrigation and the use of domesticated cattle—that seem to have stimulated a minor population explosion during the following millennium.

From 7500 to 6750 B.C., the people at Ali Kosh cut small slabs of raw clay out of the ground to build small multiroom structures. The rooms excavated by archaeologists are small, seldom more than 2.1 metres by 3 metres, and there is no evidence that the structures were definitely houses where people actually spent time or slept. Instead, they may have been storage rooms. On the other hand, house rooms of even smaller size are known in other areas of the world, so it is possible that the people at Ali Kosh in its earliest phase were actually living in those tiny, unbaked

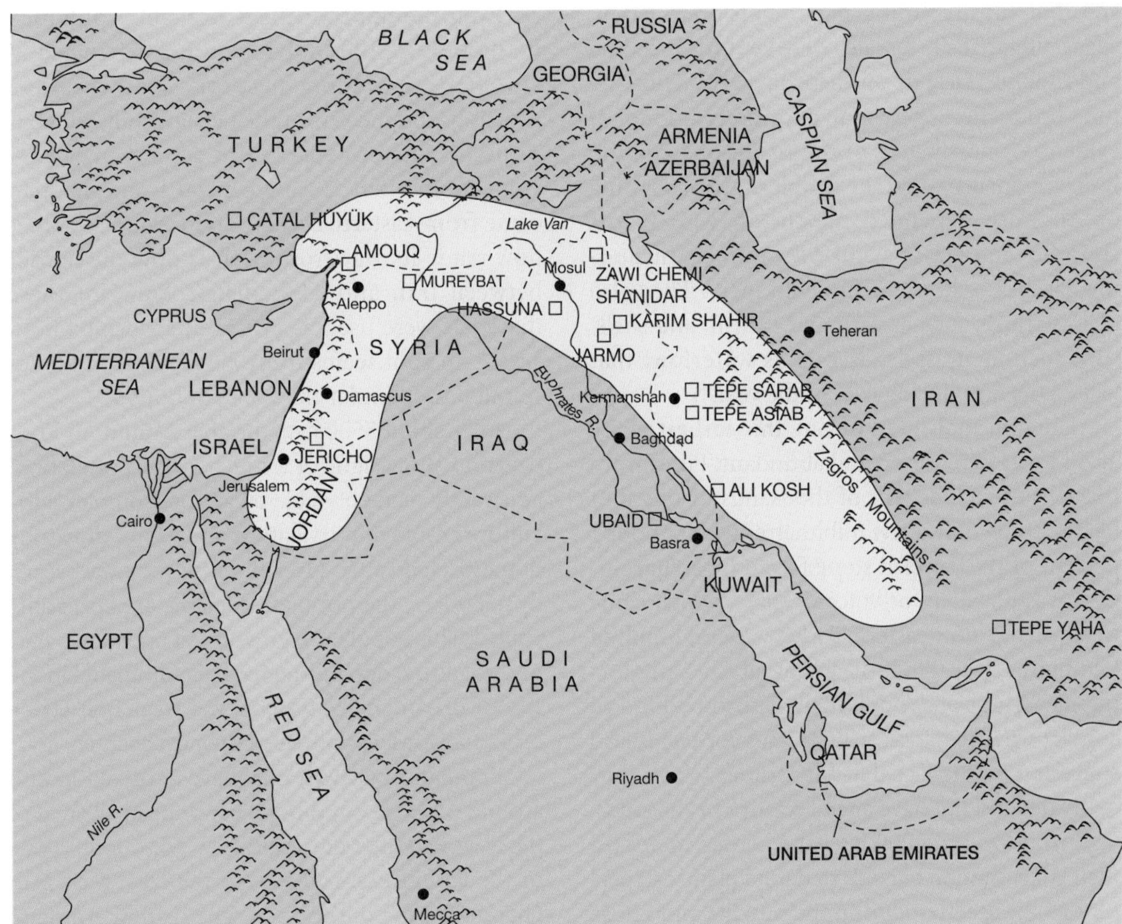

Figure 12–5 Early Agricultural Settlements in the Near East

Modern cities are represented by a dot, early settlements by a square. The yellow colour indicates the area of early agricultural settlement.

"brick" houses. There is a bit of evidence that the people at Ali Kosh may have moved over the course of the summer with their goats to nearby mountain valleys (just a few days' walk away), perhaps in search of more grassy habitats.

We have a lot of evidence about what the people at Ali Kosh ate. They got some of their food from cultivated emmer wheat and a barley variety. However a considerable amount of protein was derived from domesticated goats. We know the goats were domesticated because wild goats do not seem to have lived in the area. Also, the fact that virtually no bones from elderly goats were found in the site suggests that the goats were domesticated and herded rather than hunted. Moreover, it would seem from the horn cores found in the site that mostly young male goats were eaten, suggesting that the females were kept for breeding and milking. Despite all these signs of deliberate food production, there is an enormous amount of evidence—literally tens of thousands of seeds and bone fragments—that the people at the beginning of Ali Kosh depended mostly on wild plants (legumes and grasses) and wild animals (including gazelles, wild oxen, and wild pigs). They also collected fish, such as carp and catfish, and shellfish, such as mussels, as well as waterfowl that visited the area during part of the year.

The flint tools used during this earliest phase at Ali Kosh were varied and abundant. Finds from this period include tens of thousands of tiny flint blades, some only a few millimetres wide. About 1 percent of the chipped stone found by archaeologists was obsidian, or volcanic glass, which came from what is now eastern Turkey, several hundred kilometres away. Thus, the people at Ali Kosh during its earliest phase definitely had some kind of contact with people elsewhere. This contact is also suggested by the fact that the emmer wheat they cultivated did not have a wild relative in the area.

From 6750 to 6000 B.C., the people increased their consumption of cultivated food plants; 40 percent of the seed remains in the hearths and refuse areas were now from emmer wheat and barley. The proportion of the diet coming from wild plants was much reduced, probably because the cultivated plants have the same growing season and grow in the same kind of soil as the wild plants. Grazing by the goats and sheep that were kept may also have contributed to the reduction of wild plant foods in the area and in the diet. The village may or may not have become larger, but the multiroom houses definitely had. The rooms were now larger than 3 metres by 3 metres; the walls were much thicker; and the clay-slab bricks were now held together by a mud mortar. Also, the walls now often had a coat of smooth mud plaster on both sides. The stamped-mud house floors were apparently covered with rush or reed mats (you can see the imprints of them). There were courtyards with domed brick ovens and brick-lined roasting pits. Understandably, considering the summer heat in the area, none of the ovens found were inside a house.

Even though the village probably contained no more than 100 individuals, it participated in an extensive trading network. Seashells were probably obtained from the Persian Gulf, which is some distance to the south; copper may have come from what is now central Iran; obsidian came from eastern Turkey; and turquoise somehow made its way from what is now the border between Iran and Afghanistan. Some of these materials were used as ornaments worn by both sexes—or so it seems from the remains of bodies found buried under the floors of houses.

After about 5500 B.C., the area around Ali Kosh began to show signs of a much larger population, apparently made possible by a more complex agriculture employing irrigation and plows drawn by domesticated cattle. Over the next thousand years, by 4500 B.C., the population of the area probably tripled. This population growth was apparently part of the cultural developments that culminated in the rise of urban civilizations in the Near East (Hole et al., 1969), as we will see in the next chapter.

Population growth may have occurred in and around Ali Kosh but did not continue in all areas of the Near East after domestication. For example, one of the largest early villages in the Near East, 'Ain Ghazal (on the outskirts of what is now Amman, Jordan), suffered a decline in population and standard of living over time, perhaps because the environment around 'Ain Ghazal could not permanently support a large village (Simmons et al., 1988).

Çatal Hüyük. On a windswept plateau in the rugged, mountainous region of southern Turkey stand the remains of a mud-brick town known as Çatal Hüyük (see Figure 12–5). Hüyük is the Turkish word for a mound formed by a succession of settlements, one built on top of another.

About 5600 B.C., Çatal Hüyük was an adobe town. Some 200 houses have been excavated, and they are interconnected in *pueblo fashion* (each flat-roofed structure housed a number of families). The inhabitants decorated the walls of the houses with imaginative murals, and their shrines with symbolic statuary. The murals depict what seem to be religious scenes and everyday events. Archaeologists peeling away frescoes found layer upon layer of murals, indicating that old murals were plastered over to make way for fresh paintings. Several rooms are believed to have been shrine rooms. They contain many large bull murals and clay bull figurines and have full-sized clay heads of cattle on the walls. Other "shrine-room" murals depict scenes of life and death, painted in red and black, respectively. Clay statuettes of a pregnant woman and of a bearded man seated on a bull have also been found in these rooms.

Farming was well advanced at Çatal Hüyük. Lentils, wheat, barley, and peas were grown in quantities that produced a surplus. Archaeologists were astonished at the richly varied handicrafts, including beautifully carved wooden bowls and boxes that the people of the town produced. These people also had obsidian and flint daggers, spearheads, lance heads, scrapers, awls, and sickle blades. Bowls, spatulas, knives, ladles, and spoons were made from bone. The houses contained belt hooks, toggles, and pins carved from bone. Evidence also suggests that men and women wore jewellery fashioned from bone, shell, and copper and that they used obsidian mirrors (Mellaart, 1964). (See Figure 12–6 on page 294 for similar tools and ornaments in Neolithic Switzerland.)

Since Çatal Hüyük is located in a region with few raw materials, the town evidently depended on exchange with other areas to secure the rich variety of materials it used. Shells were procured from the Mediterranean, timber from the hills, obsidian from 80 kilometres away, and marble from western Turkey.

Domestication in Mesoamerica

A very different pattern of domestication is seen in Mesoamerica. Here the semi-nomadic Archaic hunting-and-gathering lifestyle persisted long after people first domesticated plants (Flannery, 1986;

Excavation in one of the pueblo-like structures of Neolithic Çatal Hüyük.

CURRENT RESEARCH AND ISSUES

Did Dogs (and Cats) Domesticate Themselves?

Early evidence of a close relationship between dogs and people comes from an archaeological site in northern Israel dating to nearly 12 000 years ago. At that site, archaeologists found the grave of an elderly woman, lying on her right side with her legs folded up, with a dog under her left hand. Do any of the attributes we associate with this common household pet explain why humans all over the world have had domesticated descendants of wolves around the house for the last 10 000 to 15 000 years?

Dogs were probably the first animals domesticated by humans, some thousands of years before plants, sheep, and goats were domesticated in the Near East. Humans were starting to settle down in semi-permanent camps and villages as they began to depend less on big game (which they had to follow over big distances) and more on relatively stationary food resources, such as fish, shellfish, small game, and wild plants rich in carbohydrates, proteins, and oils.

Why would humans have been interested in taming wolves at that time? One theory is that humans were shifting their prey from large animals to small, and they needed dogs for tracking wounded game or for retrieving killed game from bodies of water or underbrush. Dogs might also have been useful as alarm-givers in case predators came close. Finally, dogs might have helped to keep a camp clean, by scavenging garbage.

It is possible that this last use of dogs suggests an alternative theory of dog domestication. Perhaps it wasn't so much that humans domesticated dogs, but that some wolves domesticated themselves by hanging around human camps. Why would wolves be interested in those humans who were first settling down? It couldn't have been the possibility of a human dinner, because that would have been a possibility for millions of years before. So perhaps something else lured wolves to those early settled camps and villages. What was different about those early settlements? For the first time in human history, people were staying in one place for considerable periods—months at a time, *year after year*—because they could count on being able to "harvest" and live on the wild resources of the area for long periods of time. If they lived there for years, even if only seasonally, they would eventually have had a problem with garbage.

The residues of meals, in particular, would have been a problem. They might not only come to stink; they might also attract rodents and bigger threats to health and children. What could the people do about this problem? Well, as any camper nowadays realizes, they could have buried the garbage so that its scent would not attract unwelcome visitors. Eventually they would have run out of room for garbage pits in or close to the settlement. Of course, they could have moved the settlement, but maybe they didn't want to.

Pringle, 1998). How can this be? Don't people have to settle near their crops to take care of them? Once they have domesticated plants, don't they stop collecting wild plants? The answer is no. In Mesoamerica, people sowed a variety of plants, but after doing so they went on with their seasonal rounds of hunting and gathering, and came back later to harvest what they had sown. Many of the early domesticates in Mesoamerica were not basic to subsistence, even if they were highly desirable. Domestication may have been a way for Archaic peoples to make desirable plants more common in their environment. For example, one of the first domesticates was the bottle gourd. These were not eaten but were used to carry water. Joyce Marcus and Kent Flannery hypothesize that the bottle gourd was domesticated by people deliberately planting them in areas where they did not grow naturally, so that as groups moved through those areas, they always had access to gourds for carrying water (Marcus and Flannery, 1996).

Bottle gourds are only one of many early domesticates from Highland Mesoamerica. Others include tomatoes, cotton, a variety of beans and squashes, and, perhaps most importantly, maize. The earliest domesticated form of maize (corn), dating from about 5000 B.C., has been found in Tehuacán, Mexico. Genetic studies of maize show that it was domesticated from teosinte, a tall wild grass that still grows widely in Mexico (see Figure 12–6) (Flannery,

After all, they had spent a lot of time and effort building permanent houses that were warm in the winter and dry in the rains. And they had a lot of things stored there. So what *could* they do?

Maybe people didn't have to do anything. Maybe those wolves hanging around the neighbourhood solved the problem for our ancestors. How? By scavenging, which is something most dogs (particularly larger ones, like the first domesticated dogs) do quite naturally and efficiently. So even a few tame wolves or domesticated dogs could have kept a garbage pit or pile from stinking and growing. And the people "feeding" that pit or pile could stay in one place for a long time, safe from smells, vermin, and disease. Dogs may have mostly domesticated themselves because it was good for some of them as well as for those Mesolithic humans.

A similar theory may explain the domestication of cats. Cats are especially good at catching and killing mice. Masses of mice skeletons (of the house mouse) begin to appear in basements of Near East dwellings after the emergence of agriculture. It is possible that humans purposely tried to domesticate cats to catch mice, but it is more likely that cats would have domesticated themselves by adapting to life near or in a granary or storage cellar. Of course, humans might have helped the process of domestication a little, by killing the more ferocious wild cats that were attracted to the settlement. The same was probably true for the wolves attracted to garbage. Even if you didn't at first want to "pet" the canids or felids that were hanging around, you wouldn't want them to attack humans. Wolves in the wild have a dominance-submission hierarchy, so they would be pre-adapted to heeding a "dominant" human; those that were not sufficiently submissive could be killed.

How could these theories of dog and cat domestication be tested? If dogs domesticated themselves as scavengers, archaeologists should find evidence of dog domestication (for example, changes in anatomy) only in sites that were occupied for a good part of the year over a period of years. Only under those circumstances would garbage be a problem and dogs a solution. Similarly, evidence of cat domestication should be found only in sites that show signs of year-to-year storage of grain. Only then would rodents be a problem and cats a solution. Perhaps archaeologists will make these tests in the future.

Sources: Budiansky S. 1992. The Covenant of the Wild: Why Animals Chose Domestication. New York: William Morrow.

Clutton-Brock J. 1984. Dog. In: Mason IL. Evolution of Domesticated Animals. New York: Longman. pp 198–210.

Clutton-Brock J. 1992. Domestication of Animals. In: Jones S, Martin R, Pilbeam D, editors. The Cambridge Encyclopedia of Human Evolution. New York: Cambridge University Press. pp 380–385.

Hole F. 1992. Origins of Agriculture. In: Jones S, Martin R, Pilbeam D, editors. The Cambridge Encyclopedia of Human Evolution. New York: Cambridge University Press. pp 373–379.

Robinson R. Cat. In: Mason IL. Evolution of Domesticated Animals. New York: Longman. pp 217–225.

1986). Indeed, these genetic studies suggest that changes occurred in only two genes, one related to the kernel glumes (outer casing), and one related to the stalk shape (Fedoroff, 2003). The genes of modern corn were already established 4000 to 6000 years ago.

Teosinte is quite different from maize in several important ways, but small genetic changes led to major phenotypic changes. The genetic malleability of maize may be one reason it has become one of the most important domesticated crops on earth. Teosinte stalks do look a lot like maize, but teosinte has a "spike" to which 7–12 individual seeds are attached in a single row, unlike the maize cob, which has many seeds in many rows. Each teosinte seed has its own brittle shell, whereas the entire maize cob is covered with a tough husk. However, early maize was also considerably different from modern maize. The oldest maize cobs—dating to about 7000 years ago—are tiny, only about 3 centimetres long. They have only a half-dozen rows of seeds, and each seed is tiny. One interesting fact about both ancient and modern maize is that it is almost completely dependent on humans to reproduce—the shift from seeds with brittle coats to cobs with a tough husk meant that someone had to open the husk without damaging the seeds in order for them to be dispersed and reproduce (Flannery, 1986; Marcus and Flannery, 1996).

Like maize and the bottle gourd, beans and squash were probably domesticated by simple manipulation of wild varieties. Runner beans, for example, grow naturally in the soils on the slopes outside of rock shelters and caves. It is not a stretch of the imagination to envision Archaic peoples harvesting these beans (for their roots to begin with—non-domestic runner bean seeds are tiny and probably were not eaten) and selectively planting those with desired qualities, like large seeds. Similarly, only the seeds of wild squashes were likely eaten by Archaic peoples, as the flesh of wild squashes often has an unattractive smell and taste. But they may have selectively planted mutants with good-tasting flesh and larger seeds, eventually producing the domestic varieties over time (Marcus and Flannery, 1996).

People who lived in Mesoamerica, Mexico, and Central America are often credited with the invention of planting maize, beans, and squash together in the same field. This planting strategy provides some important advantages. Maize takes nitrogen from the soil; beans, like all legumes, put nitrogen back into the soil. The maize stalk provides a natural pole for the bean plant to twine around, and the low-growing squash can grow around the base of the tall maize plant. Beans supply people with the amino acid lysine, which is missing in maize. Thus, maize and beans together provide all the essential amino acids that humans need to obtain from food. Whether teosinte was or was not the ancestor of maize, it may have provided the model for this unique combination since wild runner beans and wild squash occur naturally where teosinte grows (Flannery, 1986).

Guila Naquitz. The Guila Naquitz cave, excavated in the 1960s by Kent Flannery, provides a good picture of early domestication in Highland Mesoamerica. Here small groups of people, probably only a single family at a time, lived intermittently (and probably seasonally) over a period of 2000 years (ca. 8900 B.C.–6700 B.C.), the period during which

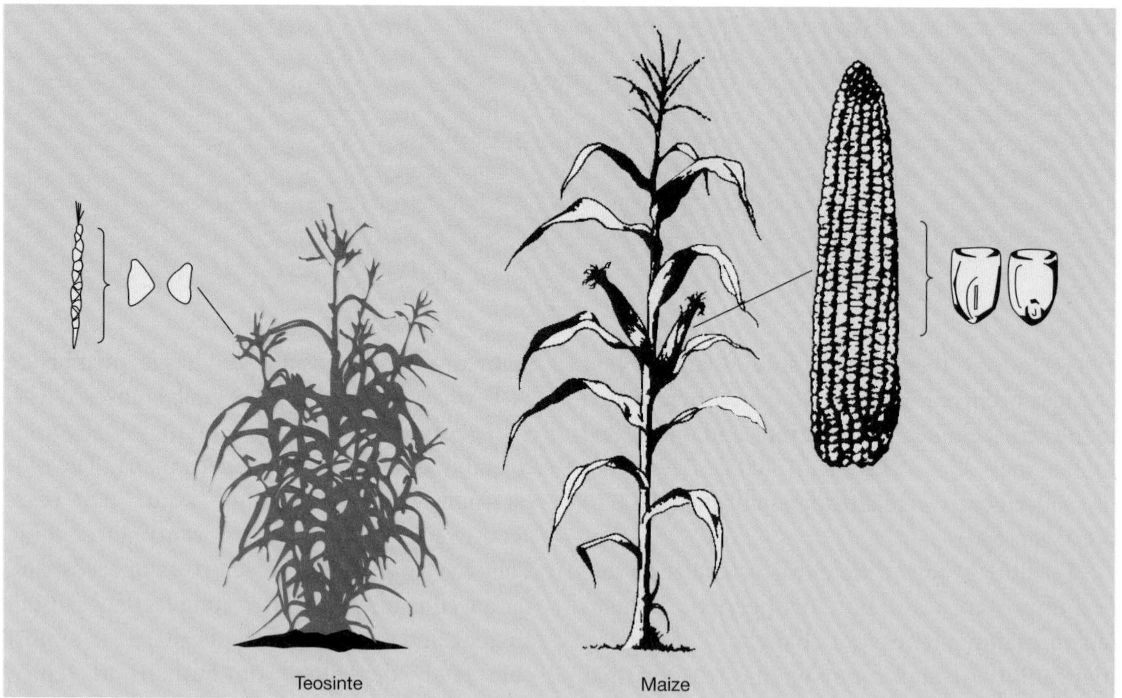

Figure 12–6 Teosinte Plant and Seeds and Maize Plant, Cob, and Kernels

Note how much larger the domesticated maize cob and kernels are compared with the teosinte spike and seeds.

Source: Feder K. 2000. Past in Perspective. Second edition. Mountain View, CA: Mayfield. Copyright © 2000 by Mayfield Publishing Company. Reprinted by permission of the publisher.

plants were domesticated. The cave itself is located in the thorn forest of the upper piedmont above the floor of the Valley of Oaxaca. The residents of Guila Naquitz hunted deer and peccary (a wild pig-like animal) with spears and spear-throwers, and trapped small animals such as rabbits. They also collected plant foods from the surrounding area, particularly prickly pear fruits, cherries, acorns, and piñion nuts from the forests above the cave, along with agave hearts, onions, and various other nuts and fruits from a variety of thorn forest plants (Flannery, 1986).

Also found in Guila Naquitz cave are the remains of domesticated plants, including bottle gourd and several varieties of squashes. How did these come to be in the cave? Were the inhabitants planting fields of squashes? Probably not in the way one thinks of planting a field today. Squashes are common wild plants in Highland Mesoamerica, and thrive in disturbed soils such as those outside of caves. It may be that the inhabitants of the Guila Naquitz cave knew squashes would grow easily near their cave, and so actively planted some with better-tasting flesh or larger seeds than those that might naturally grow there (Flannery, 1986). Domestication and the use of domesticated plants would be rather informal—a supplement to a diet already rich in animal and plant species. This picture seems much different from that at Near Eastern sites such as Ali Kosh and Çatal Hüyük. Domestication in Guila Naquitz appears to have been accomplished by hunters and gatherers who supplemented their basic diet with some desired plants (squashes with tasty flesh, for example); there was no "revolution" that enabled the people to rely on domesticated plants.

Domestication Elsewhere in the World

South America and the Eastern United States.

Outside of Mesoamerica, evidence of independent domestication of plants comes from at least two areas in the New World: South America and the eastern United States. The first plants to be domesticated in the New World were members of the cucurbit family, including the bottle gourd and a variety of squashes, all probably domesticated some time after 7500 B.C. In addition to these and other plants domesticated in Mesoamerica, we can trace more than 200 domesticated plants to the Andes in South America, including potatoes, lima beans, peanuts, amaranth, and quinoa. The first clear domesticates were squashes and gourds that may date back to 8000 B.C., which makes domestication in the Andes about as old as in Mesoamerica. The origins of the root crops manioc and sweet potato are less certain, but those crops probably originated in lowland tropical forest regions of South America (MacNeish, 1991; Hole, 1992).

Many of the plants grown in North America, such as corn, beans, and squash, were apparently introduced from Mesoamerica. However, at least three seed plants were probably domesticated independently in North America at an earlier time—sunflowers, sumpweed, and goosefoot. Sunflowers and sumpweed contain seeds that are highly nutritious in terms of protein and fat; goosefoot is high in starch and similar to corn in food value (Smith, 1992b). Sumpweed is an unusually good source of calcium, rivalled only by greens, mussels, and bones. It is also a very good source of iron (better than beef liver) and thiamine (Asch and Asch, 1978). These plants may have been cultivated in the area of the plains around the lower Ohio, Tennessee, and mid-Mississippi River valley beginning around 2000 B.C. (corn was introduced about A.D. 200).

All of the pre-corn domesticates are nutritionally superior to corn, so why did North American agriculturalists switch to a reliance on corn in the last 1000 years (Smith, 1992a; Smith, 1992b)? In the archaeologist Bruce Smith's words, "With the exception of the sunflower, North American seed crops are not exactly household words" (Smith, 1992b). Crop yields of corn would have had to be quite high to surpass the yields of those other crops, so perhaps the crucial factors were the time of harvest and the amount of effort required. Goosefoot, for example, was comparable to corn nutritionally. Harvesting and preparing it for storage though, took a lot of work and had to be done during the fall, the time of year when deer could be hunted intensively. So perhaps the incompatibility of goosefoot production and deer hunting, and the ease of harvesting corn and preparing it for storage, explain the switch to corn (Smith, 1992b).

On the whole, domestic animals were less important economically in the New World than they were in many parts of the Old World. In North America, dogs and turkeys were the main domesticated animals before the arrival of the Spaniards. Dogs in North and South America probably descended from the North American wolf and were domesticated relatively early. Domesticated turkeys from about A.D. 500 have been found in pueblos in the American Southwest (Clutton-Brock, 1988). Their feathers were used for arrows, ornaments, and weaving, and their bones for tools; but they do not seem to have been used frequently for food. However, turkeys were an important food in Mexico, where they may have been independently domesticated, and in Central America. When Cortés came to Mexico in 1519, he found domesticated turkeys in great quantities (Crawford, 1984).

The central Andes was the only part of the New World where domesticated animals were a significant part of the economy. Used for meat, transportation, and wool, llamas and alpacas (members of the camel family) were domesticated as early as 5000 B.C. in the Andes (Clutton-Brock, 1988). Guinea pigs, misnamed because they are neither pigs nor from Guinea, are rodents that were domesticated in the Andes sometime later. They were an important source of food even before domestication (Müller-Haye, 1984). Since they were domesticated, they have been raised in people's dwellings.

Animal domestication in the New World differed from that in the Old World because different wild species were found in the two hemispheres. The Old World plains and forests were the homes for the wild ancestors of the cattle, sheep, goats, pigs, and horses we know today. In the New World, the Pleistocene herds of horses, mastodons, mammoths, and other large animals were long extinct, allowing few opportunities for domestication of large animals (Wenke, 1984).

East Asia. The archaeological record for the domestication of seed crops is better known than for soft-flesh crops because the latter do not preserve well. The earliest clear evidence of cereal cultivation outside the Near East is from China. Late in the sixth millennium B.C. in north China there were sites where foxtail millet was cultivated. Storage pits, storage pots, and large numbers of grinding stones suggest that millet was an enormously important item in the diet. The wild-animal bones and the hunting and fishing tools that have been found suggest that people still depended on hunting and fishing somewhat, even though domesticated pigs (as well as dogs) were present. In south China, from about the same time, archaeologists have found a village by the edge of a small lake where people cultivated rice, bottle gourds, water chestnuts, and the date-like fruit called jujube. The people in south China also raised water buffalo, pigs, and dogs. And, as in the north China sites, some of their food came from hunting and fishing (Chang, 1981; MacNeish, 1991).

Mainland Southeast Asia may have been a place of domestication as early as the Near East was. The dating of domestication in Southeast Asia is not yet clear; the dates of the oldest site with probable domesticates—Spirit Cave in northwest Thailand—range from about 9500 B.C. to 5500 B.C. Some of the plants found at Spirit Cave are not clearly distinguishable from wild varieties, but others, such as gourds, betel nut, betel leaf, and water chestnut, were probably domesticates (MacNeish, 1991).

Most of the early cultivation in mainland Southeast Asia seems to have occurred in the plains and low terraces around rivers, although the main subsistence foods of early cultivators were probably the fish and shellfish in nearby waters. The first plants to be domesticated probably were not cereal grains, as they were in the Near East. Indeed, some early cultivated crops may not have been used for food at all. In particular, bamboo may have been used to make cutting tools and for a variety of building purposes, and gourds were probably used as containers or bowls. We do not know yet exactly when rice was first domesticated, but there is definite evidence of cultivated rice in the Yangzi Valley in China around 8500–8000 B.P. (Higham and Lu, 1998).

Bananas and taro may have been first domesticated in New Guinea. Recent analyses of soils from archaeological deposits at Kuk Swamp have identified phytoliths (small silica crystals formed between plant cells that are unique to particular species of plants) from bananas and taro dating from almost 7000 years ago (Denham et al., 2003; Neumann 2003). Archaeologists have known that agricultural fields with soil mounds and irrigation features have a long history in New Guinea, dating back as far as 10 000 years. The new findings of very early taro and banana cultivation suggest that New Guinea may have been the location where these plants were first domesticated. Other major food plants were domesticated first in Southeast Asia, including root crops, such as taro and yams, and tree crops, such as breadfruit, coconuts, and bananas (MacNeish, 1991; Hole, 1992).

Africa. Some plants and animals were domesticated first in Africa. Most of the early domestications probably occurred in the wide, broad belt of woodland-savannah country south of the Sahara and north of the equator. Among the cereal grains, sorghum was probably first domesticated in the central or eastern part of this belt, bulrush millet and a kind of rice (different from Asian rice) in the western part, and finger millet in the east. Groundnuts and yams were first domesticated in West Africa (Phillipson, 1993). We do know that farming became widespread in the northern half of Africa after 6000 B.C.; investigators continue to debate whether the earliest crops grown there were indigenous or borrowed from the Near East. There is little doubt, however, that some of the plant foods were first domesticated in sub-Saharan Africa because the wild varieties occur there (MacNeish, 1991; Phillipson, 1993). Many of the important domestic animals in Africa today—cattle, sheep, and goats—probably were domesticated first in the Near East; most likely the donkey and guinea fowl were first domesticated in Africa (Clutton-Brock, 1988).

A man harvesting sorghum in Burkina Faso. Sorghum is one of several plant species domesticated in Africa.

Why Did Food Production Develop?

We know that an economic transformation occurred in widely separate areas of the world beginning after about 10 000 years ago, as people began to domesticate plants and animals. The question is, why did domestication occur? And why did it occur independently in many different places within a period of a few thousand years? Considering that people depended only on wild plants and animals for millions of years, the differences in exactly when domestication first occurred in different parts of the world seem small. The spread of domesticated plants seems to have been more rapid in the Old World than in the New World, perhaps because the Old World spread was more along an east–west axis (except for the spread to sub-Saharan Africa), whereas the New World spread was more north–south. Spreading north and south may have required more time to adapt to variation in day lengths, climates, and diseases (Diamond, 1997). (Figure 12–1 on page 274 shows a timeline for domestication of plants and animals in the Old and New Worlds.)

There are many theories of why food production developed; most have tried to explain the origin of domestication in the area of early agriculture. Gordon Childe's theory, popular in the 1950s, was that a drastic change in climate caused domestication in the Near East (MacNeish, 1991). According to Childe, the postglacial period was marked by a decline in summer rainfall in the Near East and northern Africa. As the rains decreased, people were forced to retreat into shrinking pockets, or oases, of food resources, which were surrounded by desert. The lessened availability of wild resources provided an incentive for people to cultivate grains and to domesticate animals, according to Childe.

Robert Braidwood criticized Childe's theory for two reasons. First, Braidwood believed that the climate changes may not have been as dramatic as Childe had assumed, and therefore the "oasis incentive" may not have existed. Second, the climatic changes that occurred in the Near East after the retreat of the last glaciers had probably occurred at earlier interglacial periods too, but there had never been a similar food-producing revolution before. Hence, according to Braidwood, there must be more to the explanation of why people began to produce food than simply changes in climate (Braidwood, 1960).

Braidwood and Gordon Willey claimed that people did not undertake domestication until they had learned a great deal about their environment and until their culture had evolved enough for them to handle such an undertaking: "Why did incipient food production not come earlier? Our only answer at the moment is that culture was not ready to achieve it" (Braidwood and Willey, 1962).

Most archaeologists now think we should try to explain why people were not "ready" earlier to achieve domestication. Both Lewis Binford and Kent Flannery suggested that some change in external circumstances must have induced or favoured the changeover to food production (Binford, 1971; Flannery, 1971). As Flannery pointed out, there is no evidence of a great economic incentive for hunter-gatherers to become food producers. In fact, some contemporary hunter-gatherers may actually obtain adequate nutrition with far less work than many agriculturalists. So what might push food collectors to become food producers?

Binford and Flannery thought that the incentive to domesticate animals and plants might have been a desire to reproduce what was wildly abundant in the most bountiful or optimum hunting and gathering areas. Because of population growth in the optimum areas, people might have moved to surrounding areas containing fewer wild resources. It would have been in those marginal areas that people might have first turned to food production in order to reproduce what they used to have.

The Binford-Flannery model seems to fit the archaeological record in the Levant, the southwestern part of the earliest agriculture, where population increase did precede the first signs of domestication (Wright, 1971). However, as Flannery admitted, in some regions, such as southwestern Iran, the optimum hunting-gathering areas do not show population increase before the emergence of domestication (Flannery, 1986).

The Binford-Flannery model focuses on population pressure in a small area as the incentive to turn to food production. Mark Cohen theorizes it was population pressure on a global scale that explains why so many of the world's peoples adopted agriculture within the span of a few thousand years (Cohen, 1977a; Cohen, 1977b). He argues that hunter-gatherers all over the world gradually increased in population so that by about 10 000 years ago the world was more or less filled with food collectors. Thus, people could no longer relieve population pressure by moving to uninhabited areas. To support their increasing populations, they would have had to exploit a broader range of less desirable wild foods; that is, they would have had to switch to broad-spectrum collecting, or they would have had to increase the yields of the most desirable wild plants by weeding, protecting them from animal pests, and perhaps deliberately planting only the most productive among them. Cohen thinks that people might have tried a variety of these strategies but would generally have ended up depending on cultivation because that would have been the most efficient way to allow more people to live in one place.

Recently, some archaeologists have returned to the idea that climatic change (not the extreme variety that Childe envisaged) might have played a role in the emergence of agriculture. It seems clear from the evidence now available that the climate of the Near East about 13 000 to 12 000 years ago became more seasonal: the summers got hotter and drier than before and the winters became colder. These climatic changes may have favoured the emergence of annual species of wild grain, which archaeologically we see proliferating in many areas of the Near East (Byrne, 1987; Henry, 1989; Blumler and Byrne, 1991; McCorriston and Hole, 1991). People such as the Natufians intensively exploited the seasonal grains, developing an elaborate technology for storing and processing the grains and giving up their previous nomadic existence to do so. The transition to agriculture may have occurred when sedentary foraging no longer provided sufficient resources for the population. This could have happened because sedentism led to population increase and therefore resource scarcity (Henry, 1989), or because local wild resources became depleted after people settled down in permanent villages (McCorriston and Hole, 1991). In the area of Israel and Jordan where the Natufians lived, some of the people apparently turned to agriculture, probably to increase the supply of grain, whereas other people returned to nomadic food collection because of the decreasing availability of wild grain (Henry, 1989).

Change to a more seasonal climate might also have led to a shortage of certain nutrients for food collectors. In the dry seasons certain nutrients would have been less available. For example, grazing animals get lean when grasses are not plentiful, so meat from hunting would have been in short supply in the dry seasons. Although it may seem surprising, some recent hunter-gatherers have starved when they had to rely on lean meat. If they could have somehow increased their carbohydrate or fat intake, they might have been more likely to get through the periods of lean game (Speth and Spielmann, 1983). So it is possible that some wild-food collectors in the past thought of planting crops to get them through the dry seasons when hunting, fishing, and gathering did not provide enough carbohydrates and fat for them to avoid starvation.

Mesoamerica presents a very different picture, because the early domesticates were not important to subsistence. Theories about population pressure and nutrient shortage don't seem to fit Mesoamerica well. However, there were apparently shortages of desired plants, such as bottle gourds, and domestication may well have occurred as humans actively sowed these desired plants. The difference between this model and the ones described above is that humans in Mesoamerica were apparently not forced into domestication by climate change or population pressure, but actively turned to domestication to obtain more of the most desired or useful plant species. The most interesting case is maize, which only became a staple food some 2500 or more years after it was first domesticated. Why did it become a staple? Probably both because it was a suitable staple crop (especially when intercropped with beans and squash, as discussed earlier) and because people liked it, so they grew it in large quantities. Over time, and perhaps because of conflict, population pressure, and other forces similar to those that apparently led to domestication in the Near East, people in Mesoamerica and later North and South America came to rely on maize as their dietary mainstay.

Consequences of the Rise of Food Production

We know that intensive agriculture (permanent rather than shifting cultivation) probably developed in response to population pressure, but we do not know for sure that population pressure was even partly responsible for plant and animal domestication in the first place. Still, population growth certainly accelerated after the rise of food production (see Figure 12–8). There were other consequences too. Paradoxically, perhaps, health seems to have declined. Material possessions, though, became more elaborate.

Environmental Restraints

How much does the physical environment affect food-getting? Anthropologists have concluded that the physical environment by itself has a restraining, rather than a determining, effect on the major types of subsistence. Since they have very short growing seasons, cold regions of the earth are not particularly conducive to the growing of plants. No society we know of has practised agriculture in the Arctic; instead, people who live there rely primarily on animals for food. Nevertheless, both food collection (as among the Inuit) and food production (as among the Lapps) can be practised in cold areas.

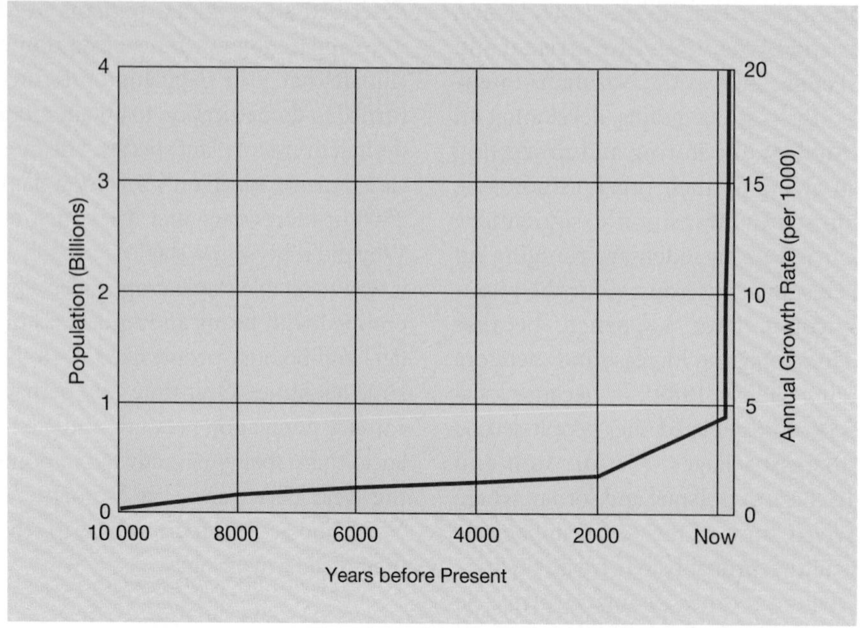

Figure 12–7 Population Growth since 10 000 Years Ago

The rate of population growth accelerated after the emergence of farming and herding 10 000 years ago. The rate of growth has accelerated even more dramatically in recent times.

Source: Adapted from Coale AJ. 1974. The History of the Human Population.

Indeed, cross-cultural evidence indicates that neither food collection nor food production is significantly associated with any particular type of habitat (Anonymous, 1967).

We know that food collection has been practised at one time or another in almost all areas of the earth. The physical environment does seem to have some effect on what kind of food collection is practised, that is, on the extent to which food collectors will depend on plants, animals, or fish. Farther away from the equator, food collectors depend much less on plants for food and much more on animals and fish (Binford, 1990; Low, 1990). Lewis Binford argues that fishing becomes increasingly important in cold climates because food collectors need non-portable housing in severe winters to protect themselves from the cold. Therefore, they cannot rely on large animals, which usually have to feed themselves by moving over considerable distances in the winter. Fishing is more localized than hunting, and therefore food collectors who rely on fishing can stay in their non-portable houses in winter (Binford, 1990).

When we contrast horticulture and intensive agriculture, the physical environment appears to explain some of the variation. Approximately 80 percent of all societies that practise horticulture or simple agriculture are in the tropics, whereas 75 percent of all societies that practise intensive agriculture are not in tropical forest environments (Anonymous, 1967). Tropical forests have abundant rainfall. Despite the attractiveness of lush vegetation and brilliant colouring, tropical forest lands do not usually offer favourable environments for intensive agriculture. Perhaps this is because the heavy rainfall quickly washes away certain minerals from cleared land. Also, the difficulty of controlling insect pests and weeds, which abound in tropical forests (Carneiro, 1968; Janzen, 1973), may make intensive agriculture less productive.

Whatever the reasons for the switch to food production, we still need to explain why food production has supplanted food collection as the primary mode of subsistence. We cannot assume that collectors would automatically adopt production as a superior way of life once they understood the process of domestication. After all, as we have noted, domestication may entail more work and provide less security than the food-collecting way of life.

The spread of agriculture may be linked to the need for territorial expansion. As a sedentary, food-producing population grew, it may have been forced to expand into new territory. Some of this territory may have been vacant, but much of it was probably already occupied by food collectors. Although food production is not necessarily easier than collection, it is generally more productive per unit of land. Greater productivity enables more people to be supported in a given territory. In the competition for land between the faster-expanding food producers and the food collectors, the food producers may have had a significant advantage: they had more people in a given area. Thus, the foraging groups may have been more likely to lose out in the competition for land. Some groups may have adopted cultivation, abandoning the foraging way of life in order to survive. Other groups, continuing as food collectors, may have been forced to retreat into areas not desired by the cultivators. Today, as we have seen, the small number of remaining food collectors inhabit areas not particularly suitable for cultivation—dry lands, dense tropical forests, and polar regions.

Just as prior population growth might account for the origins of domestication, so would further population growth and ensuing pressure on resources at least partly explain the transformation of horticultural systems into intensive agricultural systems at later periods. However, just as the environment can affect the mode of subsistence, so, too, can the mode of subsistence affect the environment. We are all too familiar with the destruction of the world's tropical rain forests. It is estimated that 31 million hectares of global rain forest is destroyed each year. However, all human behavioural patterns associated with subsistence affect the environment (see Applied Anthropology, "The Effect of Food-Getting on the Environment"). Some environments may make it difficult to adopt certain subsistence practices. For example, intensive agriculture cannot supplant horticulture in some tropical environments and horticulture continues to be practised in these regions.

Accelerated Population Growth

As we have seen, sedentism (even before the rise of food production) may have increased the rate of human population growth. But population growth definitely accelerated after the emergence of farming and herding, possibly because the spacing between births was reduced and therefore fertility increased. Increased fertility may have been an advantage, because of the greater value of children in farming and herding economies; there is evidence from recent population studies that fertility rates are higher where children contribute more to the economy (Kasarda, 1971; White, 1973). Not only may parents desire more children to help with chores; the increased workload of mothers may also (but inadvertently) decrease birth spacing. The busier a mother is, the less frequently she may nurse and the more likely her baby will be given supplementary food by other caretakers such as older siblings (Ember, 1983). Less frequent nursing (Konner and Wortman, 1980) and greater reliance on other food may result in the earlier resumption of ovulation after the birth of a baby. (Farmers and herders are likely to have animal milk to feed to babies, and also cereals that have been transformed by cooking into soft, mushy porridges.) Therefore, the spacing between births may have decreased (and the number of births per mother, in turn, increased) when mothers got busier after the rise of food production.

Declining Health

Although the rise of food production may have led to increased fertility, this does not mean that health generally improved. In fact, it appears that health declined at least sometimes with the transition to food production. The two trends may seem paradoxical, but rapid population growth can occur if each mother gives birth to a large number of babies, even if many of them die early because of disease or poor nutrition.

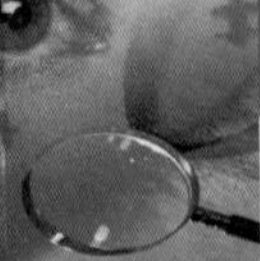

APPLIED ANTHROPOLOGY

The Effect of Food-Getting on the Environment

Many people are now aware of industrial pollution—the dumping of industrial wastes in the ground or into rivers, the spewing of chemicals into the air through smokestacks—but we don't often realize how much humans have altered the environment by the ways they collect and produce food. Consider irrigation. There are various ways to capture water for irrigation. Water can be channelled from rivers; rainwater can be caught in terraces carved out of hillsides; ancient water can be pumped up from vast underground reservoirs called aquifers. But not all of the water drawn for irrigation seeps into the ground. Much of it evaporates, leaving behind minerals and salts. And the more a piece of land has been irrigated, the saltier the ground becomes. Eventually, the soil becomes too salty to grow crops effectively.

Some archaeologists have suggested that the accumulation of toxic salts in the soil at least partly explains the doom or decline of various groups in the past. For example, salinization may have contributed to the decline of the earliest city-states in Mesopotamia, present-day southern Iraq, and southwestern Iran. The Hohokam farmers who lived in what is now Arizona had about 240 kilometres of canals for irrigation; some of their ditches were 4.5 metres deep and 7.6 metres wide. In fact, their irrigation networks were comparable to those that served the Aztecs in pre-Columbian Mexico City. The Hohokam seem to have vanished around A.D. 1400, perhaps because the salty soil poisoned their crops. Today much of the soil is still too salty for cultivation.

The lessons of history may not have been learned yet. The San Joaquin Valley of California, perhaps the most productive agricultural area in the world, now has a serious salinization problem. One solution in many of the areas of the Great American Desert is to pump water up from underground. Indeed, in many places there is a great deal of water underground. For example, the Ogallala aquifer, which underlies parts of Nebraska, Kansas, Texas, Oklahoma, Colorado, and New Mexico, contains water left from the Ice Ages. The pumping solution, if it is a solution, is only a short-term fix though, for the huge Ogallala aquifer is also the fastest-disappearing aquifer. The only question is how long it will take to disappear totally.

Too many people raising too many animals can also have serious effects on the environment. We can easily imagine how the possibility of profit might inspire people to try to raise more animals than the land will support. For example, 300 years ago the Great American Desert looked like a vast grassland. It supported large herds of buffalo, which in the next 200 years were all but exterminated by overhunting. The white settlers soon discovered they could raise cattle and sheep on this grassland, but many parts of it were overgrazed. It took the swirling dust storms of the 1930s to make people realize that overgrazing as well as poor farming practices could be disastrous. These problems are not new. The Norse colonized Greenland and Iceland around A.D. 800; but overgrazing of pasture undoubtedly contributed to soil erosion and the disappearance or decline of the colonies by A.D. 1500.

Are environmental problems associated only with food production? Although food producers may be the worst offenders, there is reason to think that foragers may also have sometimes overfished, overgathered, or overhunted. For example, some scholars suspect that the movement of humans into the New World was mainly responsible for the disappearance of the mammoth. Unfortunately, there is little evidence that humans have been good conservers in the past. That does not mean that humans cannot do better in the future—but they have to want to.

Sources: Dirks R. 1998. Hunger and Famine. In: Ember CR, Ember M, Peregrine PN, editors. Research Frontiers in Anthropology. Upper Saddle River, NJ: Prentice Hall. Prentice Hall/Simon & Schuster Custom Publishing.

Plundering Earth Is Nothing New. 12 June 1994. Los Angeles Times News Service as reported in the New Haven Register. pp A18–19.

Reisner M. 1993. Cadillac Desert: The American West and Its Disappearing Water. Revised edition. New York: Penguin.

The evidence that health may have declined sometime after the rise of food production comes from studies of the bones and teeth of some prehistoric populations, before and after the emergence of food production. Nutritional and disease problems are indicated by such features as incomplete formation of tooth enamel, non-accidental bone lesions (incompletely filled-in bone), reduction in stature, and decreased mean age at death.

In a recent review of the impact of agriculture, Clark Larsen refers to a variety of studies that have observed lower mean ages at death for agricultural populations as compared with earlier hunter-gatherer samples (Larsen, 1995). This, he notes, has been interpreted as a reflection of increased mortality and decreased life expectancy associated with the shift to agriculture. This hypothesis was the central focus of the 1984 volume of papers *Palaeopathology at the Origins of Agriculture* (Cohen and Armelagos, 1984a), in which osteological evidence for demographic patterns and indicators of health are presented for several regions of the world. Many of the prehistoric populations that were studied relied heavily on agriculture and seemed to show less adequate nutrition and higher infection rates than populations living in the same areas before agriculture. Some of the agricultural populations were of shorter stature and had lower life expectancies (Cohen and Armelagos, 1984b; Roosevelt, 1984; Cohen, 1987; Wood et al., 1992; Cohen, 1998). The general conclusions drawn from studies throughout the 1970s and 1980s was that the shift to an agricultural subsistence and economy was associated with increases in mortality and the prevalence of infectious diseases. However, for populations that were undergoing moderate growth or decline, the effects of changes in mortality are negligible, while the effects of birth rate, and therefore fertility, are significant (Larsen, 1995). As discussed in Chapter 3, this is critical since life expectancy derived from skeletal samples depends on the simple assumption of mean age at death being approximately equivalent to life expectancy at birth.

Given these arguments, the observed decline in mean age at death among agricultural populations in the archaeological record is more likely a reflection of their rapid population growth (Howell, 1986). The extent to which fertility and mortality increased or decreased with a shift to agriculture is a key question, which as yet remains unsolved (Johansson and Horowitz, 1986). However, given the wide range of ecological conditions in which various populations adopted agricultural practices, there may have been a similarly broad spectrum of demographic responses to this shift with respect to mortality and fertility (Jackes et al., 1997a; Jackes et al., 1997b).

Understanding the biological impact of the Mesolithic–Neolithic transition is in fact not an easy task. Most of the evidence for apparent health declines associated with agriculture comes from Nubia in the Nile Valley and the American Southwest. However, examining this question is difficult since regions with reasonably large samples of Mesolithic skeletons followed immediately by large, well-preserved Neolithic samples are fairly rare (Jackes et al., 1997a; Jackes et al., 1997b). Mary Jackes, David Lubell, and Chris Meiklejohn have studied large samples of Mesolithic and Neolithic skeletal material from central and southern Portugal (Jackes et al., 1997a; Jackes et al., 1997b). In their study of three Mesolithic and eight Neolithic sites, these researchers observed little increase in rates of skeletal infection over this period. They don't find it surprising, however, since the Mesolithic populations show evidence of being relatively sedentary, and the Neolithic populations continued to show some evidence of seasonal foraging (Jackes et al., 1997a; Jackes et al., 1997b). Despite this continuity, there was some apparent increase in fertility and population growth in the Neolithic period. In contrast to the evidence from the Near East, they concluded from their study that there was "no evidence that the comfortable way of life of the Portuguese Mesolithic was replaced by a wretched and unhealthy Neolithic existence" (Jackes et al., 1997a).

The question of a decline in health associated with earlier agricultural populations remains a topic of debate. Greater malnutrition can result from an over-dependence on a few dietary staples that lack some necessary nutrients. Over-dependence on a few sources of food may also increase the risk of famine because the fewer the staple crops, the greater the danger to the food supply posed by a weather-caused crop failure. However, some or most nutritional problems may be the result of social and political factors, particularly the rise of different socio-economic classes of people and unequal access, between and within communities, to food and other resources (Roosevelt, 1984). Social stratification or considerable socio-economic inequality seems likely to have developed after the rise of food production. The effects of stratification and political dominance from afar on the general level of health may be reflected in the skeletal remains of prehistoric Native Americans who died in what is now Illinois between A.D. 950 and 1300, the period spanning the changeover in that region from hunting and gathering to agriculture. The agricultural people living in the area of Dickson's Mounds—burial sites named after the doctor who first excavated them—were apparently in much worse health than their hunter-gatherer ancestors. Curiously, archaeological evidence suggests that they were still also hunting and fishing. A balanced diet was apparently available, but who was getting it? Possibly it was the elite at Cahokia, 177 kilometres away, where perhaps 15 000 to 30 000 people lived, who were getting most of the meat and fish. The individuals near Dickson's Mounds who collected the meat and fish may have acquired luxury items such as shell necklaces from the Cahokia elite, but many of the people buried at Dickson's Mounds clearly did not benefit nutritionally from the relationship with Cahokia (Goodman et al., 1984a; Goodman and Armelagos, 1985; Cohen, 1998).

The Elaboration of Material Possessions

Every society makes use of a *technology* to convert raw materials to food and other goods. Technology includes tools, constructions (such as fish traps), the required skills (such as how and where to set up a fish trap), and also the political organization required to extract, process, and redistribute resources. Societies vary considerably in their technologies and in the way access to technology is allocated. For example, food collectors and pastoralists typically have fairly small tool kits. They must limit their tools, and their material possessions in general, to what they can comfortably carry with them, or to those that can be expediently manufactured at the place where they are needed.

The tools most needed by food collectors are weapons for the hunt, digging sticks, and receptacles for gathering and carrying. Andaman Islanders

As this reconstruction shows, transforming grain into flour was a "daily grind," putting a great deal of stress on the lower back and knees of women. Studies of Neolithic skeletons of women show marks of stress on bone and arthritis, probably reflecting their long hours of work at the grinding stone.

used bows and arrows for hunting game and large fish. Australian aborigines developed two types of boomerangs: a heavy one for a straight throw in killing game and a light, returning one for playing games or for scaring birds into nets strung between trees. The Semang of Malaya used poisoned darts and blowguns. The Mbuti Pygmies of the Congo River basin still trap elephants and buffalo in deadfalls and nets. Of all food collectors, the Inuit probably had the most sophisticated weapons, including harpoons, compound bows, and ivory fish hooks. Yet the Inuit also had relatively fixed settlements with available storage space and dog teams and sleds for transportation (Service, 1979).

Societies with intensive agriculture and industrialized societies are likely to have tools made by specialists, which means that tools must be acquired by trade or purchase. Probably because complex tools have greater value, they are less likely than simple tools to be shared except by those who contributed to their production.

In the more permanent villages that were established after the rise of food production about 10 000 years ago, houses became more elaborate and comfortable, and construction methods improved. The materials used in construction depended on whether timber or stone was locally available or whether a strong sun could dry mud bricks. Modern architects might find to their surprise that bubble-shaped houses were known long ago in Neolithic Cyprus. Families in the island's town of Khirokitia made their homes in large, domed, circular dwellings shaped like beehives and featuring stone foundations and mud-brick walls. Often, more space was created by dividing the interior horizontally and firmly propping a second floor on limestone pillars.

Sophisticated ceramics like this 5000-year-old Chinese funeral urn first appeared in the Neolithic era as part of the elaboration of material possessions.

Sizable villages of solidly constructed, gabled wood houses were built in Europe on the banks of the Danube and along the rims of Alpine lakes (Clark and Piggott, 1965). Many of the gabled wooden houses in the Danube region were long, rectangular structures that apparently sheltered several family units. In Neolithic times these longhouses had doors, beds, tables, and other furniture that closely resembled those in modern-day societies. We know the people had furniture because miniature clay models have been found at their sites. Several of the chairs and couches seem to be models of padded and upholstered furniture with wooden frames, indicating that Neolithic European artisans were creating fairly sophisticated furnishings (Clark and Piggott, 1965). Such furnishings were the result of an advanced tool technology put to use by a people who, because they were staying in one area, could take time to make and use furniture.

For the first time, apparel made of woven textile appeared. This development was not simply the result of the domestication of flax (for linen), cotton, and wool-growing sheep. These sources of fibre alone could not produce cloth. It was the development by Neolithic society of the spindle and loom for spinning and weaving that made textiles possible. True, textiles can be woven by hand without a loom, but to do so is a slow, laborious process, impractical for producing garments.

The pottery of the early Neolithic was similar to the plain earthenware made by some Mesolithic groups and included large urns for grain storage, mugs, cooking pots, and dishes. To improve the retention of liquid, potters in the Near East may have been the first to glaze the earthenware's porous surface. Later, Neolithic ceramics became more artistic. Designers shaped the clay into graceful forms and painted colourful patterns on the vessels.

It is probable that virtually none of these architectural and technological innovations could have occurred until humans became fully sedentary. Nomadic hunting and gathering peoples would have found it difficult to carry many material goods, especially fragile items such as pottery. It was only when humans became fully sedentary that these goods would have provided advantages, enabling villagers to cook and store food more effectively and to house themselves more comfortably.

There is also evidence of long-distance trade in the Neolithic, as we have noted. Obsidian from southern Turkey was exported to sites in the Zagros Mountains of Iran and to what are now Israel, Jordan, and Syria in the Levant. Great amounts of obsidian were exported to sites about 300 kilometres from the source of supply; more than 80 percent of the tools used by residents of those areas were made of this material (Renfrew, 1969). Marble was sent from western to eastern Turkey, and seashells from the coast were traded to distant inland regions. Such trade suggests a considerable amount of contact among various Neolithic communities.

About 3500 B.C., cities first appeared in the Near East. These cities had political assemblies, kings, scribes, and specialized workshops. The specialized production of goods and services was supported by surrounding farming villages, which sent their produce to the urban centres. A dazzling transformation had taken place in a relatively short time. People had not only settled down but also become "civilized," or urbanized. (The word *civilized* literally means to make "citified" [Anonymous, 1988].) Urban societies seem to have developed first in the Near East and somewhat later around the eastern Mediterranean, in the Indus Valley of northwestern India, in northern China, and in Mexico and Peru. In the next chapter we turn to the rise of these earliest civilizations.

Summary

1. Food collection or foraging—hunting, gathering, and fishing—depends on wild plants and animals and is the oldest human food-getting technology. Food collectors can be found in various physical habitats and most are nomadic and with low population density.
2. In the period before plants and animals were domesticated (called the Mesolithic period in regard to Europe and the Near East), there seems to have been a shift in many areas of the world to less dependence on big-game hunting and greater dependence on what is called broad-spectrum collecting. The broad spectrum of available resources frequently included aquatic resources such as fish and shellfish and a variety of wild plants and deer and other game. Climatic changes may have been partly responsible for the change to broad-spectrum collecting.
3. In some sites in Europe, the Near East, Africa, and Peru, the switch to broad-spectrum collecting seems to be associated with the development of more permanent communities. In other areas, such as the semi-arid highlands of Mesoamerica, permanent settlements may have emerged only after the domestication of plants and animals.
4. The shift to the cultivation and domestication of plants and animals has been referred to as the Neolithic revolution, and it occurred, probably independently, in a number of areas. To date, the earliest evidence of domestication comes from the Near East about 8000 B.C. Dating for the earliest domestication in other areas of the Old World is not so clear, but the presence of different domesticated crops in different regions suggests that there were independent centres of

domestication in China, Southeast Asia (what is now Malaysia, Thailand, Cambodia, and Vietnam), and Africa sometime around or after 6000 B.C. In the New World, there appear to have been several early areas of cultivation and domestication: the highlands of Mesoamerica (about 7000 B.C.), the central Andes around Peru (about the same time), and the Eastern Woodlands of North America (about 2000 B.C.).

5. Theories about why food production originated remain controversial, but most archaeologists think that certain conditions must have pushed people to switch from collecting to producing food. Some possible factors include (1) population growth in regions of bountiful wild resources (which may have pushed people to move to marginal areas where they tried to reproduce their former abundance); (2) global population growth (which filled most of the world's habitable regions and may have forced people to turn to a broader spectrum of wild resources and to domesticate plants and animals); and (3) the emergence of hotter and drier summers and colder winters (which may have favoured sedentism near seasonal stands of wild grain; population growth in such areas may have forced people to plant crops and raise animals to support themselves).

6. Regardless of why food production originated, it seems to have had important consequences for human life. Populations generally increased substantially after plant and animal domestication. Even though not all early cultivators were sedentary, sedentism did increase with greater reliance on agriculture. Somewhat surprisingly, some prehistoric populations that relied heavily on agriculture seem to have been less healthy than prior populations that relied on food collection. In the more permanent villages that were established after the rise of food production, houses and furnishings became more elaborate, and people began to make textiles and to paint pottery. These villages have also yielded evidence of increased long-distance trade.

Glossary Terms

domestication (p. 287)
food collection (p. 276)
food production (p. 277)
foragers (p. 276)
horticulture (p. 277)
intensive agriculture (p. 279)
Neolithic (p. 287)
rachis (p. 287)
sedentism (p. 275)
shifting cultivation (p. 277)
slash-and-burn techniques (p. 278)
subsistence technology (p. 276)

Critical Questions

1. What might cause people to work harder to get food?
2. How might people have domesticated sheep, goats, and cattle?
3. Why might foragers be less likely then intensive agriculturalists to suffer from food shortages?

Internet Exercises

1. Visit the Çatal Hüyük website **www.catalhoyuk.com/** and learn about the ongoing excavations. Write a brief summary of the most current discoveries.
2. Domestication of wild plants is not without its difficulties. Look at the description of attempts to cultivate wild rice at **www.hort.purdue.edu/newcrop/proceedings1993/v2-235.html**. Explore the problems of shattering seed casings and increased disease with cultivation.

Suggested Reading

Cohen MN. 1998. Were Early Agriculturalists Less Healthy Than Food Collectors? In: Ember CR, Ember M, Peregrine PN, editors. Research Frontiers in Cultural Anthropology. Upper Saddle River, NJ: Prentice Hall. Prentice Hall/ Simon & Schuster Custom Publishing. This article is a specially written chapter for an undergraduate audience, reviewing the evidence for a decline in health with the advent of agriculture.

Cowan CW, Watson PJ, editors. 1992. The Origins of Agriculture: An International Perspective. Washington, DC: Smithsonian Institution Press. Summarizes the geography, climate, botany, and archaeology of the events associated with the emergence of plant cultivation in different parts of the Old and New Worlds.

Henry DO. 1989. From Foraging to Agriculture: The Levant at the End of the Ice Age. Philadelphia: University of Pennsylvania Press. An examination and discussion of theories about the origins of agriculture, with particular reference to the areas bordering the eastern Mediterranean.

MacNeish RS. 1991. The Origins of Agriculture and Settled Life. Norman: University of Oklahoma Press. After reviewing previous theories about the origins of agriculture, the author puts forward his own model and reviews the archaeological sequences in each of the early regions of domestication in order to evaluate his theory.

Price TD, Brown JA, editors. 1985. Prehistoric Hunter-Gatherers: The Emergence of Cultural Complexity. Orlando, FL: Academic Press. A volume of papers by archaeologists on the beginnings of social complexity among hunter-gatherers. The scope is global; most of the papers deal comparatively or cross-archaeologically with the various adaptations of hunter-gatherers in the past.

Thorp IJ. 1999. The Origins of Agriculture in Europe. Routledge. The author presents a comparative analysis from recent literature and archaeological evidence of the late Mesolithic and early Neolithic periods.

ORIGINS OF CITIES AND STATES

13

CHAPTER OUTLINE

From the time agriculture first developed until about 6000 B.C., people in the Near East lived in fairly small villages. There were few differences in wealth and status from household to household, and apparently there was no governmental authority beyond the village. There is no evidence that these villages had any public buildings or craft specialists or that one community was very different in size from its neighbours. In short, these settlements had none of the characteristics we commonly associate with "civilization."

Sometime around 6000 B.C., in parts of the Near East—and at later times in other places—a great transformation in the quality and scale of human life seems to have begun. For the first time we can see evidence of differences in status among households. For example, some are much bigger than others. Communities began to differ in size and to specialize in certain crafts, and there are signs that some political officials had acquired authority over several communities, that what anthropologists call "chiefdoms" had emerged.

Somewhat later, by about 3500 B.C., we can see many, if not all, of the conventional characteristics of **civilization**: the first inscriptions, or writing; cities; many kinds of full-time craft specialists; monumental architecture; great differences in wealth and status; and the kind of strong, hierarchical, centralized political system we call the **state**.

This type of transformation has occurred many times and in many places in human history. The most ancient civilizations arose in the Near East around 3500 B.C., in northwestern India after 2500 B.C., in northern China around 1750 B.C., in the New World (Mexico and Peru) just over 2000 years ago, and in tropical Africa somewhat later (Anonymous, 1978; Connah, 1987; Wenke, 1990). At least some of these civilizations evolved independently of the others—for example, those in the New World and those in the Old World. Why did they do so? What conditions favoured the emergence of centralized, state-like political systems? What conditions favoured the establishment of cities? We ask this last question separately, because archaeologists are not yet certain that all the ancient state societies had cities when they first developed centralized government. In this chapter we discuss some of the things archaeologists have learned or suspect about the growth of ancient civilizations. Our discussion focuses primarily on the Near East and Mexico because archaeologists know the most about the sequences of cultural development in those two areas (see Figure 13–1).

Archaeological Inferences about Civilization

The most ancient civilizations have been studied by archaeologists rather than historians because those civilizations evolved before the advent of writing. How do archaeologists infer that a particular people in the preliterate past had social classes, cities, or a centralized government?

As we have noted, it appears that the earliest Neolithic societies were **egalitarian**; that is, people did not differ much in wealth, prestige, or power. Differences in prestige and social power that existed in the Neolithic were conferred upon individuals as a function of respect (status) that was earned through a lifetime of demonstrated skills and accomplishments. This status was not transferable to descendants. Some later societies show signs of social inequality, indicated by burial finds. Archaeologists generally assume that inequality in death reflects inequality in life, at least in status and perhaps also in wealth and power. Thus, we can be fairly sure that a society had differences in status if only some people were buried with special objects, such as jewellery or pots filled with food. Further, we can be fairly

Civilization: urban society, from the Latin word for "city-state."

State: a political unit with centralized decision-making affecting a large population. Most states have cities with public buildings; full-time craft and religious specialists; an "official" art style; a hierarchical social structure topped by an elite class; and a governmental monopoly on the legitimate use of force to implement policies.

Egalitarian Society: a society in which all persons of a given age-sex category have equal access to economic resources, power, and prestige.

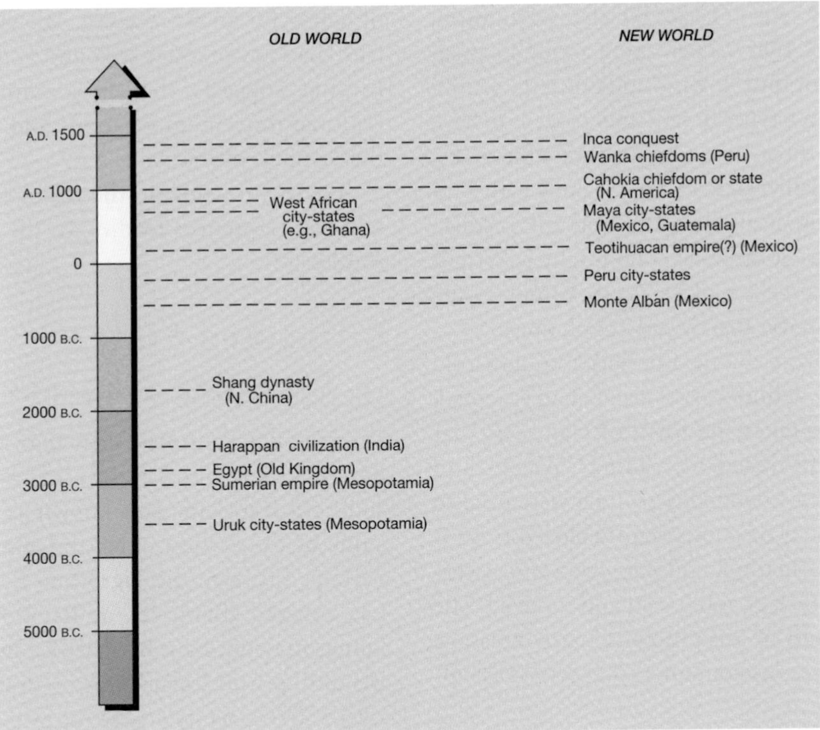

Figure 13–1 The Emergence of Civilization

sure that high status was assigned at birth rather than achieved in later life if we find noticeable differences in children's tombs. For example, some (but not all) child burials from as early as 5500 to 5000 B.C. at Telles-Sawwan in Iraq, and from about 800 B.C. at La Venta in Mexico, are filled with statues and ornaments, suggesting that some children had high status from birth (Flannery, 1972). However, burials indicating differences in status do not necessarily mean a society had significant differences in wealth. It is only when archaeologists find other substantial differences, as in house size and furnishings, that we can be sure the society had different socioeconomic classes of people.

Some archaeologists think that states first evolved around 3500 B.C. in Greater Mesopotamia, the area now shared by southern Iraq and southwestern Iran. Archaeologists do not always agree on how a state should be defined, but most think that hierarchical and centralized decision-making affecting a substantial population is the key criterion. Other characteristics are usually, but not always, found in these first states. They usually have cities with a substantial part of the population not involved directly in the collection or production of food (which means that people in cities are heavily dependent on people elsewhere); full-time religious and craft specialists; public buildings; and often an official art style. There is a hierarchical social structure topped by an elite class from which the leaders are drawn (Flannery, 1972; Redman, 1978).

How can archaeologists tell, from the information provided by material remains, whether a society was a state or not? This depends in part on the individual criteria for a state. For example, Henry Wright and Gregory Johnson defined a state as a centralized political hierarchy with at least three levels of administration (Wright and Johnson, 1975). How might archaeologists infer that such a hierarchy existed in some area? Wright and Johnson suggested that the way settlement sites differ in size is one indication of how many levels of administration there were in an area.

During the early Uruk period (just before 3500 B.C.) in what is now southwestern Iran, there were some 50 settlements that seem to fall into three groups in terms of size (Wright and Johnson, 1975; Johnson, 1987). There were about 45 small villages, three or four "towns," and one large centre, Susa. These three types of settlements seem to have been part of a three-level administration hierarchy, since many small villages could not trade with Susa without passing through a settlement intermediate in size. Because a three-level hierarchy is Wright and Johnson's criterion of a state, they think a state had emerged in the area by early Uruk times.

Evidence from the next period, middle Uruk, suggests more definitely that a state had emerged. This evidence takes the form of clay seals that were apparently used in trading (Wright and Johnson, 1975). *Commodity sealings* were used to keep a shipment of goods tightly closed until it reached its destination, and *message sealings* were used to keep track of goods sent and received. The clay seals found in Susa include many message seals and *bullae*, clay containers that served as bills of lading for goods received. The villages, in contrast, had few message seals and *bullae*. Again, this finding suggests that Susa administered the regional movement of goods and that Susa was the "capital" of the state.

Reconstruction of the ornaments found with a royal burial from the Sumerian city of Ur. The headdress is made of gold and the necklaces include gold and lapis lazuli. Archaeologists assume that such special treatment indicates elite status.

Let us turn now to the major features of the cultural sequences leading to the first states in southern Iraq.

Cities and States in Southern Iraq

Farming communities older than the first states have not been found in the arid lowland plains of southern Iraq—the area known as Sumer, where some of the earliest cities and states developed. Perhaps silt from the Tigris and Euphrates rivers has covered them. Or, as has been suggested, Sumer may not have been settled by agriculturalists until people learned how to drain and irrigate river-valley soils otherwise too wet or too dry for cultivation. At any rate, small communities depending partly on agriculture had emerged in the hilly areas north and east of Sumer early in the Neolithic. Later, by about 6000 B.C., a mixed herding-farming economy developed in those areas.

The Formative Era

Elman Service called the period from about 5000 to 3500 B.C. the *formative era*, for it saw the coming together of many changes that seem to have played a part in the development of cities and states. Service suggested that with the development of small-scale irrigation, lowland river areas began to attract settlers. The rivers provided not only water for irrigation but also molluscs, fish, and water birds for food, and they provided routes by which to import needed raw materials, such as hardwood and stone that were lacking in Sumer.

Changes during this period suggest an increasingly complex social and political life. Differences in status are reflected in the burial of statues and ornaments with children. Different villages specialized in the production of different goods—pottery in some, copper and stone tools in others (Flannery, 1972). Temples were built in certain places that may have been centres of political as well as religious authority for several communities (Service, 1975). Furthermore, some anthropologists think that chiefdoms, each having authority over several villages, had developed by this time (Flannery, 1972; Service, 1975).

Sumerian Civilization

By about 3500 B.C., there were quite a few cities in the area of Sumer. Most were enclosed in a fortress wall and surrounded by an agricultural area. About 3000 B.C. all of Sumer was unified under a single government. After that time, Sumer became an empire, with great urban centres. Imposing temples, commonly set on artificial mounds, dominated the cities. In the city of Warka the temple mound was about 45 metres high. The empire was very complex and included an elaborate system for the administration of justice, codified laws, specialized government officials, a professional standing army, and even sewer systems in the cities. Among the many specialized crafts were brick making, pottery, carpentry, jewellery making, leatherworking, metallurgy, basket making, stonecutting, and sculpture. Sumerians learned to construct and use wheeled wagons, sailboats, horse-drawn chariots, and spears, swords, and armour of bronze (Kramer, 1963).

A partially restored ziggurat, or temple tower, in what was the Sumerian city of Ur in 2100 B.C.

Chiefdom: a political unit, with a chief at its head, integrating more than one community but not necessarily the whole society or language group.

As economic specialization developed, social stratification became more elaborate. Sumerian documents describe a system of social classes: nobles, priests, merchants, craft workers, metallurgists, bureaucrats, soldiers, farmers, free citizens, and slaves. Slaves were common in Sumer; they often were captives, brought back as the spoils of war.

We see the first evidence of writing around 3000 B.C. The earliest Sumerian writings were in the form of ledgers containing inventories of items stored in the temples and records of livestock or other items owned or managed by the

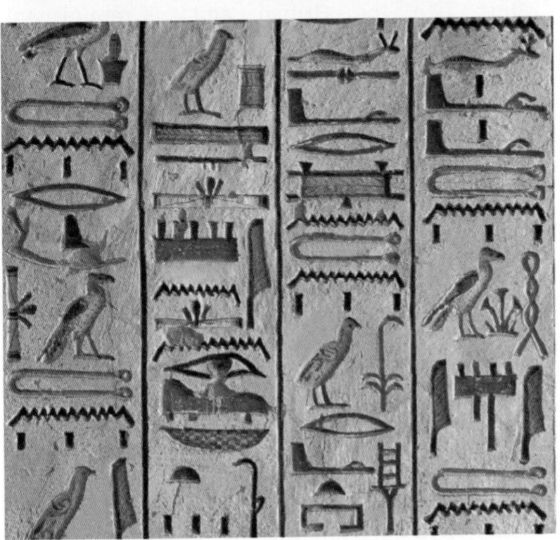

Examples of two of the earliest writing systems on earth. On the left is a cuneiform tablet and on the right is a section of a hieroglyphic panel.

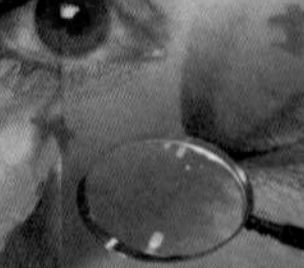

APPLIED ANTHROPOLOGY

Imperialism, Colonialism, and the State

The first city-states in the world seem to have emerged during the Uruk period, roughly the fourth millennium B.C., in the river valleys of southern Mesopotamia, now southern Iraq. From their very beginnings, these first city-states had "foreign trade." This trade may have been indispensable; the riverine environment, though fertile when drained and irrigated, lacked necessary raw materials such as hardwood and stone. The trade with other areas could have been peaceful and balanced, as between equals. After all, it is possible that when one area has something that another wants, and vice versa, the people on both sides could voluntarily arrange to satisfy each other's needs by bargaining and negotiating. However, the archaeological evidence available from the preliterate Uruk period, as well as the documentary evidence available for shortly afterward, suggests that the first city-states in Mesopotamia were engaged in imperialism and colonialism from their very beginnings.

Just like the British and French, who first came to North America to explore and trade and often used force to protect their settlements and access to trade items, the Uruk city-states seem also to have dominated their peripheral, less-developed trading "partners." For example, before 3000 B.C. there were fortified towns with Uruk-style pottery and administrative artifacts at river junctions in the north of Mesopotamia. Why did the Uruk people go there? One possibility is that they deliberately built outposts to secure their access to needed trade goods, including hides and dried meat.

There was no single state involved in this imperialism and colonialism. Not until after 3000 B.C. was southern Mesopotamia (Sumer) politically unified. Rather, the various Uruk-period polities of the Tigris and Euphrates river valleys seem to have been intensely competitive. The walls around the cities indicate that they were probably subject to attack by their rivals at any time. This imagined scenario is reminiscent of the Greek city-states described by Thucydides. It is also like the impression we get from the hieroglyphic writings of the Mayan city-states in and around southern Mexico (A.D. 300–800), which, in a mixture of history and propaganda, extol the triumphs of the various rivalrous rulers. And, of course, we all are familiar with how Britain and Spain and Holland and France were rivalrous before and after the New World was discovered.

We know that the Greek city-states were imperialistic colonizers because we have historical evidence of the fact. Greek-speakers, from Athens and other polities, established colonies all over the Mediterranean—Syracuse in Sicily and Marseilles in France, for example. But what about the Uruk city-states? Why should we think they, too, were imperialistic colonizers? The archaeologist Guillermo Algaze recently reviewed the evidence. First there was the colonization of the plains of southwestern Iran, which people could get to from southern Mesopotamia in seven to ten days by foot or donkey caravan. Then, and maybe overlapping with

temples. Sumerian writing had wedge-shaped characters, or **cuneiform**, formed by pressing a stylus against a damp clay tablet. For contracts and other important documents, the tablet was fired to create a virtually permanent record. Egyptian writing, or **hieroglyphics**, appeared about the same time. Hieroglyphics were written on rolls woven from papyrus reeds, from which our word *paper* derives.

Cuneiform: wedge-shaped writing invented by the Sumerians around 3000 B.C.

Hieroglyphics: "picture writing," as in ancient Egypt and in Mayan sites in Mesoamerica (Mexico and Central America).

Cities and States in Mesoamerica

Cities and states emerged in Mesoamerica—now Mexico and Central America—later than they did in the Near East. The later appearance of civilization in Mesoamerica may be linked to the later emergence of agriculture in the New World, as we saw in the last chapter, and possibly to the near-absence of large animals such as cattle and horses the expansion into southwestern Iran, the Uruk polities established outposts or took over already-existing settlements to the north and northwest, on the plains of what are now northern Iraq and Syria; these latter settlements were apparently all located at intersections of the important waterways and overland routes.

According to Algaze, the Uruk enclaves and outposts outside southern Mesopotamia fit what the comparative historian Philip Curtin calls "trade diaspora." Curtin thinks that such movements developed after the emergence of cities, with their vulnerable populations. (An urban population is vulnerable because a city, by definition, is inhabited mostly by people who are dependent for their food on people who live outside the city.) Diasporas have taken various forms, but they all represent ways to organize exchange between areas with different but complementary resources. At one end of the range of possibilities—involving little or no political organization—commercial specialists remove themselves from their own society and settle as aliens somewhere else. At the other end of the range of variation—the most politically organized end—the expanding polity is involved from the beginning in the founding of outposts that secure the required trade.

Algaze thinks that the Uruk expansion was motivated by a lack of resources in southern Mesopotamia, but is that a complete explanation? Other areas of the world, at the time and since, have lacked resources, but they did not all become imperialistic colonizers. So what else, in addition to the need for external resources, might explain the Uruk expansion? And how can we explain why it eventually stopped? Algaze notes that when the Uruk settlers moved into southwestern Iran, they were entering an area that was not so densely settled, so they may have encountered only minimal resistance. Indeed, the various Uruk-period enclaves and outposts outside southern Mesopotamia were apparently larger and more complex than any previous communities in the peripheral areas. Perhaps, then, imperialism and colonialism are possible only in a world of unequals.

Years ago, the anthropologist Stanley Diamond argued that "imperialism and colonialism are as old as the State." Does this mean that states are likely to practice imperialism and colonialism if they can get away with it? Or are only some conditions likely to predispose states to imperialism and colonialism? How strongly are imperialism and colonialism linked to state organization anyway? What makes a humane state possible? Perhaps future research, particularly cross-cultural and cross-historical research, will tell us.

Sources: Algaze G. 1993. The Uruk World System: The Dynamics of Expansion of Early Mesopotamian Civilization. Chicago: University of Chicago Press.

Curtin PD. 1984. Cross-Cultural Trade in World History. Cambridge: Cambridge University Press.

Diamond S. 1974. In Search of the Primitive: A Critique of Civilization. New Brunswick, NJ: Transaction Books.

Marcus J. 1998. Maya Hieroglyphs: History or Propaganda? In: Ember CR, Ember M, Peregrine PN, editors. Research Frontiers in Anthropology. Upper Saddle River, NJ: Prentice Hall. Prentice Hall/Simon & Schuster Custom Publishing.

Zeder MA. 1994. After the Revolution: Post-Neolithic Subsistence in Northern Mesopotamia. American Anthropologist 96:97–126.

that could be domesticated (Diamond, 1989). We focus primarily on the developments that led to the rise of the city-state of Teotihuacán, which reached its height almost 2000 years ago. Teotihuacán is located in a valley of the same name, which is the northeastern part of the larger Valley of Mexico.

The Formative Period

The formative period in the area around Teotihuacán (1000–300 B.C.) was characterized initially by small, scattered farming villages on the hilly slopes just south of the Teotihuacán Valley. There were probably a few hundred people in each hamlet, and each of these scattered groups was probably politically autonomous. After about 500 B.C., there seems to have been a population shift to settlements on the valley floor, probably in association with the use of irrigation. Between about 300 and 200 B.C. small "elite" centres emerged in the valley; each had an earthen or stone raised platform. Residences or small temples of poles and thatch originally stood on these platforms. That some individuals, particularly those in the elite centres, were buried in special tombs supplied with ornaments, headdresses, carved bowls, and a good deal of food indicates some social inequality (Helms, 1975; Sanders et al., 1979). The various elite centres may indicate the presence of chiefdoms.

The City and State of Teotihuacán

About 150 B.C. no more than a few thousand people lived in scattered villages in the Teotihuacán Valley. In A.D. 100 there was a city of 80 000. By A.D. 500, well over 100 000 people, or approximately 90 percent of the entire valley population, seem to have been drawn or coerced into Teotihuacán (Millon, 1967; Wenke, 1990).

The layout of the city of Teotihuacán, which shows a tremendous amount of planning, suggests that from its beginning the valley was politically unified under a centralized state. Mapping has revealed that the streets and most of the buildings are laid out in a grid pattern, where each grid square measures 57 square metres. Residential structures are often squares of this size, and many streets are spaced apart according to multiples of the basic unit. Even the river that ran through the centre of the city was channelled to conform to the grid pattern. Perhaps the most outstanding feature of the city is the colossal scale of its architecture. Two pyramids dominate the metropolis, the so-called "Pyramid of the Moon" and the "Pyramid of the Sun." At its base the latter is as big as the great Pyramid of Cheops in Egypt.

The thousands of residential structures built after A.D. 300 follow a standard pattern. Narrow streets separate the one-storey buildings, each of which has high, windowless walls. Patios and shafts provide interior light. The layout of rooms suggests that each building consisted of several apartments; more than 100 people may have lived in one of these apartment compounds. There is variation from compound to compound in the size of rooms and the elaborateness of interior decoration, suggesting considerable variation in wealth (Millon, 1976).

Like any major city, Teotihuacán attracted migrants from the surrounding areas. Researchers at the University of Western Ontario are currently examining the question of how migrant populations maintained their ethnic identity within Teotihuacán. Around A.D. 200, a small population of about 1000 Zapotecs emigrated from the Valley of Oaxaca, 400 kilometres southeast of Teotihuacán (Spence, 1992). These people settled in an enclave (Tlailotlacan) at the edge of the city, maintaining their identity for over 500 years (Spence, 1992).

When the Temple of Quetzalcoatl in Teotihuacán was built in A.D. 200, more than 200

The city of Teotihuacán, which had its peak in A.D. 500, was a planned city built on a grid pattern. At the centre was the Pyramid of the Sun shown here.

individuals were sacrificed. A collaborative effort between Mike Spence at the University of Western Ontario and Mexican physical anthropologists is being undertaken to conduct an osteological analysis of 160 skeletons associated with this event. Using a variety of methods including analysis of ancient DNA, stable isotopes, and skeletal traits, anthropologists hope to be able to paint a clear picture of the health and nutrition, and origin and relationships of those who died.

At the height of its power (A.D. 200–500), the metropolis of Teotihuacán encompassed an area larger than imperial Rome (Millon, 1967). Much of Mesoamerica seems to have been influenced by Teotihuacán. Archaeologically, its influence is suggested by the extensive spread of Teotihuacán-style pottery and architectural elements. Undoubtedly, large numbers of people in Teotihuacán were engaged in production for, and the conduct of, long-distance trade. Perhaps 25 percent of the city's population worked at various specialized crafts, including the manufacture of projectile points and cutting and scraping tools from volcanic obsidian. Teotihuacán was close to major deposits of obsidian, which was apparently in some demand over much of Mesoamerica. This fine-grained volcanic stone was used to produce a variety of items in Teotihuacán (projectile points, knives, scrapers, drills, figurines, etc.) that were distributed at times over distances of more than 1000 kilometres (Spence, 1996). Materials found in graves indicate that there was an enormous flow of foreign goods into the city, including precious stones, feathers from colourful birds in the tropical lowlands, and cotton (Helms, 1975; Weaver, 1993).

The City of Monte Albán

Teotihuacán probably was not the earliest city-state in Mesoamerica: there is evidence of political unification somewhat earlier, about 500 B.C., in the Valley of Oaxaca, in southern Mexico, with the city of Monte Albán at its centre. Monte Albán presents an interesting contrast to Teotihuacán. Whereas Teotihuacán seems to have completely dominated its valley, containing almost all its inhabitants and craftspeople, Monte Albán did not. The various villages in the Valley of Oaxaca seem to have specialized in different crafts, but Monte Albán did not monopolize craft production. After the political unification of the valley, cities and towns other than Monte Albán remained important; the population of Monte Albán grew only to 30 000 or so. Unlike Teotihuacán, Monte Albán was not an important commercial or market centre, it was not laid out in a grid pattern, and its architecture was not much different from that of other settlements in the valley in which it was located (Blanton, 1981; Marcus, 1983).

Monte Albán did not have the kinds of resources that Teotihuacán had. It was located on top of a mountain in the centre of the valley, far from either good soil or permanent water supplies that could have been used for irrigation. Even finding drinking water must have been difficult. No natural resources for trade were nearby, nor is there much evidence that Monte Albán was used as a ceremonial centre. Because the city was at the top of a steep mountain, it is unlikely that it could have been a central marketplace for valley-wide trade.

Why, then, did Monte Albán rise to become one of the early centres of Mesoamerican civilization? Richard Blanton suggested it might have originally been founded in the late formative period (500–400 B.C.) as a neutral place where representatives of the different political units in the valley could reside to coordinate activities affecting the whole valley. Thus, Monte Albán may have been like the cities of Brasília, Washington, D.C., and Athens, all of which were originally founded in "neutral," non-productive areas. Such a centre, lacking obvious resources, would not, at least initially, threaten the various political units around it. Later it might become a metropolis dominating a more politically unified region, as Monte Albán came to do in the Valley of Oaxaca (Blanton, 1976; Blanton, 1978).

Other Centres of Mesoamerican Civilization

In addition to Teotihuacán and Oaxaca, there were other Mesoamerican state societies, which developed somewhat later. For example, there are a number of centres with monumental architecture, presumably built by speakers of Mayan languages, in the highlands and lowlands of modern-day Guatemala and the Yucatán Peninsula of modern-day Mexico. On the basis of surface appearances, the Mayan centres do not appear to have been as densely populated as Teotihuacán or Monte Albán. It is now evident though that these other Mayan centres were more densely populated and more dependent on intensive agriculture than was once thought (Turner, 1970; Harrison and Turner, 1978), and recent translations of Mayan picture writing indicate a much more developed form of writing than previously thought (Houston, 1988). It is apparent now that Mayan urbanization and cultural complexity were underestimated by earlier archaeologists because of the dense tropical forest that now covers much of the area of Mayan civilization.

The First Cities and States in Other Areas

So far we have discussed the emergence of cities and states in southern Iraq and Mesoamerica whose development is best, if only imperfectly, known archaeologically. But other state societies probably arose more or less independently in many other areas of the world as well (see Figure 13–2). We say "independently" because such states seem to have emerged without colonization or conquest by other states.

Almost at the same time as the Sumerian empire, the great dynastic age was beginning in the Nile Valley in Egypt. The Old Kingdom, or early dynastic period, began about 3100 B.C., with a capital at Memphis. The archaeological evidence from the early centuries is limited, but most of the population appears to have lived in largely self-sufficient villages. Many of the great pyramids and palaces were built around 2500 B.C. (Wenke, 1984).

Elsewhere in Africa, states also arose. In what is present-day Ethiopia, the Axum (or Aksum) state evolved beginning sometime early in the 1st millennium A.D., and ultimately became a centre of trade and commerce between Africa and the Arabian Peninsula. Among the unique accomplishments of the Axum state were multistorey stone residences built in a singular architectural style. Axum is also notable as being perhaps the first officially Christian state in the world (Connah, 1987).

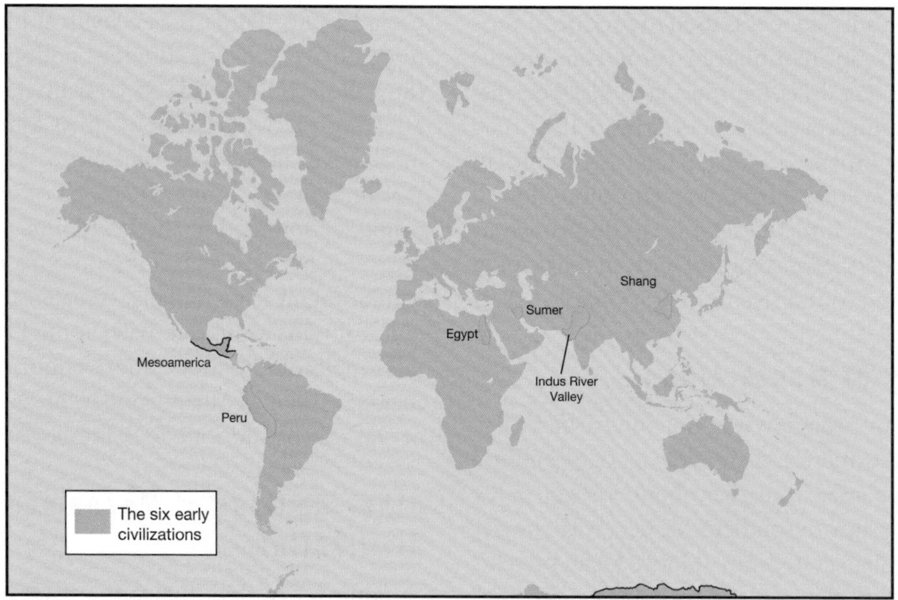

Figure 13–2 Six Early Civilizations

Source: Adapted from Service ER. 1975. Origins of the State and Civilization: The Process of Cultural Evolution. New York: Norton. By permission of W. W. Norton & Company, Inc. Copyright © 1975 by W. W. Norton & Company, Inc.

One of the cities of the Harappan civilization in the Indus Valley was Mohenjodaro. Seen here is an excavated large "bath" with surrounding rooms. Columns originally surrounded the pool. (Modern buildings appear in the background.) In contrast to other early civilizations, there was little display of grandeur. All Harappan cities were laid out according to the same plan.

In sub-Saharan Africa, by A.D. 800, the savannah and forest zones of western Africa had a succession of city-states. One of them was called Ghana, and it became a major source of gold for the Mediterranean world, as did other states in what came to be known as the "Gold Coast" (Fagan, 1989: 428). In the Congo River basin, a powerful kingdom had evolved by A.D. 1200, with cities described as having tens of thousands of residences and a king that was recognized as an equal by the Portuguese king in the early 1500s (Connah, 1987). Farther south, states apparently arose in several areas early in the 2nd millennium A.D. One of these was responsible for the large, circular stone structures known today as the Great Zimbabwe (Vogel, 2002).

In the Indus Valley of northwestern India, a large state society had developed by 2300 B.C. This Harappan civilization did not have much in the way of monumental architecture, such as pyramids and palaces, and it was also unusual in other respects. The state apparently controlled an enormous territory—over a million square kilometres. There was not just one major city but many, each built according to a similar pattern and with a municipal water and sewage system (Wenke, 1984).

The Shang dynasty in northern China (1750 B.C.) has long been cited as the earliest state society in East Asia. Recent research suggests that an even earlier one, the Xia dynasty, may have emerged in the same general area by 2200 B.C. (Chang, 1981). In any case, the Shang dynasty had all the earmarks of statehood: a stratified, specialized society; religious, economic, and administrative unification; and a distinctive art style (Chang, 1986).

In South America, a group of distinct state societies may have emerged as early as 2500 B.C. in the Supe and Pativilca valleys north of Lima, Peru. The valley contains a group of large cities that seem to have been interdependent—cities on the coast supplied inland cities with fish, while inland cities served as political and economic centres. The cities contain plaza areas and large pyramids, which are thought to be temple structures (Haas et al., 2004; Solis et al., 2001). After 200 B.C. the major river valleys leading from the Andes to the sea witnessed the development of a complex agricultural system dependent on irrigation. The separate, but similar, states participated in a widespread system of religious symbols and beliefs called Chavín. The various states included the well-known Moche state, creators of some of the most remarkable effigy ceramics ever known, and the Nazca state, the people of which constructed a huge landscape of intaglios (inscribed images and lines) on the hard ground of highland deserts. By A.D. 700, these regional states were integrated into a large, militaristic empire called Wari or Huari (Lumbreras, 1974).

And in North America, a huge settlement, with over 100 earthen mounds (one of them, Monk's Mound, is the largest pre-Columbian structure north of Mexico), and covering an area of more than 13 square kilometres, developed near present-day St. Louis late in the 1st millennium A.D. The site is called Cahokia, and it was certainly the centre of a large and powerful chiefdom. Whether it had achieved a state level of organization is controversial. There is evidence for religious and craft specialists and there is clear social stratification, but whether or not the leaders of Cahokian society were able to govern by force is still unclear (Fowler, 1975).

Theories about the Origin of the State

We have seen that states developed in many parts of the world. Why did they evolve when and where they did? A number of theories have been proposed to explain the origins of the state. We consider those that have been discussed frequently by archaeologists (Cohen and Service, 1978; Zeder, 1991).

Irrigation

Irrigation seems to have been important in many of the areas in which early state societies developed. Irrigation made the land habitable or productive in parts of Mesoamerica, southern Iraq, the Nile Valley, and other areas. It has been suggested that the labour and management needed for the upkeep of an irrigation system led to the formation of a political elite, in effect, the overseers of the system, who also eventually became the governors of the society (Wittfogel, 1957). Proponents of this view believe that both the city and civilization were outgrowths of the administrative requirements of an irrigation system.

Critics note that this theory does not seem to apply to all areas where cities and states may have emerged independently. For example, in southern Iraq, the irrigation systems serving the early cities were generally small and probably did not require extensive labour and management. Large-scale irrigation works were not constructed until after cities had been fully established (Adams, 1960; Wright, 1986). Thus, irrigation could not have been the main stimulus for the development of cities and states in Sumer. Even in China, for which the irrigation theory was first formulated, there is no evidence of large-scale irrigation as early as Shang times (Wheatley, 1971).

Although large-scale irrigation may not always have preceded the emergence of the first cities and states, even small-scale irrigation systems could have resulted in unequal access to productive land and so may have contributed to the development of a stratified society (Adams, 1960). In addition, irrigation systems may have given rise to border and other disputes between adjacent groups, thereby prompting people to concentrate in cities for defence and stimulating the development of military and political controls (Adams, 1981). Finally, as Robert Adams and Elman Service both suggested, the main significance of irrigation, either large- or small-scale, may have been its intensification of production, a development that in turn may have indirectly stimulated craft specialization, trade, and administrative bureaucracy (Service, 1975; Adams, 1981).

Population Growth, Circumscription, and War

Robert Carneiro has suggested that states may emerge because of population growth in an area that is physically or socially limited. Competition and warfare in such a situation may lead to the subordination of defeated groups, who are obliged to pay tribute and to submit to the control of a more powerful group (Sanders and Price, 1968; Carneiro, 1970). Carneiro illustrated his theory by describing how states may have emerged on the northern coast of Peru.

After the people of that area first settled into an agricultural village life, population grew at a slow, steady rate. Initially, new villages were formed as population grew. However, in the narrow coastal valleys—blocked by high mountains, fronted by the sea, and surrounded by desert—this splintering-off process could not continue indefinitely. The result, according to Carneiro, was increasing land shortage and warfare between villages as they competed for land. Since the high mountains, the sea, and the desert blocked any escape for losers, the defeated villagers had no choice but to submit to political domination. In this way, chiefdoms may have become kingdoms as the most powerful villages grew to control entire valleys. As chiefs' power expanded over several valleys, states and empires may have been born.

Carneiro noted that physical or environmental circumscription may not be the only kind of barrier that gives rise to a state. Social circumscription may be just as important. People living at the centre of a high-density area may find that their migration is blocked by surrounding settlements just as effectively as it could be by mountains, sea, and desert.

Marvin Harris suggested a somewhat different form of circumscription. He argued that the first states with their coercive authority could emerge only in areas that supported intensive grain agriculture (and the possibility of high food production) and were surrounded by areas that could not support intensive grain agriculture. So people in such areas might tolerate the coercive authority of a state because they would suffer a sharp drop in living standards if they moved away (Harris, 1979; Wenke, 1990).

Carneiro suggested that his theory applies to many areas besides the northern coast of Peru, including southern Iraq and the Indus and Nile valleys. Although there were no geographic barriers in areas such as northern China or the Mayan lowlands on the Yucatán Peninsula, the development of states in those areas may have been the result of social circumscription. Carneiro's theory seems to be supported for southern Iraq, where there is archaeological evidence of population growth, circumscription, and warfare (Young, Jr., 1972). And there is evidence of population growth before the emergence of the state in the Teotihuacán Valley (Sanders and Price, 1968).

Population growth does not necessarily mean population pressure though. For example, the populations in the Teotihuacán and Oaxaca valleys apparently did increase prior to state development, but there is no evidence that they had even begun to approach the limits of their resources. More people could have lived in both places (Brumfiel, 1976; Blanton et al., 1981; Feinman et al., 1985). Nor is population growth definitely associated with state formation in all areas where early states arose. For example, according to Wright and Johnson, there was population growth long before states emerged in southwestern Iran, but the population apparently declined just before the states emerged (Wright and Johnson, 1975; Carneiro, 1988; Hole, 1994).

In addition, Carneiro's circumscription theory leaves an important logical question unanswered: Why would the victors in war let the defeated populations remain and pay tribute? If the victors wanted the land so much in the first place, why wouldn't they try to exterminate the defeated and occupy the land themselves, which has happened many times in history?

Local and Long-Distance Trade

It has been suggested that trade was a factor in the emergence of the earliest states (Polanyi, 1957; Sanders, 1968). Wright and Johnson theorized that the organizational requirements of producing items for export, redistributing the items imported, and defending trading parties would foster state formation (Wright and Johnson, 1975). Does the archaeological evidence support such a theory?

In southern Iraq and the Mayan lowlands, long-distance trade routes may indeed have stimulated bureaucratic growth. In the lowlands of southern Iraq, as we have seen, people needed wood and stone for building, and they traded with highland people for those items. In the Mayan lowlands, the development of civilization seems to have been preceded by long-distance trade.

Farmers in the lowland regions traded with people in faraway places in order to obtain salt, obsidian for cutting blades, and hard stone for grinding tools (Rathje, 1971). In southwestern Iran, long-distance trade did not become very important until after Susa became the centre of a state society, but short-distance trade may have played the same kind of role in the formation of states.

Kwang-chih Chang put forward a similar theory for the origin of states in China. He suggested that Neolithic societies in the Yellow River valley developed a long-distance trade network, which he called an *interaction sphere*, by about 4000 B.C. Trade spread cultural elements among the societies in the interaction sphere, so that they came to share some common elements. Over time, these societies came to depend on each other both as trade partners and as cultural partners, and around 2000 B.C. they unified into a single political unit under the Shang dynasty (Chang, 1986). Thus, Chang sees political unification in China as an outgrowth of a pre-existing system of trade and cultural interaction.

The Various Theories: An Evaluation

Why do states form? As of now, no one theory seems to fit all the known situations. The reason may be that different conditions in different places may have favoured the emergence of centralized government. After all, the state, by definition, implies an ability to organize large populations for a collective purpose. In some areas, this purpose may have been the need to organize trade with local or far-off regions. In other cases, the state may have emerged as a way to control defeated populations in circumscribed areas. In still other instances, a combination of factors may have fostered the development of the state type of political system (Brumfiel, 1983).

The Consequences of State Formation

We have considered several areas where states arose, as well as a number of theories to explain the origin of states. But what were the consequences for the people living in those societies? The consequences seem to have been dramatic.

One of the ways states change the lifestyles of people is by allowing for larger and denser populations (Johnson and Earle, 2000). As we have already seen, agriculture itself gives populations the potential to grow, and the development of a state only furthers that potential. Why? Because a state is able to build infrastructure—irrigation systems, roadways, markets—that allows both the production and distribution of agricultural products to become more efficient. States are able to coordinate information as well, and can use that information to manage agricultural production cycles and to anticipate or manage droughts, blights, or other natural disasters. States are also able to control access to land (through laws and a military) and thus can both maintain farmers on the land and prevent others (from either within or outside of the state) from removing the farmers or interfering with their ability to produce food.

With increased efficiency of agricultural production and distribution, states also allow many (if not most) people in the society to be relieved of food production. These people are freed to become craftspeople, merchants, and artists, as well as bureaucrats, soldiers, and political leaders. People may also live apart from agricultural fields, and thus cities with dense populations can arise. Cities can also arise in locations that are not suited to agriculture but that perhaps are suited to trade (such as the cities on rivers in southern Mesopotamia) or defence (such as on top of a mountain, as in the case of Monte Albán). Art, music, and literature often flourish in such contexts, and these too are often consequences of the rise of states. Organized religion also often develops after states appear. Thus, all the hallmarks we associate with civilization can be seen as resulting from the evolution of states (Childe, 1950).

The development of states can have many negative impacts as well. When states develop, people become governed by force and are no longer able to say no to their leaders. Police and military forces can become instruments of oppression and terror (Service, 1975). On a less obvious level, the class stratification of states creates differences in access to resources and an underclass of poor, uneducated, and frequently unhealthy people. Health issues are exacerbated by the concentration of people in cities, an environment in which epidemic diseases can flourish (Diamond, 2003). Without direct access to food supplies, people in cities also face the threat of malnutrition or outright starvation if food production and distribution systems fail (Dirks, 1993).

All states appear to be expansionistic, and the emergence of state warfare and conquest seems one of the most striking negative impacts of the evolution of states. In fact, more human suffering can probably be linked to state expansion than to any other single factor. Why do states expand? One basic reason may be that they are simply able to. States have standing armies ready to fight or be sent to conquer enemies. Another reason for state expansion might be related to the threat of famine and disease, which is more likely with intensive agriculture (Johnson and Earle, 2000).

A third answer to the question of why states tend to expand might be that belligerence is simply part of the nature of states. States often arise through military means, and it may be vital to the continuation of some states that military power be continually demonstrated (Ferguson and Whitehead, 1992). Regardless of the causes, war and conquest are the consequences of state formation. Often, too, defeat in war is the fate of states.

The Decline and Collapse of States

All of the most ancient states collapsed eventually. None of them maintained their power and influence into historic times. Why? Might the reasons for their fall tell us something about why they rose in the first place? For example, if a particular factor was partly responsible for the rise of an ancient state, its disappearance or deterioration may partly explain the decline of that state. Then again, the reasons for the decline of states may be quite different from the reasons for the growth of states.

One suggested explanation for the decline and collapse of states, that is, environmental degradation, is perhaps relevant to state development. If states originally arose where the environment was conducive to intensive agriculture and harvests big enough to support social stratification, political officials, and a state type of political system, then perhaps environmental degradation—declining soil productivity, persistent drought, and the like—contributed to the collapse of ancient states. The archaeologist Harvey Weiss has suggested that persistent drought helped to bring about the fall of the ancient Akkadian empire, in the Near East. By 2300 B.C., the Akkadians had established an empire stretching 1300 kilometres from the Persian Gulf in what is now Iraq to the headwaters of the Euphrates River in what is now Turkey. A century later the empire collapsed. Weiss thinks that a long-term drought brought the empire down, as well as other civilizations that existed at that time too. Many archaeologists doubted there was such a widespread drought, but evidence recently presented at a meeting of the American Geophysical Union indicates that the worst dry spell of the past 10 000 years began just as the Akkadians' northern stronghold was being abandoned. The evidence of the drought—windblown dust in sediment retrieved from the bottom of the Persian Gulf—indicates that the dry spell lasted 300 years. Other geophysical evidence suggests that the drought was worldwide (Kerr, 1998).

Environmental degradation may occur for other reasons than natural events. The behaviour of humans may sometimes be responsible. Consider the collapse of Cahokia, a city of at least 15 000 people that thrived for a while in the area where the Missouri and Mississippi rivers converge. In the 12th century A.D., Cahokia had large public plazas, a city wall constructed from some 20 000 logs, and massive mounds. But within 300 years only the mounds were left. Silt from flooding covered former croplands and settled areas. The geographer Bill Woods thinks that overuse of woodlands for fuel, construction, and defence led to deforestation, flooding, and persistent crop failure. The result was the abandonment of Cahokia. Timber depletion is also indicated by studies of charcoal from excavations in the area. Apparently the quality of wood used in construction declined over time, suggesting that choice trees became scarcer. Cahokia is just one example of degradation that may have been caused by human behaviour. Another example is the increasing saltiness of soils caused by evaporation of water from fields that

NEW PERSPECTIVES ON GENDER

Effects of Imperialism on Women's Status

Archaeologists, particularly those who are women, have begun to pay attention to the gender implications of archaeological materials. Do the findings from excavated houses imply anything about what women and men did where they lived? What do the findings in houses and other places suggest about the division of labour by gender? Can archaeology tell us about women's status in the culture and how it may have changed over time? Research suggests that if you look for gender-related results, you often can find some. For example, the archaeologist Cathy Costin has studied the effects of Inca imperialism on women's status in a conquered area.

Costin participated in a research project that studied culture change in the Yanamarca Valley of highland Peru. The project focused on the development of chiefdoms among the indigenous Wanka ethnic group between A.D. 1300 and 1470 and on the effects of the Inca conquest at the end of that period. According to the archaeology, most people before the Inca conquest were farmers, but some households specialized part time in the production of pottery, stone tools, and perhaps textiles. Documents written after the arrival of the Spaniards suggest that the Wanka had developed chiefdoms at about A.D. 1300, possibly as a result of intensified warfare among the various communities. A high level of conflict is inferred from the locations and configurations of the settlements: most people lived in fortified (walled) communities located on hills above the valley floor. According to the documentary sources, the Wanka chiefs had achieved their positions because of success as war leaders.

We know from documents that the Inca conquered the Wanka during the reign of the emperor Pachakuti (about A.D. 1470). The Wanka region became a province within the Inca empire, and bureaucrats from the capital at Cuzco came to govern the Wanka. The Inca conquerors, including military personnel, formed the highest class in the valley. The Wanka chiefs became vassals of the Inca state and imitators of Inca ways, using Inca-like pottery and building Inca-style additions to their homes. The economy of the valley became more specialized, apparently to meet the needs of the Inca. People in some villages still mostly farmed, but in other villages most households specialized in the production of pottery, stone tools, and other crafts. Skeletal remains indicate that the commoners became healthier and lived longer after the Inca conquest.

How did the Inca conquest affect the status of women? One key to an answer was suggested by the presence in the excavations of several thousand perforated round ceramic objects. They were spindle whorls, weights used in spinning to keep the thread tight and even. The thread (from llama and alpaca wool)

Monk's Mound at Cahokia.

was made into cloth, which became the major form of tax payment after the Inca took over. Each village had to produce a certain amount of cloth for the state tax collectors. The cloth collected was used to clothe men serving in the army and to "pay" other government personnel. The burden of producing the cloth fell on the traditional spinners and weavers, who we know from the post-Spanish documents were females of all ages.

All excavated households, dated to just before the Inca conquest, had spindle whorls, indicating that the female occupants in all households spun and made cloth. More whorls were found the farther up the mountain the house was located, indicating that women who lived closer to the high grasslands, where the flocks of llamas and alpacas were kept, spun more thread than did women who lived farther down from the pastures. We might expect that elite women would do less work. But, to the contrary, the women in elite households seem to have produced more cloth than the women in commoner households; the elite households had twice as many whorls on average as the commoner households had.

After the Inca conquest, households appear to have produced twice the amount of thread they did before, because there are twice the number of recovered spindle whorls. There is no indication, archaeological or documentary, that the women were freed from other tasks to make more time for spinning, so it would appear that women had to work harder under Inca domination to produce thread and cloth. However, the producers do not appear to have benefited from the increased cloth production. Much if not most of the cloth produced was removed from the villages and taken to Inca storage facilities in the capital and redistributed from there.

In addition to working harder for the Inca, women seem to have fared worse than the men when it came to nutrition. Christine Hastorf's chemical analysis of bones from Inca-period graves suggests that women ate less maize (corn) than did men. It seems that the men were "eating out" more than women. Maize was often consumed as *chicha* beer, a key component of state-sponsored feasts, which were probably attended more by men than women. Men also worked more in state-organized agricultural and production projects, where they probably were rewarded with meat, maize, and *chicha* for their service to the state.

Sources: Brumfiel EM. 1992. Distinguished Lecture in Archeology: Breaking and Entering the Ecosystem—Gender, Class, and Faction Steal the Show. American Anthropologist 94:551–567.

Costin CL. 1998. Cloth Production and Gender Relations in the Inka Empire. In: Ember CR, Ember M, Peregrine PN, editors. Research Frontiers in Anthropology. Upper Saddle River, NJ: Prentice Hall. Prentice Hall/Simon & Schuster Custom Publishing.

Gero JM, Conkey MW, editors. 1991. Engendering Archaeology: An Introduction to Women and Prehistory. Oxford: Basil Blackwell.

Hastorf C. 1991. Gender, Space, and Food in Prehistory. In: Gero JM, Conkey MW, editors. Engendering Archaeology: An Introduction to Women and Prehistory. Oxford: Basil Blackwell.

have been irrigated over long periods of time, as in what is now southern Iraq (Anonymous, 1996).

Civilizations may sometimes decline because human behaviour has increased the incidence of disease (see discussion on page 301). For example, many lowland Mayan cities were abandoned between A.D 800 and 1000. Explanations of this collapse have ranged from overpopulation to resource depletion. In fact, another factor may have been increasing incidence of yellow fever. The clearing of forests and the consequent increase of breeding sites for mosquitoes may have favoured the spread of the disease from areas farther south in Central America. Or the planting of particular trees by the Mayans in their urban areas may have increased the populations of co-resident monkeys who carried the disease (which mosquitoes transmitted to people) (Wilkinson, 1995).

Another reason that some states have collapsed appears to be overextension. This is often one of the reasons given for the decline of the Roman Empire. By the time of its fall, beginning in the 2nd century A.D., the empire had expanded throughout the Mediterranean region and into northwestern Europe. That huge area may simply have been too large to administer. "Barbarian" incursions on the peripheries of the empire went unchecked because it was too difficult, and too costly, to reinforce these far-flung frontiers. Sometimes these incursions became wholesale invasions that were exacerbated by famines, plagues, and poor leadership. By the time the last Roman emperor of the West was deposed in A.D. 476, the empire had withered to virtually nothing (Tainter, 1988).

The history of Ephesus, a former city lying in ruins in what is now western Turkey, illustrates the waxing and waning of states and empires. From about 1000 B.C. to 100 B.C., it was controlled by the Greeks, Lydians, Persians, Macedonians, and Romans, among others.

Many other ideas have been put forward to explain collapse, ranging from catastrophes to almost mystical factors such as "social decadence," but, as with theories for the origin of states, no single explanation seems to fit all or even most of the situations. While it is still not clear what specific conditions led to the emergence, or collapse, of the state in each of the early centres of civilization, the question of why states form and decline is a lively focus of research today. More satisfactory answers may come out of ongoing and future investigations.

Summary

1. Archaeologists do not always agree on how a state should be defined, but most seem to agree that hierarchical and centralized decision-making affecting a substantial population is the key criterion. Most states have cities with public buildings, full-time craft and religious specialists, an official art style, and a hierarchical social structure topped by an elite class from which the leaders are drawn. Most states maintain power with a monopoly on the use of force. Force or the threat of force is used by the state to tax its population and to draft people for work or war.
2. Early state societies arose within the Near East in what is now southern Iraq and southwestern Iran. Southern Iraq, or Sumer, was unified under a single government just after 3000 B.C. It had writing, large urban centres, imposing temples, codified laws, a standing army, wide trade networks, a complex irrigation system, and a high degree of craft specialization.
3. The earliest city-state in Mesoamerica probably developed around 500 B.C. in the Valley of Oaxaca, with a capital at Monte Albán. Somewhat later, in the northeastern section of the Valley of Mexico, Teotihuacán developed. At the height of its power, A.D. 200–500, the city-state of Teotihuacán appears to have influenced much of Mesoamerica.

4. City-states arose early in other parts of the New World: in Guatemala, the Yucatán Peninsula of Mexico, Peru, and possibly near St. Louis. In the Old World, early states developed in Egypt, the Indus Valley of India, northern China, and West Africa.
5. There are several theories of why states arose. The irrigation theory suggests that the administrative needs of maintaining extensive irrigation systems may have been the impetus for state formation. The circumscription theory suggests that states emerge when competition and warfare in circumscribed areas lead to the subordination of defeated groups, who are obliged to submit to the control of the most powerful group. Theories involving trade suggest that the organizational requirements of producing exportable items, redistributing imported items, and defending trading parties would foster state formation. Which is correct? At this point, no one theory is able to explain the formation of every state. Perhaps different organizational requirements in different areas all favoured centralized government.

Glossary Terms

chiefdoms (p. 313)
civilization (p. 310)
cuneiform (p. 314)
egalitarian (p. 310)
hieroglyphics (p. 314)
state (p. 310)

Critical Questions

1. Cities and states did not appear until after the emergence of food production. Why might food production be necessary, but not sufficient, for cities and states to develop?
2. As with the emergence of food production, the earliest cities and states developed within a few thousand years of each other. What might be the reasons?
3. How has colonialism shaped today's society? Do colonialism and imperialism still shape society today, and if so in what manner?
4. Can you imagine a future world without states? What conditions might lead to that "state" of the world?

Internet Exercises

1. Visit **www.maya-archaeology.org/** for an overview of Mayan archaeology resources.
2. Visit **http://archaeology.asu.edu/teo/** and read about the city of Teotihuacán.
3. Visit **www.jhu.edu/digitalhammurabi/** and read about the Digital Hammurabi Project. How is this technology helping us to understand more about the past.

Suggested Reading

Blanton RE, Kowalewski SA, Feinman G, Appel J. 1993. Ancient Mesoamerica: A Comparison of Change in Three Regions. Second edition. Cambridge: Cambridge University Press. A comparison and analysis of cultural development, and particularly the development of states, in three regions of Mesoamerica—the Valley of Oaxaca, the Valley of Mexico, and the eastern (Mayan) lowlands.

Burenhult G, editor. 1994. Old World Civilizations: The Rise of Cities and States. St. Lucia, Queensland, Australia: University of Queensland Press. A gorgeous book of colour photographs, surveying many of the ancient civilizations in Asia, Africa, and Europe.

Daniel G. 2004. The First Civilizations: The Archaeology of Their Origins. Phoenix Press, Limited. An overview of the earliest civilizations in Mesopotamia, Egypt, the Indus Valley, and China in the Old World, and Mexico, Yucatan, and Peru in the New World.

Diamond J. 2005. Collapse. Penguin. A popular account of environmental degradation and the collapse of complex societies.

Feinman GM, Marcus J, editors. 1998. States. Santa Fe, NM: School of American Research Press. This collection of papers discusses the rise and fall of the ancient states in the Near East, India and Pakistan, Egypt, Mesoamerica, and the Andes, and presents some key questions for future research.

Tainter JA. 1988. The Collapse of Complex Societies. Cambridge: Cambridge University Press. Comprehensive description of the theory of collapse as a function of declining marginal returns in complex systems.

Wenke RJ. 1999. Patterns in Prehistory: Humankind's First Three Million Years. Fourth edition. New York: Oxford University Press. Chapters 7 to 15 provide an up-to-date review of what is known and what is controversial about the origins of cities and states around the world.

Name Index

L

M

N

O

P

Q

R

Subject Index

Note: Entries for figures are followed by "*f*"

F

H